FATAL SWITCH

Murder on the Panama Road

Louise Stanton Warren

Olivette-Crooke, LLC

Fernandina Beach, Florida

Copyright © 2022 by Louise Stanton Warren

All rights reserved. No part of this book may be reproduced or transmitted in any form or by any means, electronic or mechanical, including photocopying and recording, or by any information storage and retrieval system, without permission in writing from the publisher at, 2417 Los Robles Dr., Fernandina Beach, FL 32034, or contact the author at www.LouiseStantonWarren.com.

Book design by Sagaponack Books & Design

ISBNs
979-8-9860380-0-1 (softcover)
979-8-9860380-1-8 (hardcover)
979-8-9860380-2-5 (e-book)

Library of Congress Catalog Card Number: 2022911716

Summary: Marie Louise Gato was allegedly murdered by Edward Pitzer in Jacksonville, Florida in 1897. The infamous murder trial of Edward Pitzer recorded the justice system of the time. Napoleon Bonaparte Broward, Duval County Sheriff, future governor of Florida, and riverboat pilot owned the *Three Friends*, a filibustering ship. The Jacksonville filibustering fleet, the *Three Friends*, the *Dauntless* and the *Commodore* ran guns, money, soldiers, food, etc. to Cuba during its War of Independence from Spain.

TRU002000 True Crime / Murder
TRU010000 True Crime / Historical
HIS036120 History / US / State & Local / South
HIS058000 History / Women
BIO002030 Biography & Autobiography / Cultural, Ethnic & Regional / Hispanic & Latino

Olivette-Crooke, LLC
Fernandina Beach, Florida

Printed and bound in United States of America
First Edition

Dedicated to

MARY CROOKE WARREN

Beautiful   Cheerful   Loving

Cigar Box Art

The truth does not change according to our ability to stomach it.

—Flannery O'Connor

Contents

Prologue ix

Part I. The Murder
1. Marie Louise is Shot 1
2. Police Arrive at Pitzers' 10
3. Police Arrive at Gatos' 14
4. Pitzer Surrenders 16

Part II. Past Experiences

Marie Louise's Family 25
1. Pearl of the Caribbean 29
2. José and Catalina 35
3. Jacksonville 1880s 42
4. Springfield 46
5. Edward Pitzer 54
6. Domingo Herrera 57
7. Marie's Shopping 61
8. Dinner and Duel 65
9. Marie's Letters 70
10. Three Friends 76

Part III. The Second Murder
1. Lt. William Gruber, Jacksonville Police Department . . . 83
2. Gruber Nightlife 87
3. The Death of Lieutenant Gruber 91
4. Search of the Murder Scene 95
5. Gruber Inquest 98

Part IV. The Pitzer Trial

Court Officers 104
1. Trial Opening 107
2. Neal Mitchell, M.D. 114
3. Trolleys Passing 121
4. Serena Field and Drucilla Bryant 127
5. Mrs. Eliza Huau 136
6. Georgia Gato 141
7. Fritz Aberdeen 147
8. Lulu and Malvina 150
9. Mr. and Mrs. Sanchez 155

10. Henry Guinard 158
11. Ernest Benton. 160
12. Mrs. Eliza Huau Recalled. 164
13. Gabriel H. Gato 166
14. Dying Declaration 171
15. An Additional Ante Mortem Statement 179
16. Defense Direct Rebuttal Witnesses. 183
17. William Arpen 191
18. Lycurgus Bigger 193
19. John Bigger 200
20. Mrs. Cornelia Pickett 209
21. Mrs. Cornelia Pickett's Affidavit & Miss Cornelia Pickett 212
22. Mrs. Rachel Bixler 215
23. Mrs. Rachel Bixler Recalled 224
24. Edward Pitzer. 227
25. Pitzer Cross-Examination. 234
26. Mrs. Enriqueta Gato 241
27. Fletcher's Closing Argument 244
28. St. Clair-Abrams' Closing Argument 248
29. Hartridge's Closing Rebuttal 253
30. Judge Call's Jury Instructions. 257
31. The Last Night 265
32. Verdict 269

Epilogue 273

Acknowledgments. 275

Endnotes. 281

Bibliography 293

Contemporary Cousins. 299

Index 301

About the Author 305

Prologue

April 22, 1897, Thursday, 4:30 p.m.

A whipped branch, a whirl of sand. Preternatural silence. As the still before a hurricane, the world watched the day close on the irrevocable, the inconceivable. Only the pealing church bells shattered the quiet and called forth the gathering.

Tucked in the rear of the sanctuary, according to church dictates, the children stood in a double semi-circle by the coffin. Tears streaked down their cheeks. The older children held the slight shoulders of the smaller ones who stood before them. Gabriel H. Gato, the father, with swollen eyes and tightly pulled mouth, set tight with controlled rage and sorrow, greeted visitors who filed by. Family, friends, and voyeurs, whom no one knew, passed Marie Louise Gato's silk-lined casket uttering sounds of mourning. Enriqueta, the young woman's mother, lay at home in bed, sobbing into her pillow, clawing at her mattress. From a small chair in the corner, a friend watched over her in silence.

Marie's cousin, Katie Huau Lorraine, waited in the vestibule to join the family procession behind the small casket as it moved forward through the nave of the church. Alphonso Fritot, another cousin, waited with Katie until the priest called him to help carry the coffin. Their parents and siblings also stood in the vestibule, speaking of nothing much in soft voices.

Finally, the casket was borne tenderly up the aisle, preceded by the rector reading the opening lines of the solemn service of the Episcopal Church. The presence of The Rt. Reverend Edwin Weed, Bishop of Florida, assisting in the services, indicated the importance and respect afforded this family.[1] The full choir, swathed in flowing robes, also participated.

From his jail cell a block away, Edward Pitzer heard the bells of the St. John's Episcopal Church tolling the girl's funeral. "It would have meant a lot to me," he said listening to the bells, "if I could have attended her funeral."

That morning, his mother had fainted at the coroner's hearing when Georgia, Marie's older sister, weeping, testified she had recognized Pitzer two nights before at her front gate with a gun in his hand.

JACKSONVILLE GIRL SHOT.

Struck by Five Bullets Fired from Ambush—Her Lover Under Arrest.

JACKSONVILLE, Fla., April 20.—Miss Mary Louise Gato, a beautiful woman about twenty years old, was shot and seriously wounded about 6:30 o'clock this evening. Edward Pitzer, the lover of the girl, is under arrest, charged with the crime, although he denied it.

Just as the girl was about to enter her home she was fired upon from ambush, the first bullet passing through her left arm. Another bullet entered the right side of the back, penetrating the liver, and another the left side, passing through the lung. A fourth bullet in the back was stopped by a steel rib in the woman's corset. Another bullet went through her hat.

Pitzer and the girl had been friendly about three years, but it is said that she did not wish to marry him. He is the son of a prominent merchant.

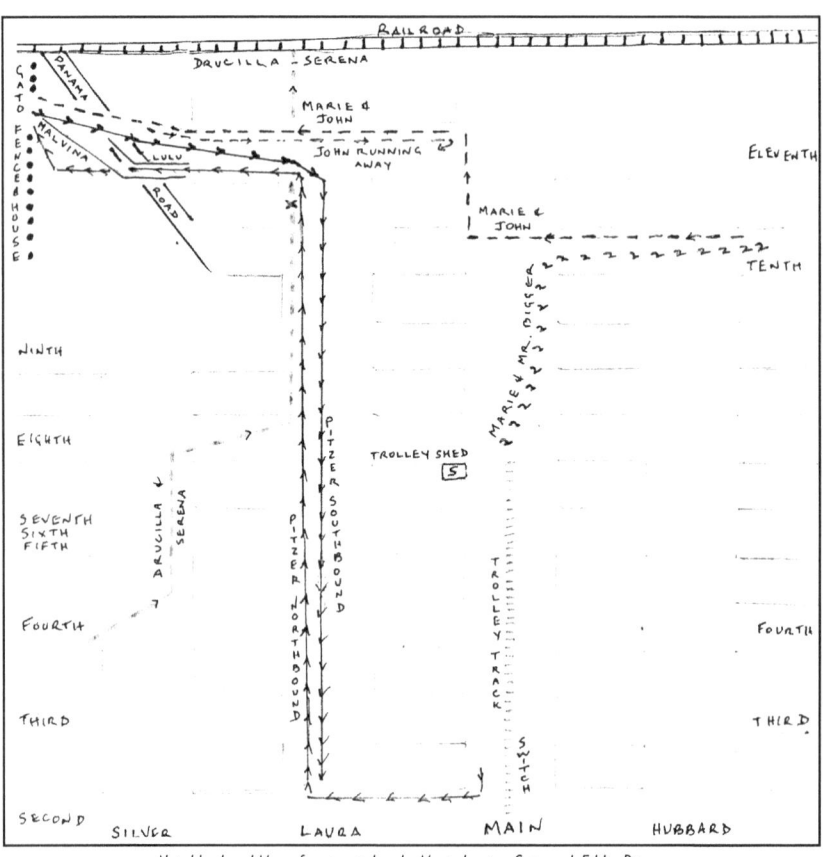

Neighborhood Map of routes taken by Marie Louise Gato and Eddie Pitzer
Map created by Christine Andow-Farley

PART I

THE MURDER

Bay Street, Jacksonville 1891, Gala Week

Main Street Trolley southbound, approaching Second Street switch

Part I – Chapter 1
MARIE LOUISE IS SHOT

April 20, 1897, 6:30 p.m.

The St. Johns River, the most prominent view from the courthouse, flowed north through the city to the Atlantic Ocean. Primarily a wooden town, Jacksonville, Florida, possessed the usual liveries, hotels, factories, stores, an opera house, a yacht club and residences from shacks to mansions. Some downtown streets were paved with bricks but most were dirt roads, which regularly stopped traffic due to being too wet or too dry. The city boasted a bicycle racetrack, a new phenomenon, where the Wheelmen, a local bicycle club, staged national events.

Jacksonville was a tourist town, with hotels serving multicourse meals of game and fish on white tablecloths, including alligator, oysters, and green turtle soup. Famous orchestras played nightly balls. Tourists and locals alike chugged in open steamboats or sailing skiffs through palm-draped waters, trolling fishing lines and shooting at alligators.

The town also embraced a large Cuban population fleeing the Ten Years War in Cuba that had begun in 1868. Marie Louise Gato's father and uncles owned huge Cuban cigar factories. As many as fifteen existed in the city, but theirs were by far the largest.[1]

The lovely Marie, not yet the voluptuous Latina with full power of her long eyelashes and provocative eyes, might someday have adorned a Cuban cigar box in the traditional style. Her cousin, the bewitching Katie Huau Lorraine, opined that Marie's features, at eighteen, were still too soft and round. Could she really seduce a man into buying a cigar? In time, Marie could have become the beautiful "cigar girl" of historic dimensions, her portrait surrounded by primary colors and gold medallions. But Marie Louise's entrancing charms were never displayed on a cigar box. On the evening of April 20th, 1897, she collapsed over her knees, quivering with pain, a beautiful girl with .38 caliber bullets in her liver.[2]

* * *

Late that afternoon, through a palm-lined esplanade, Marie Louise Gato had left downtown and motored by trolley northward towards home. The trees on the Main Street esplanade were not the storied coconut palms or royal palms, charms of subtropical south Florida, but chunky cabbage palms with fortitude, serious-minded, like the city itself. The trolley wobbled and clanked up the street through scenes memorialized on postcards. The dwindling sun peeked through long fronds and rough curved bark ears. On both sides of Main Street, mansions with Greek columns and black iron fences stood in grand repose. Victorian Springfield, Jacksonville's first suburb, only lasted a few blocks and soon gave way to more bucolic scenes.

Occasionally, frightened horses squealed, shying at the clanging bell and the metallic screech of shifting rails at the switch, but Marie Louise saw another rolling diversion. A cluster of local Wheelmen pedaled hard on their two-wheelers past the streetcar heading north toward Trout Creek. The northern curve of the Panama Road running through Panama Mills led to the bicycle racetrack. The cyclers turned to look when Marie Louise called out to Willie, her older brother, who, embarrassed by her attention, raced away to avoid her and swerved off the road, stalled in grass and dirt.

"What's the matter with you, Gato? Scared of your gorgeous sister?" yelled other riders, happy to see Marie Louise. She greeted them with a practiced smile, her chin angled and slightly uplifted, then she waved goodbye as the boys pulled away.

The trolley ride ended at West 8th Street and Main, and scrub country began. She exited at the West 8th Street terminal, where there was a nearby footpath she normally walked through a forested patch toward her house. Scraggly oaks and Spanish bayonets covered the ground among pines and live oaks. The path opened onto fields and pastures and crossed the southern end of the Panama Road.

Gabriel Gato's house from the front

Two blocks north, her white clapboard house stood isolated in the fields thirty feet back from the dirt road. A white picket fence bordered the house, a narrow deep structure cooled by passing breezes and the shade trees surrounding it.

Gabriel Gato's house from the side. Grape arbor in foreground.

Marie's usual walk would take her beside the road between the yard fence and an old, broken plank fence once used for livestock. Sometimes as she approached her house, through the front window she could see the family gathered at the elongated table for dinner. They would be sitting beneath a Tiffany lamp, or a very good impression, that hung from the dining room ceiling.

That day however instead of walking straight home, she approached Lycurgus Bigger, a neighbor and fellow passenger who also exited at West 8th Street. Marie Louise told him she was nervous about an unfamiliar dark man who had also departed the trolley; he had taken her normal path, then paused to look back at her. Or so Bigger later claimed, she said.

According to Bigger, Marie Louise had said to him, "Something's wrong. Would you walk me home?" Bigger later was to tell police that Marie Louise had remarked, "A nigger wouldn't pay a nickel for that short ride. I don't trust him."

Bigger said because he was tired and carrying heavy packages, he didn't want to walk the extra distance. "If you come to my house," he told her, "my son will walk with you." Bigger also said he had not noticed the man and thought Marie was mistaken.

He turned away, leaving her by the tracks. Marie Louise lifted her hem above the dirt of the rutted road and hurried after him. She trotted behind him several feet until they reached his house, a block east of Main and a few blocks north. She waited outside on Bigger's porch for his son, John.

The sixteen-year-old boy came out the front door grinning, not the protection she sought, but he walked beside her and not two steps ahead. She thought about the father's rudeness walking in front of her. Some people in the town preferred a lighter skin color than hers. Perhaps he was one.

After ten minutes through the countryside and down the road to her gate, they stopped in front of her house. "I hope you felt safe," John said, grinning again, and with a tip of his fingers to his forehead, he departed, headed for home, kicking dust in the dirt road as he went.

7 p.m.

Marie tangled with a new latch on the front yard gate that Fritz, the Gatos' gardener, had mounted that day. Almost as defective as the previous one, it was equally hard to release. As she struggled against it, she smelled the sweet-scented jasmine newly in bloom and admired the white blossoms.

Scanning the area quickly, she sensed more than saw, a head and torso enmeshed in the leaves beside her. Eddie Pitzer, on his knees behind a rose bush at the front path, held a .38 pistol in both hands, aimed directly at her. She flinched, her sight on the gun. Pitzer often hid in the Gato shrubbery. He spied on the family, especially her, but that evening, pointing a gun at her, this was unique.

"What are you doing?" she shouted. At that moment the gate latch came loose and the entryway swung open. She stepped into the yard. Pitzer rose higher, but still on his knees, and aimed the gun at her head. "That's not funny, Eddie," she screamed at him.

Crossing her arms to protect her face, "Put the gun down," she shouted again as he pulled the trigger.

His first bullet grazed her temple, piercing the brim of her skimmer. The hat tumbled backwards to the ground. "Eddie, *estás loco*? Stop it."

She stepped back, her arms still lifted to shield her face. He crept closer, circling the bush on his knees. He fired another shot. It happened fast.

"*Imbécil!*" she called as his second bullet pierced her left elbow. It traveled through the uplifted arm, exited her hand, blew off her thumb, leaving a bloody lump.

A bag of candy she'd bought in town scattered when it flew from her hands. With a light splash, pieces plopped into the decorative fountain in the yard. She turned to run, but Pitzer moved forward on his knees, grabbed her skirt and held her in place.

She pulled against his restraint, but it only tightened his grasp. The hooks at her waistband bent open and her skirt fell. Pitzer held on, while she struggled against his grip, arms thrashing, legs straining. Still on his knees, close beside her, he angled three more bullets into her back. Marie Louise lurched forward, bent double.

The Gato family, eating dinner at the dining room table, annoyed at Marie's lateness, heard night calls of birds and insects floating through the open windows. Then gunfire exploded in the front yard. A scream streaked into the window behind it.

"That's Marie Louise," yelled Georgia Gato, Marie's older sister, scraping her chair back from the table.

"It can't be," said their mother, "she planned to stay in town at the Huau's tonight. Their step-grandmother, Eliza Huau, eating dinner with the family that night, leaped up, knocking her chair to the floor with a crash.

"She obviously changed her mind," said Georgia rushing behind her grandmother. Both Eliza and Georgia raced from the dining room to the entry hall. Mrs. Huau slammed open the front door, hitting the wall behind it and pushed past Georgia to the yard. The rest of the family tumbled out hurrying behind the grandmother.

Marie's body angled forward. Her head turned towards the house, she saw the family clamber down the piazza steps. Her mother, stately, all in white for dinner, stopped to steady herself on a balustrade.

"That's Edward Pitzer. I see you, Eddie," shrieked Georgia from the piazza as Pitzer, fumbling with Fritz's new latch, his back to the house, shoved a gun in his pocket. He had known the old latch well. Finally, the gate swung open. He dashed down the Panama Road then toward Laura which was paved with sidewalks towards town.

"Eddie has shot Sister," Georgia yelled from the porch.

Eliza Huau reached Marie first. "Oh, my darling, whatever happened? Look at me," she said, placing her hands on the girl's face, turning it towards her.

"*Abuelita*," said Marie, staring up at her grandmother, her eyes straining to focus, her pupils dilated. "Mama," Marie said softly to herself, swaying, still bowed at the waist. She held an arm across her abdomen and stared at the stub of her thumb, at the spring of her blood.

"Who did this, darling?" Eliza cried. "Who did this, Marie?" She cradled the girl's waist to prevent her falling.

"Eddie," Marie whispered. She gasped for air. "Eddie shot me."

Fritz Aberdeen, the gardener, eating his dinner in the kitchen at the back of the house, had heard the gunshots in front. He raced from the kitchen, across the side porch and yard, past the climbing grape arbor in time to see Marie stooped over, grasping her midsection, as her grandmother ran towards her. Edward Pitzer stood tussling with the new latch.

"Little one," Fritz said, speaking with an accent. "You will be fine. Soon." He scrambled to her. Over her shoulder, he saw Pitzer running. He knew he could catch him but he stayed with Marie instead.

"Help me, Fritz." Marie turned towards his voice. He and Eliza lifted her shoulders and with tiny steps, she crept between them toward the house. She swayed. Her feet dragged and wandered. Georgia held open the heavy front door and the family trailed in behind Marie. Enriqueta, the mother, replaced Eliza Huau beside her wounded daughter.

"Mama, Eddie did it. He was hiding behind the bush," said Marie.

Enriqueta nudged the clustering children away. Fritz helped guide Marie into the parlor. He lowered her carefully to the couch. Willie, arriving home, watched from the foot of the hall stairs.

"William, get blankets and the eiderdown," Enriqueta ordered. "Take the children upstairs and call Dr. Mitchell."

He rushed his brother and sisters up the steps and brought back the comforter.

Enriqueta unbuttoned Marie's dress and drew it over her head. The girl moaned as her mother slipped off Marie's chemise and untied her corset. Bullet holes the size of dimes, punctured her lower back. Enriqueta covered her mouth. A small amount of blood had pinked the edge of the three small red holes. No exit wounds. The bullets were still in her body. Enriqueta and Eliza looked at each other, rolling eyes, neither speaking.

Willie grabbed the telephone receiver from the wall and asked the operator for Dr. Mitchell. The doctor was sick, the office told him. Dr. Dean would come instead.

"I don't like that," Enriqueta whispered to Eliza. "Gabriel will call again when he comes home."

Marie reached for her mother's arm. Her gaze wandered up her mother's dress, resting on her face. "It hurts so bad, Mama." she whined. "Make it stop."

Eliza steadied the girl's shoulders, while Enriqueta arranged the comforter and bandaged her hand. A small string of pink froth bubbled on her forehead where the first bullet had grazed her. With a damp cloth, Georgia gently bathed the blood away.

A strong knock banged on the door. Startling them all, Dr. Dean had arrived. The sandy haired young doctor walked directly to Marie Louise. She felt him hold her wrist for a pulse. She felt his hand on her forehead.

Dean whispered to Enriqueta, "She's in shock and obviously, much pain. I'll give her a small dose of morphia to soothe her."

At 11th Street, a half-block south of the Gatos', the Panama Road crossed towards town. At the corner, John Bigger, walking home after accompanying Marie Louise, jerked still at the sound of shots. He turned to the Gato yard and saw flashes in the twilight. He fled from the corner, racing east on 11th Street and slammed into Charlie Flynn, a younger boy, who lived on the street. Charlie was running toward the commotion.

"You're not scared are you, John?" Charlie said, seeing John Bigger running away. "Come on. We have to see what's happened." As they headed toward the Gato house, John heard Gabriel Gato's horse and carriage turning from Main to 11th. When the carriage rumbled by, John grabbed the horse's bridle. It tossed its head and pawed to a stop. Gato frowned down from his carriage.

"There's been a shooting at your place," said John. "You better hurry," he called up to Gato. "We're heading there to see if we can help." In the background Charlie hooted, "Coward," at John.

"*Que demonios*? Sweet Mother of God!" Gato yelled as he entered the house. Enriqueta placed her hand on his arm. Marie Louise saw her father's dark mustache and whiskers. She reached up to touch him and he gathered her gently close to his chest. "Who did this, Marie Louise?" he whispered.

"Eddie Pitzer, Papa." Her voice was soft. "He did it from behind the bush."

"Darling girl," he said. "You will be fine." Turning to Enriqueta, his voice quiet, but tight and ferocious, "He will pay," he said. He noticed the doctor beside the couch. "Where's Mitchell?" He glared at the man.

"Dr. Dean," said Enriqueta, stepping in front of Gabriel. "Dr. Mitchell is a particular friend of ours," she said. Her voice was mild. "My husband will ring him to see if he is recovered enough to call on Marie. Please remain with us, also."

"I will be happy to assist," said Dean.

After calling the Mitchell house, Gato returned to say Dr. Mitchell would arrive shortly.

Aunts, uncles and cousins entered soon after. Enriqueta's brother, José Huau, took a chair close to Marie. The family gathered in the parlor on the chairs and the floor. The younger Gato children, frightened and still, snuggled in the laps of the older girls. Joe, the youngest, wept. Neighbors gathered in the yard.

Enriqueta paced through the house with a handkerchief in her hand, her long skirts rustling against the furniture. When she composed herself, checking her sobs, she returned to her daughter. She touched Marie Louise's cheek and kissed her.

Neal Mitchell, the town's most prominent doctor, arrived to examine Marie Louise.[3] Sitting beside her on a short stool, he pressed her wounds with flattened fingers. She did not react to his touch and seemed not to feel it.

"Her heart is racing. Her pulse is 185," said Mitchell. "Her blood pressure is very low. She suffers severe shock and is bleeding internally. We will not probe for bullets until she is stronger."

"I gave her a bit of morphine," Dean said. Mitchell nodded.

Neighbors and townspeople, restless for news, pushed into the bushes and fences. Uncle Huau explained the circumstances to them from the piazza, Georgia beside him. The trees in the distance faded in darkness. The night breezes blew.

Inside, gas lamps flickered. Electric bulbs shone in the hallway and kitchen. The children's tears flowed quietly. They could hear their sister struggle to breathe, but could barely hear her words. Other siblings had died as infants or youths, coughing and fevered, or never managing to breathe at all. None had died from a bullet. Then, Marie Louise lurched up and forward, regurgitating a stream of dark blood spoiled her clothes. It was a consistency of fine gravel. A guttural shriek flew out a window. Eliza Huau had screamed.

A collective gasp rose in the yard. The crowd grew silent. The death watch had begun in earnest.

Part I – Chapter 2

Police Arrive at Pitzers'

8 p.m.

The Jacksonville Police Chief, a burly fat man with a full head of white hair, wore his matching mustache in a catenary curve above his lip. A local hero, Chief John Keefe could easily lift grown men above his head.[1] Shot in the chest with buckshot and armed with only his club, he'd once subdued a gang of rioting mill workers, forced an assailant to his knees, and singly carried the man to jail.

A report to the police at 7:58 p.m. on April 20 relayed that Edward Pitzer had shot Marie Louise Gato in front of her house. The call rang in as the night squad rolled out. They headed straight to the Gatos' home.

Meanwhile, Eliza Huau answered Chief Keefe's telephone call at the scene. She strained to reach the receiver. "Yes, sir. It is definitely true," she said. "Dr. Mitchell is here now, as is Dr. Dean. There's a crowd in the yard. Eddie Pitzer did it. I saw him."

Not knowing Pitzer, Keefe consulted a city directory. He telephoned the home. "Are you Edward Pitzer?" he asked the man who answered.

"I am James Pitzer, his father."

"The Jacksonville Police Department here," the chief growled. "Where is he?"

"I don't know. Maybe at supper. He usually dines at Pigniolo's."

"He is accused of shooting Marie Gato. I'm coming to your house. Don't leave, James."

Pitzer hung up the receiver and stared at the phone, considering the call, before reporting to his wife. "That was the police department," he said to Tillie. "They have something to say about Edward."

"It better be something nice," she said.

James Pitzer's father, John, an Old West pioneer, had founded the town of Winterset, Iowa.[2] He owned sizeable acreage there, the first hotel in Winterset and the first store. He'd served as county treasurer and county judge. James, working in his father John's store in Winterset, had always been a shopkeeper. Now, Eddie, also the son of a shopkeeper, worked for James at his home goods store on Bay Street.

Keefe and Deputy Sheriff Vinzant drove the police wagon to East Beaver Street, the outskirts of town where the streets were dirt and bay trees grew plentifully. Keefe had sent a man to the Union Station to monitor who boarded trains.

Several blocks south of the Gatos' residence, the Pitzers rented a small frame house on a large estate where they had lived for a decade, moving to Jacksonville when Eddie was ten. He had played with the Gato children on their rambling acreage. The girls, especially, teased and chased him. When he poured a pail of water over Willie's head, they didn't like him for awhile. He didn't mind. He always went back.

Tillie Pitzer, Eddie's mother, had been Matilda Jane Cubbage, who came from Carnegie, Pennsylvania, across the Monogahela River from Pittsburgh. To be a Cubbage in that section meant respect from the neighbors and respectability.[3][4] It meant dressing well, never starving, never working in a mine and, sometimes, it meant real wealth. Tillie's grandfather, James, from County Down, Ireland, settled there in 1806. With that legacy, Matilda Jane maintained a fine sense of herself.

In the doorway of the Pitzer house, Chief Keefe addressed James Pitzer. "Your son is accused of shooting Marie Louise Gato. She's seriously wounded," Keefe said, his guttural voice, filling the hall "I'm here to arrest him."

Cubbage sisters of Carnegie, PA
Sarah Cubbage Hosack, Eddie's aunt, (far left), Matilda Jane Cubbage (Tillie), Eddie's mother (far right)

"Please," James whispered. "You've got to be wrong. You've made a mistake." His whisper was desperate. "My son doesn't shoot people, especially Marie. You're very wrong."

"Who is it, James?" Tillie called, pretending ignorance.

"My wife has heart disease. Please don't upset her," said Pitzer. "Don't come out here, Tillie."

"What do you mean 'don't come out here'?" A full-figured woman in a long print dress hurried into the hall, swinging her shoulders and arms. She clomped in sturdy shoes to stand by her husband, a thin man, slightly taller than she.

"They think Eddie shot Marie Louise," James said.

The short vertical lines above her lip hardened. "Are you mad? My son would never do such a thing. You dare not say otherwise. Perhaps you should leave."

To Tillie, there was no incongruity that Eddie, her son, the son of a small shopkeeper, attempted to woo Marie Louise. The fact that she was the daughter of a Cuban aristocrat, a well-known entrepreneur, who gave Christmas parties for 500 people, did not concern her. The Cuban girl's status remained beneath her son's. Tillie understood Marie was pretty, but Eddie could not love a dark-skinned foreigner. She would never be white enough.

"Tillie," said James, quietly, to placate his wife. "Come in, please," he said to the policemen.

"Eddie is a good boy and never touches alcohol," said Tillie, an active member of the temperance movement, judging things accordingly.

"Where is your son, Mrs. Pitzer?" asked Keefe, removing his cap.

"I don't know. He may be at the store or his rented room with Mrs. Pickett. He could be there." She loosed a hollow echoing sob, and James dug in his pocket for his handkerchief to give her.

"If my son killed Miss Gato," he said, patting his wife's shoulder, "he has killed himself. I would go look for him if I could leave his mother."

Keefe nodded. "Where would you look?"

"The store. Mrs. Pickett's boarding house or even the Gato place."

Searching the Pitzer house, finding nothing, the officers left. "If you see your son, call the station," the chief said.

Tillie Pitzer slammed the door behind them. "Yes, definitely count on our call," she muttered.

Part I – Chapter 3

Police Arrive at Gatos'

Leaving Pitzer's, crossing east on 10th Street to the Panama Road, the officers headed north to the Gato place. A few lights shone through the pine forest as they drove in the dark. They hitched the wagon to a side fence, next to Gabriel's carriage. Crossing to the front entry gate, past the bush where the shooter had hidden, Keefe strode through the crowd. More gawkers spread in the street.

"You're walking through the crime scene," one yelled.

"Don't step on clues," another bellowed. Raucous laughter surrounded him.

People hurried up Laura Street from town and down the Panama Road to join the throng. Lanterns and torches cast shadows through the trees. Cuban cigar workers, neighbors, and families gathered. People unknown to the Gatos, and the family unknown to them, paraded across the city to gape. Children were tucked under their mothers' arms. Prayers rose in the dusk and signs of the cross appeared.

At the edge of the crowd, two colored girls leaned together, eyes wide. Mouths shut tight. Their heads done up in do-rags, wearing often-scrubbed faded clothes, they worked cleaning the house across the road.

"Is this Pitzer a cigar man?" asked a Cuban, who stood in the crowd.

"No. He's white," someone answered and pointed. "He lived just there for years and years. And he's still around."

At the front door, Keefe turned, his deputy at his side. "Quiet," he yelled at the crowd. He lifted his kepi and smoothed his white hair. "Watch yourselves. I can hear, you know. It's no problem to scoop you up for a trip downtown."

When the door opened, Gabriel Gato flushed dark with anger. Georgia scrambled up from the floor. She pushed in front of her father. "Eddie did it," she blurted to Keefe. "Eddie Pitzer. Sister said so." Short and sturdy, she punched out her words. "I despise that boy."

Gabriel placed his hand on his daughter's shoulder. "He has annoyed us all for some time," he said, his accent loud and strong.

"I assume you're saying Edward Pitzer is not here. Where is he?"

"Ha! Yes, I saw where he went!" said Georgia. "I saw him run out the gate pushing a gun in his pocket. He scampered towards town like a scared mouse."

Keefe, from the hallway entrance, saw Marie on the couch in the parlor. He walked slowly toward her. Not knowing what to say, he rubbed the side of his nose and stared at her.

"Miss Gato, I am John Keefe, the police chief. How do you feel?" he asked in a voice softer than normal.

"Not very well," she whispered. Her eyes opened, but were narrow and drifting.

"I'm sorry you feel so bad, miss." He cleared his throat. "I'm also sorry to ask you, but did you see who shot you?"

"Eddie Pitzer did it," Marie said, hardly audible. "He was hiding behind a bush at the gate. He did it."

"Do you have any doubt about that, Miss Gato?"

"No, sir. I do not."

"Thank you, miss. I'm glad you are certain. Now, our job is to find the young man. Do you know where he might be?"

Before she responded, the telephone rang. Lieutenant William Gruber at the station had important news for the chief.

Part I – Chapter 4

Pitzer Surrenders

8:30 p.m.

Edward Pitzer usually closed his father's home goods store on Bay Street before 8 p.m., leaving early for the night. Most small stores like Pitzer's remained open as long as a customer lingered.

It was a soft, spring evening, good for walking. Wearing his derby, Eddie passed the barber shop next door to the Pitzer store. Beside the red and white barber pole, George Clark, the barber's son, leaned on the shop window. In his hand, he held a cigar on its way to his mouth. When he saw Pitzer, his jaw dropped and the cigar fell to the sidewalk.

"What are you doing sauntering around?" Clark protested, squatting to rescue the smoldering tobacco. "People are saying you shot Marie Louise. She might die and she says you did it."

"Say that again! That's stupid," responded Pitzer.

"You're stupid strolling about, because that's the word," said Clark. "Is she all right?"

Clark spread his hands, lifted his shoulders. Leaning back on the window, he'd said all he knew.

Pitzer returned to his father's store, as if he'd been there for hours. He locked the shop door behind him before he grabbed the phone from the wall to ring the Gato place. Willie Gato answered, not recognizing Pitzer's voice.

"She's been shot. Ed Pitzer did it." Willie's voice wobbled. "They're looking for Pitzer now." Pitzer hung up the receiver. For long seconds, he stared at the phone, circling the mouthpiece with his finger.

"You're right," Pitzer said to Clark outside. "I'm going to turn myself in. Those crazy Cubans will kill me." Clark watched Pitzer head east toward the police station. Store lights and streetlights crystallized ahead of him in the darkness. Eddie knew Marie would never say he shot her. He was convinced of that.

At the police station, Lieutenant Gruber worked on his nightly reports at his rolltop desk. His dark frock coat was draped on a hook beside him and his kepi and holstered pistol rested on the nearby shelf. When Pitzer arrived, Gruber looked up and waited for him. A photograph of the police squad hung above the front counter and Pitzer paused, staring at it. The lieutenant, on the front row in the picture, blonde, fine-looking, sprawled in his chair beside the other officers. Rank cops, horses and wagon assembled behind them. The squad room remained quiet except for the grind of Gruber's swivel chair.

"Is this new?" asked Pitzer.

"Last year. What do you want?"

"I'm not sure what to do."

"I'm not surprised," said Gruber. He knew of the Gato shooting and the allegation against Pitzer, but didn't recognize Pitzer from a wandering bone. Finally, the visitor said, "My name is Edward Pitzer. I think you're looking for me.

"I have a room at Mrs. Pickett's boarding house," he continued to blurt. "I have been at Pickett's since a little before seven this evening. I was talking to Cornelia, her daughter."

Gruber effortlessly, without noise or change of expression, rose and moved smoothly to Pitzer's side. He patted the young man's clothing for a gun. Without Pitzer realizing it, Gruber had blocked him against the counter.

"Those Cubans will come for me with everything they've got," Pitzer said. "Knives, guns, ropes, anything. I need protection." His voice rose. "I want someone to escort me out there so I can exonerate myself."

"You do?" said Gruber, tilting his head. "Let me get right to it." Pitzer nodded.

Then, Gruber twirled the lightweight Pitzer, pinning his wrists behind him, snapping handcuffs on his wrists. He snatched Pitzer's derby from his head. "I'll lock you in a cell but not for your protection," said Gruber. "You're a prisoner, not a ward. No exoneration tonight."

"I didn't do it. I didn't," Pitzer whined. "Ask Marie. Marie will tell you I didn't. Take me out there. I should have gone there first," he wailed. "But sometimes they're unfriendly. They might have shot me. Let me ask Marie. She'll tell you I didn't do it. You needn't take my word."

"If I drive you out there, they might shoot me, too," Gruber drawled. "So we'll skip that." He escorted Pitzer to the holding cell, taking his shirt, cuffs, collar and braces for storage. After shutting him away, he telephoned the Pitzer residence for the police chief, who had already departed. He reached him finally at the Gato home.

"Pitzer's here at the station, sir. Just dropped in, it seems. He's afraid of the girl's family and he wants protection to come out there. He's convinced the girl will say he's innocent."

"Interesting," said Keefe. "I'd like to see what happens between them." Gabriel, overhearing from the parlor, nodded his head in agreement. "Bring him out," said Keefe. "But be sure you're armed."

"Lucky you," Gruber said to Pitzer, at the holding cell. "They've agreed to let you come out."

"Good," Pitzer exulted. "You'll see. She'll say I never did such a thing. Has she recovered yet?" he stuttered.

"She's seriously injured, now that you mention it." Gruber unlocked the cell door. Pitzer began to cry quiet tears.

Gruber jerked him from the cell.

"Have you sent word to my mother yet?" asked Pitzer.

"No, I haven't done that. Actually, I won't be doing it."

"Please do," said Pitzer, crying harder. Whimpers, then a sob. "Tell her I didn't do it. Tell her I'm all right and not to worry."

Outside, a reporter watched Gruber and Pitzer board the back of the police buggy while a patrolman drove the horses. The reporter wrote that Pitzer seemed to labor under great mental excitement and acted much insane.[1]

At the Gato house, the chief met the carriage and led Pitzer up the front path by his elbow.

"Lynch him!" someone yelled, shoving towards Pitzer. A crowd packed behind him. "Lynch him or shoot him, like he did her." Patrolmen encircled the prisoner, thrusting their clubs at the crowd. Keefe elbowed a path for Pitzer and the wall of police surrounding him.

"I didn't do it," Pitzer pleaded to the crowd. "Ask Marie." They shook their fists and yelled. "I'll talk to Marie. She'll say it's not me," he yelled back.

"She says you shot her," Georgia screamed from the piazza.

A man in the crowd waved a pistol. Keefe grabbed the barrel and twisted it out of his hand. Gabriel had said Eddie could talk to Marie Louise, but the crush of people stormed the prisoner. Afraid the mob would kill him, Keefe motioned to turn him back. Lifting the prisoner under his shoulders, the patrol shoved him into the police wagon and Gruber climbed in behind him.

The crowd roared. The wagon crawled through crowded streets, brightened by handheld beacons. The whole city stirred. Clutched on porches, on corners and sidewalks, groups parsed gossip. Police patrolled dark downtown streets.

After Pitzer was removed, several men in suits and ties climbed the Gato porch steps, removing their hats as they entered the house. Justice of the Peace A. O. Wright, as assistant coroner, flourished a full bow tie. Dr. Mitchell had summoned Wright to evaluate Marie Louise's status. Sigo Myers, Gabriel Gato's business partner, also arrived.

Later in the evening, José Alejandro Huau, after consoling the family and talking with Marie, stood in the Gato side yard with his nephew, Alphonso Fritot. Huau leaned on the cane he normally carried as a matter of style. The sounds of whirring bats, the intermittent chirp of a restless bird stippled the night shadows. Huau rubbed his palm roughly on his forehead and bowed his head. His hat fell to the ground. Alphonso leaned to retrieve the hat. Close beside him, he heard his uncle's great sob and pretended he had not.

"I wired Domingo Herrera, the fiancé," said Alphonso in a whisper, handing back Huau's hat. "He's still in Cuba with his command. I'm sure he'll try to come."

Huau nodded.

***

John Bigger, the boy who walked Marie home from the trolley, and Enriqueta Gato, her mother, also shared the dregs of the evening. John saw her standing on the piazza and walked over to speak to her. The lady's black hair, pinned high, and her round brown eyes reflected the incandescent bulb in the hall. Even in the dim light her skin glowed hazily; the natural claret of her lips and the light café tones of her complexion warmed her expression. She leaned on the banister, despairing but gentle.

"Mrs. Gato, I have something to tell you," John said. For a moment, he felt a great love for Mrs. Gato and a great sorrow for her. With moist eyes, she turned to him.

"After walking Marie home," he said, clearing his throat, "when I turned the corner at 11th Street, I heard the shots. I didn't know if someone was shooting at me, so I ran toward Main Street. When I looked up, Eddie Pitzer raced past me. He turned right on Laura."

Enriqueta quickly stood and straightened herself. "Dios mío," she said, quietly, lifting her hand to her chest. "I cannot think it. He is more demented than I ever believed. You will tell this to the police, of course?"

"Of course," John responded. "I will help every way I can."

At that moment there was a scuffle in the Gatos' yard. They both turned to look. "No more disturbance, please," sighed Enriqueta Gato.

Chief Keefe, followed by Charlie Flynn, walked up the path. The crowd was still milling. Keefe and Charlie joined Mrs. Gato and asked to enter her house.

Lycurgus Bigger also walked up the path. He had given his statement to the police. He told them about the dark man who scared Marie Louise getting off the trolley. "John," he said, approaching his son on the piazza, "we need to talk," and gave him a rough gesture to follow him.

***

Later, in the Gato dining room, Charlie Flynn and John Bigger gave their statements to Chief Keefe. John watched and listened to Charlie recount that it was definitely Ed Pitzer who ran past them on 11th Street. Everyone in the neighborhood knew he had a crush on Marie Louise. He raced away from the Gato place, pumping hard past them.

At his turn to speak, John Bigger stared at the table and said quietly that the running man was much too big to be Edward Pitzer. Charlie spun and looked at John. "All I saw was a large dark man dressed in black," said John.

"Wait. That's not what you said before," Charlie objected.

"I made a mistake," said John. "I never was sure."

John looked up from the table. Mrs. Gato stood staring at him, perfectly poised and quiet, framed in the kitchen doorway with slightly raised eyebrows. She listened to him contradict everything he had told her earlier. At the sight of her still dark eyes, John rose, saying no more, and left the house through the hallway. His father was waiting for him outside.

* * *

Marie Louise died the following morning, April 21st, about eighteen hours after being shot. Her priest had visited. Her family surrounded her.

PART II

PAST EXPERIENCES

Marie Louise's Family

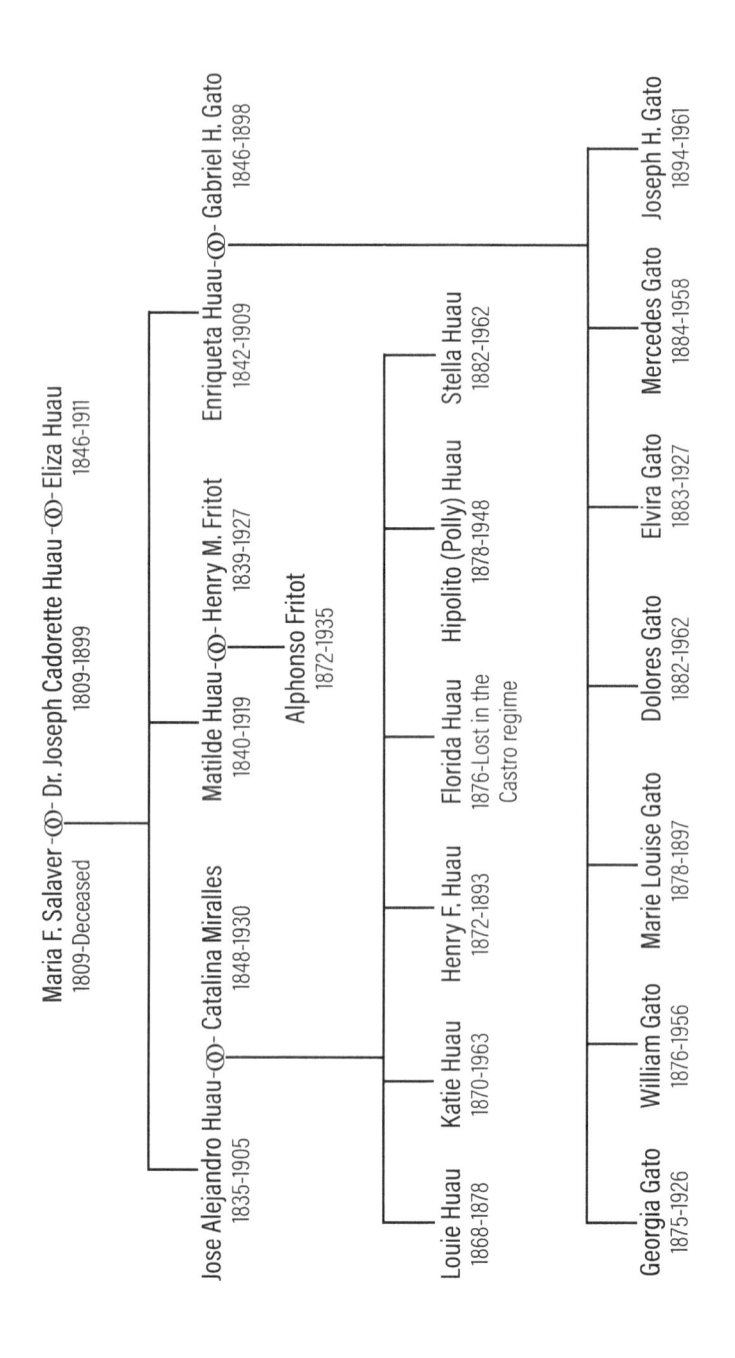

- Maria F. Salaver -ⓜ- Dr. Joseph Cadorette Huau -ⓜ- Eliza Huau
  1809-Deceased   1809-1899   1846-1911

  - Jose Alejandro Huau -ⓜ- Catalina Miralles
    1835-1905   1848-1930
    - Louie Huau
      1868-1878
    - Katie Huau
      1870-1963
    - Henry F. Huau
      1872-1893

  - Matilde Huau -ⓜ- Henry M. Fritot
    1840-1919   1839-1927
    - Alphonso Fritot
      1872-1935

  - Enriqueta Huau -ⓜ- Gabriel H. Gato
    1842-1909   1846-1898
    - Florida Huau
      1876-Lost in the Castro regime
    - Hipolito (Polly) Huau
      1878-1948
    - Stella Huau
      1882-1962
    - Georgia Gato
      1875-1926
    - William Gato
      1876-1956
    - Marie Louise Gato
      1878-1897
    - Dolores Gato
      1882-1962
    - Elvira Gato
      1883-1927
    - Mercedes Gato
      1884-1958
    - Joseph H. Gato
      1894-1961

II MARIE LOUISE'S FAMILY

Grandfather, Dr. Joseph Cadorette-Huau
1809-1899

Step-Grandmother, Eliza Huau
1846-1911

Father, Gabriel H. Gato
1846-1898

Mother, Enriqueta Huau Gato
1842-1909

Jose Alejandro Huau, uncle
1835-1905

Catalina Miralles Huau, married to Jose Huau
1848-1930

William (Willie) H. Gato, Marie's brother
1876-1956

Marie' Louise Gato
1878-1897

II   Marie Louise's Family

Alphonso William Fritot, a Fritot first cousin
1872-1935

L to R: Stella Huau Capers, Enriqueta Huau Gato,
Catalina Miralles Huau, Marie Louise Gato

Joseph Hypolito Huau (Polly),
Jose and Catalina's youngest son in WWI uniform.
1880-1948.

Stella Huau Capers, a Huau, first cousin
1882-1962

Beach Outing
From left, rear- Elvira, Joe, Enriqueta Gato; Katie, Henry, Catalina Miralles, Florida Huau; Marie Louise.
front-Dolores, Mercedes Gato; Polly Huau.

Part II – Chapter 1

Pearl of the Caribbean

Cuba 1851

The small black steam engine chugged along the short-line railroad between Bejucal and Havana, the first railroad in Latin America. One of the first in the world. Crossing green pastures and sugarcane fields, winding between the dark mountains, it hauled sugar to Havana for shipping. Returning, it carried news by rail to Don Francisco Hidalgo-Gato, the wealthy scion of an old Havana family, father of Gabriel H. Gato.[1]

The train pulled under the long covered platform, an open-air station in Bejucal. Cigar workers crowded the wooden benches waiting to travel to Havana factories. Don Francisco's farm laborers, wielding long carts with enormous wheels, loaded his tobacco aboard.

"General López was captured," the train conductor whispered to Don Francisco as the conductor dismounted his train's steps. "Every man in two small armies hanged. They garroted the general with an iron screw collar.[2] Bolted him to an iron chair and hoisted it high in the air to ridicule him and to scare insurgents." Originally from Venezuela and at one time serving in the Spanish army, Narciso Lopez' position had changed toward Spain. He hoped to preserve slavery on the island but also to annex Cuba to the American Confederacy.

The little train also brought Don Francisco news of the machete warfare of the Cuban guerrilla fighters against Spain. Although his personal views were private, slave-holding planters, such as Hidalgo-Gato, often aligned with Spain and might be guerilla targets.

The fighters, called Mambises after the Dominican General Mamby, rode in tan fatigues and straw campaign hats. When they charged, machetes aloft, their long mustaches blew across their faces. Most, farm workers and former slaves, used machetes to clear tropical jungles. Crisp chops of the blade hacked tough sugarcane like cucumber. Machetes transformed to weapons with ease.

* * *

Cuba 1860

From a hill above Bejucal, Don Francisco sat on his favorite horse. *Encanto,* a Cuban Paso, a small muscular descendant of Columbus' horses, carried Don Francisco great distances at great speeds. Don Francisco wore a flat-brimmed hat and a dark patterned bandana to search for wandering cattle in the relentless sun. As he stood near ruins of ancient battles, he watched a rising swirl of dust inch across the land below him. "It appears we have unexpected visitors," he muttered to *Encanto.* He turned the horse toward the dust cloud. *Encanto's* withers tightened.

Don Francisco watched through his small telescope. The riders turned toward his hacienda. He thought they were Mambises. His wife, children and house servants were there unarmed. He tugged *Encanto's* reins, rotating the horse's head. He prodded his spurs into its side. Armed only with a thin steel blade and a holstered long-barreled revolver, he galloped down the rocky trails.

At the bottom of the mountain, a draft horse hitched to a wooden cart waited while the wagon's occupants watched Hidalgo-Gato race towards them. Dressed simply, the people bowed their heads as *Encanto* drew closer at breakneck speed.

"*Buenas tardes, señor,*" said Gaston Barona Acosta, a local *notario.* "I think you know me, señor."

"I have seen you somewhere," said Don Francisco.

"I am a notary. I represent these people," Acosta said, sweeping his plump hand towards the group in the wagon. "Would you like to conduct business sitting down?"

"We are all sitting," said Don Francisco, wiping *Encanto's* neck.

"Very well, sir." The notary pointed to an older African woman. "That is Rosa. Rosa has a son, Toribio. She is a free woman. She wants her son to be free as well. Your slave, Samuel, fathered the boy. Toribio must have your permission for his freedom. I have drawn papers. If you sign them, the boy will be a freedman."[3]

Don Francisco considered the woman sitting in the wagon, her grey head bowed on her chest, her long straight hair braided into a rope.

"Hand me your papers." Don Francisco reached for them. "It is your custom to arrive unannounced?" he said. "Someday you may be shot."

At his barn, Hidalgo-Gato handed *Encanto's* reins to the stable boy. Micaela, his servant, opened the hacienda door for him. His boot heels struck the tile floors when he walked dim halls to his *oficina*. Plush cushions piled on dark carved furniture in his study. Numerous candles, numbers only the rich afford, stood in ornate candelabras. "Micaela," he yelled, entering the room. "There are five people in the grove who need something to drink."

Micaela responded with a questioning tilt of her head. "In the grove?"

"Do it," he replied. Her ruffled skirt, red and orange layers, swished in the quiet walkway. "And make certain Gabriel remains upstairs." Don Francisco placed the satchel on his desk. Acosta's file contained an affidavit for Don Francisco Hidalgo-Gato declaring Toribio, the son of his slave, a free person. Hidalgo-Gato remembered the birth of the boy. He remembered when Samuel told him.

Havana was the central slave market of the world. There was no incentive in Cuba to breed slaves or to keep slaves healthy. If a slave died or was maimed, a fresh slave, newly arrived on the docks, easily replaced the former. Prices were low. A buyer had only to choose a clean one, not infected in the hold of a ship. The handler would determine a slave's worth, while the family dined in the city.

Don Francisco considered the indulgence requested by Toribio. His eyes swept over the ancient swords on his walls and his ancestors' oil portraits in gold frames. His family's life had brilliant trappings, his surname, one of the three oldest in Cuba. Countless slaves were beaten, mutilated and killed at will. They lost lives and limbs in the slashing and grinding of the sugar mills, their bodies ravaged by constant labor in tobacco and sugarcane fields. Don Francisco's slaves were not. He did not approve of harshness, but he could not slow the tide of change nor could he induce it, but he would do this.

He reached for his pen and dipped the ink and wrote his name, signing the affidavit. "Micaela," he called. "Take this satchel to the fat one standing outside." She read across his shoulder. It was a dangerous thing he did, freeing the slave with no exchange. "Do it now," he said. "Return quickly. No conversation."

In the evening, Don Francisco sat with his friends on his portico, sipping an imported cognac, which the local rums could not yet match. Watching the sun slip behind the hills, apprehension grew within him. As he listened to the winds blow across the fields and brush through the palm fronds, the scent of revolution wafted again in Cuba. Gabriel, his son, watched from an upstairs room. He saw only his father relaxing with friends. He did not hear their talk.

"My land belongs to my family more generations than I could know," said a guest, seated in a spread-back wicker chair. A thin man, his legs in white suit pants, crossed sharply at his knees. His lank wrist dangled his empty glass over the arm of his chair. "If Spain went away, who would protect my land? We are happy Spain continues to embrace us. We are comfortable with her traditions, amigo. How could we be more content than to bathe in this golden sun that even now strokes us gently as it slips away until tomorrow?"

"I understand," answered Don Francisco. "But is it all right with you that Spain takes ninety percent of what is ours and spends forty percent on their army here? Get Don Tomás another drink, Micaela." Potted palms and crowds of multicolored flowers fluttered in the breeze around them. Night sounds of crickets and frogs rose from the hills. Bats swooped across the darkening terrace.

"That is all philosophy. I care nothing for it," said Don Tomás, raising his empty glass to be refilled, ignoring Micaela as she poured the cognac.

"Perhaps you prefer to think of freedoms and rights?" responded Don Francisco. "The slaves, for instance." Don Tomás drew back as if skewered by the leaves of the Spanish bayonet beside him. "You and I, we need slaves for field work and millwork. Insurrectionists need them for war. Slaves, of course, just want freedom." Don Francisco shrugged his shoulders and opened his palms. Still in his riding clothes, he scraped the heel of his boot across the ochre tile.

"This makes for dangerous times, does it not, Francisco?" said another guest. Shaded in the twilight, Hidalgo-Gato could hear the displeasure in his tone. "At least, we rest easy because slavers will always bring more imports of fresh Africans. That is right, eh, Don Francisco Hidalgo-Gato?"

His host did not respond but stared into the shadow. Don Francisco knew, in time, the *criollos*, many high-born Cubans of pure Spanish descent like himself, would engage against Spain. But it would not be tomorrow. Still, he smiled in his friend's direction. Was the man hinting at something? Could he know what transpired that afternoon with the local *notario*? He could not. Not so soon.

Don Tomás looked back and forth between the other two men, unsure of what he missed. Such things were always hard to determine. No one spoke for several moments. Don Francisco rose from his chair to leave his guests. "*Buenas tardes*," he said when he stood. "Call Micaela for anything you need, *por favor*." He bowed his head slightly to his guests, thinking, as he turned, *That was not good. I left in too much haste.*

In the descending dark, a small field mouse stuck its head over the edge of the porch. With rapid twitching of its tiny nose and quick, small jerks of its head, it scanned the tile floor. Perhaps Micaela had served some crumbs with the cognac she poured earlier. The mouse would not have minded.

Inside, the serving woman began to set places for the evening meal on the long, dark table in the dining room. The candles were lit, their shadows shifting on the walls. Silver serving pieces sparkled in the flickering light. At the end of the table, she placed two additional earthenware plates. Don Francisco heard the family upstairs preparing to descend the stairs. Micaela watched him. She had heard the group's discussion and she worried.

"Times are changing, Micaela," said Don Francisco. "Spain is losing its reason here but the barbarity will end. Slavery won't last forever. And Cuba will be free from Spain. Please, ask Gabriel to come to my office." He hesitated. "I must send him away soon," Don Francisco said in a quiet voice. In 1863, at 16 years old, Gabriel arrived in Savannah, Georgia.

He waved for the serving woman to remove the extra plates. "No dinner guests tonight," he said. "I'd rather serve a mouse."

Part II – Chapter 2

José and Catalina

Cuba 1868

An evening summer rain began. José Alejandro Huau, alone in his second-floor office, worked in the bleached stucco building of the Matanzas Railroad Company in Matanzas, a northern coast seaport town of Cuba. He listened to the full drops of water smacking the terrace outside. Scripting his resignation after a decade as a mechanical engineer, Huau was leaving the railroad.

As he worked, the door of the back hallway opened and closed. The floorboards groaned with footsteps. The Matanzas Revolutionary Committee gathered on the first floor. Heavy black ink flowed on the page Huau wrote. He had delayed his decision too long. The resignation must be done that night.

The insurgents would meet a ship from Florida at the Bay of Matanzas. Huau led the committee assembled in the building's basement, crammed between mechanical parts and lumber. His revolutionary leadership in Matanzas served him well for later filibustering activities from the United States.

José Alejandro Huau

Approaching the storage room, Huau heard the strident voices, the excitement. The night had been planned for months. "Quiet," Huau warned, opening the creaking back door. "You are not safe here. We are safer on the streets, so as to see and hear around us. Do not be caught tonight," he entreated. "Our comrades in the hills are hungry. Their horses are hungry. Tonight, if we do this right, they will have food and weapons. Rain is falling. It may ruin some explosives. There may be delays. Mountain roads may turn to mud. But rain always stops. We cannot stop. Let us go."

The Catholic Church, unpopular in the basement storage room, supported Spain, which the revolutionary group opposed. Still, several men crossed themselves. Distinguished in their suits and ties, they departed in silence, one by one. Quietly, they passed the colonial grandeur of granite and marble, limestone and stucco facades, ruined and cavernous from previous wars. Many more walls would disintegrate before Huau returned to Matanzas.

"That way," Huau ordered Henry Fritot. "Spread out."

The men slipped by La Catedral San Carlos de Borromeo, crossed the river on separate bridges, and crunched along a gravel path from town. Huau threw up his arm. They halted. Had he heard a twig snap? A patch of undue silence? If he had, lives could be lost.

A ship in faint silhouette waited close to shore. Prey to Spanish gunboats and American Coast Guard cutters, the ship would unload armaments to the rebels in Cuba. Then, shielded in darkness, she would escape to steam across the Florida Straits.

At an inlet beyond the curve of the coastline, Huau and the other revolutionaries hacked their way to the dunes through forested outgrowths and thickets of palmetto clumps. Looking down from the edge of the trees, they watched shallow waves roll across the beach below them. The shower had passed. The moon lay a ribbon of silver on the sea.

"God bless you and keep you safe," Huau whispered, as he watched the men descend the bank.

A dinghy from the cargo ship moored deep in the sand. He looked around him for peripheral movement, for unusual shapes in the moonlight. He saw nothing. The wind was up, blowing sea and sand on the American filibusterers unloading the boat for the Ten Years War.

Wooden crates, roped together, labeled "groceries" and "medicine," contained some food, guns and ammunition. The boxes creaked, pulled through the sand and up the dunes. The Matanzas men stacked them in a cavern covered by sea grass. Fighters from the mountains would retrieve the artillery soon. At the top of the hill, the men paused for a breath. Huau smiled at Fritot and slapped his back. Others shook hands. Huau's contacts from the United States, along with his brother-in-law Fritot's moneyed colleagues, had helped pay for the shipment secreted to the revolutionaries.

From the deserted beach, the sailors launched the dinghy toward the waiting ship. The two men pushing off screamed unexpectedly in the dark. Bright rifle flashes cracked nearby. Bullets powdered the sides of the dinghy and splashed high fountains of saltwater beside them. Arms in the air, blood streaming, the two sailors plunged sideways into the sea. Those in the boat scooped their oars to open water.

"Down," shouted Huau to the men of Matanzas. "Guns," he cried but he was too late. Spanish soldiers at the top of the dunes rimmed the embankment, trapping the Matanzas révolutionnaires. Huau, his arms in the air, scrambled from the shadows. "Detengan el fuego!" he shouted. "Cease fire! I am here alone. Take me and I will go anywhere."

"Señor Huau," called a ranking Spanish soldier, "Is it you? What a surprise. Why would you be sneaking about in the night?" The man approached. "Since I find you here, I am afraid I must chain you now for the long ride to Havana. Unfortunately, the ride is aboard your own train."

"You are too late, as always," shouted one of the rebels, as some of the soldiers ran down the hill. "See, now, the boat is already leaving." The man pointed to the retreating ship.

"Silencio," ordered Huau.

"You will not travel as you are accustomed, I am afraid, Señor Huau," the Spanish officer continued. "You will ride in the cow car. The cows will trust you, I know, and they will enjoy your company."

The Spanish soldiers recognized the révolutionnaires, whose arms they bound with thick, thorny rope, cutting their flesh, drawing blood. They prodded the men with the flats of their swords to hurry them through the underbrush.

"Someone more important than I will have much to say to you, Señor Huau," said the spokesman, "and he may not be so surprised that you are here tonight, sir." He turned to watch the ship at sea and motioned to it. "I am only sorry we cannot extend our invitation to them."

Sitting on the promontory at the neck of Havana Harbor, El Castillo de los Tres Reyes Magos del Morra named for the Three Magi seemed to bear no spiritual purpose. A stone edifice erected in the 1600s to protect the city from pirates and buccaneers, Morro Castle had enjoyed a moderate degree of success for that.

José Huau knew the outside of the fort. A small turret with a lighthouse projected a stark beam illuminating miles of ocean. Its odd geometry, built to conform to the shape of the outcropping where it sat, enclosed bastions, prisons, barracks, and wine cellars. Inside, imprisoned, Huau was lost in its labyrinth.

The interior walls of the castle remained cold despite the tropical sun. Human waste slid down chutes to the bay. Lanterns provided light and the smoke turned the walls black. Mold grew on the stones and prisoners snaked through the halls to avoid the slime.

Morro Castle

For nine months as a captive at the Castle, Huau lived in the dark, squatting to eat, waiting and sleeping, walking a continual circle in his cell. Then, one day, the guards came. "Levántese. Get up. Ahora, diablo." Pulling him from his cell, they handcuffed him, smearing him against the sludge on the wall, and dragged him to an open courtyard. He fell to his knees, squinting in the sunlight.

Three men sat at a scarred table. Huau raised himself to his feet and faced the magistrados, waiting for them to speak. "You will not insult us by lying about your intentions on the night you were arrested," one said.

"My intentions were clear," said Huau.

"You are safe, amigo," another said. "We will not promote your notoriety or your status, whatever it might be. Señor, you will not become a martyr through death or lengthy incarceration. You think others will follow you and become emboldened, Señor Huau? They will not. No one will follow you."

The third man rose from his seat. "You will leave this place. You will leave our country. Your name will be forgotten as if you never lived." He unlocked Huau's handcuffs. "Now, depart before we change our minds."

José's wife, Catalina, had arrived in Havana by train from Matanzas to escort José by carriage from Morro Castle. A tiny woman, younger than her husband, she knotted her black hair at the back of her neck as an older matron might do. From a wealthy family, Catalina still wore the highest quality black silk and lace while Huau was locked in Morro Castle. The ragged, thinner man, in need of a haircut, navigated the descending stone path to reunite with his beloved wife.

During her husband's imprisonment, Doña Catalina had prepared for their exit from Cuba. She said her prayers, lit candles in the basilica and visited shops along the Broad Way. She bought and sold carpets, jewelry, crystal lamps, and other fine goods. She accumulated cash and small items to conceal for the family's exodus.

"Ah, señora, a cup of tea?" the merchants had offered her when she entered their stores. They knew of Huau's imprisonment; she traded only at shops in sympathy. Her servant followed her carrying brocade bags of rich possessions.

"No tea today, gracias," she always said. "I have some special delights to show you. More interesting than tea, I think." The storekeepers locked their front doors and led her to the most comfortable chair they owned. Her servant delicately removed precious items from her bags while the storekeepers ogled. They did not examine her treasures; they knew their worth.

"Thank you, Marcos," she'd say to her servant, rising when the transactions concluded. The buyers handed her accurate stacks of pesos; she knew the numbers exactly and they never doubted she did.

Doña Catalina also had visited the better homes with her wares, often the homes of friends. They might have something marketable. Or they might desire something of hers. With them, she drank tea from porcelain services. With them, she smiled and told stories, while her sharp black eyes scanned the rooms. "This is my favorite couch in all Matanzas," she'd say, rubbing her hand in the deep velvet. Or, if she noticed a ring on her host's finger, worn for the occasion of her visit, she might murmur, "And how I love your sapphire." The stone lay in her hand before she finished her sentence.

Catalina purchased many precious jewels from her friends. People knew the days she would call. They marked the dates on her calling cards. On those days, they slung open their drapes to welcome her and to announce their presence at home.

Doña Catalina also planned their departure from Cuba. The City of Matanzas sponsored a winter ball for which lights were strung in the trees, a mariachi band played in the streets and bright burning candles lined the walkways. Inside the government building, a dance orchestra performed. Tuxedoed gentlemen gathered at the bar for a taste of good rum and a glass of Madeira to serve to the table of ladies.

In his black evening suit and stiff white shirt, José waltzed Catalina around the ballroom and out the back door. They ran to the docks. Jewels and paper money lined Catalina's ball gown. A small launch ferried them to the waiting ship, ready to embark for Baltimore.

José's sister, Señora Matilde Fritot, waited aboard ship with her boy, Alphonso, age three, who grasped her hand, too afraid to speak. She also held José's infant son, Louie, in her arms.

Alphonso remembered the night his family departed Cuba. He remembered the sound of the water lapping the sides of the wooden ship and Louie Huau sleeping throughout the journey, as babies do. No one mentioned the boy's father, who wasn't with the others, but the boy worried. Had they forgotten his father locked in the depths of Morro Castle? Quietly, Alphonso began to cry. No one noticed in the dark.

Part II – Chapter 3

JACKSONVILLE 1880s

At the corner of Bay and Main Streets in Jacksonville, Florida, a barber pole and folding sandwich sign at the door, stood the one-story brick tobacco store, C.M. De Huau's *La Favorita*. José Huau named it for his wife, Catalina Miralles De Huau. Huau's cigar manufacturing company filled an entire block, producing 6-8 million cigars a year, netting him $200,000 annually. His tobacco store and soda fountain, a favorite destination in town, added another $60,000 a year.[1]

A long awning shading the display windows, and a wooden walk ran on the front and sides of the corner store. Tall bay trees, with long shiny leaves, grew along the street that borrowed their name.

At that moment, a local merchant of estimable girth plunged through the doors of the shop, skidding on his side across the floor. Tumbling in after him, a second, equally outsized merchant followed in his sliding package of flesh, encouraged by the vice grip the first man had on his arm. One man combed a few strands of hair across his round bald pate. The other wore a sinister-appearing toothbrush mustache with flecks of grey that matched his fulsome hair.

The two men, Austrian immigrants, owning large competing dry goods stores on Bay Street, loathed each other. Face to face on the sidewalk in front of Huau's store, due to their hefty sizes, they could not pass at the same time. Neither would step aside for the other. A struggle ensued for the right of first passage, which resulted in their startling entry to *La Favorita*.

La Favorita, Huaus' tobacco shop, Bay and Pine (Main), circa 1870s. El Esmero factory owned by Huau located in the tall building on left.

Alphonso Fritot, Huau's nephew and Huau's son, Louie, played with colorful glass marbles on the wooden floor of *La Favorita*. Three years older, Alphonso was the master of the game. Alphonso, from the far side of a counter housing the shop's soda fountain, aimed his shooter toward the target marbles.

The tangle of the two large men, rolling on errant marbles, slid partially under Huau's showcase of prized meerschaum pipes, some in their leather cases. The collection, particular favorites of Huau's, sold only for handsome prices. Huau stood laughing at the collision until he realized the men had floundered under his pipe display.

Louie Huau, kneeling on the floor, saw an opportunity to beat Alphonso at the marbles game. He quickly thumbed his own shooter, popping a shiny agate by mistake at one of the merchants. The man squealed and rubbed his balding head. Huau leaned to pop Louie on his bottom, then hurried to protect his precious meerschaums. The men rose in silence, regretting their indecorous performance. Grimacing, they each bought a cigar and left.

Henry Fritot, Alphonso's father, and Gabriel Gato, Huau's brothers-in-law, also manufactured cigars but Huau's business surpassed theirs. Known throughout the state, Huau owned factories in Jacksonville and Key West. He also owned a cigar stand and souvenir shop in the Everett Hotel lobby in Jacksonville, called one of the nobbiest places in town.[2]

The Huaus and Fritots lived several blocks north of their Bay Street cigar businesses. White frame, handsome two-story dwellings, with piazzas on both floors, stood abreast. Trellises with twirling vines and tasteful white pebbles spread in the yards of brother and sister—José Huau and Matilde Fritot—his on the corner of Main and Union, hers one door south.

Jose Huau's house at Main and Union Streets. Huau stands on the first floor porch. His wife, Catalina, and children pose on second floor porches. Fritot boys stand on porch next door..

When Louie, Huau's eldest, died from a tropical fever at ten years old, Alphonso, who felt the younger boy belonged to him, locked himself in his bedroom for three days. He emerged only to follow Louie's casket up the dirt paths of the Old City Cemetery for burial.

In Dr. Joseph Hypolito Cadorette-Huau, José Huau's father, leaving his position as oculist and head of the Matanzas Military Hospitals, moved to Jacksonville with his second wife, Eliza. His daughter, Enriqueta, José's younger sister also joined them.[3]

In April 1874, Enriqueta and Gabriel Gato married. She was approximately five years older than he. The three brothers-in-law now owned separate tobacco retail and production facilities on the same commercial corridor.

José and Catalina's next child, Kathryne, called Katie, was born in Jacksonville in 1873. Two years younger than Louie, she arrived nattering, lecturing, managing. Smart and beautiful, dark and daring, Katie smiled, cajoled and threatened for whatever she wanted from the day she was born. Catalina Huau, alone, sometimes managed the girl by the strength of her own strong will.

Henry Huau, Katie's younger brother, born two years later, entered the world a natural gentleman with huge brown eyes. Katie and he resembled each other as if they were twins, both equally beautiful. Alphonso extended his caretaking duties to his younger cousins.

As they grew older, the three young people circulated in a socially smart set. The next day, the newspapers carefully reported their attendance at parties and events.[4] Articles included detailed descriptions of Katie's attire, her flowers, her carriage, and sometimes, her escort. It was also reported Alphonso and Henry always danced with the most beautiful girls at the hops.

Part II – Chapter 4
SPRINGFIELD

After the death of his father, Don Francisco, Gabriel H. Gato left Cuba for the southeastern United States with several of his former slaves. He lived in Charleston, Savannah and Fernandina before moving to Jacksonville in 1868 where he worked at Juan Garcia's cigar factory.[1] In1874, Gabriel established *La Favorita* Cigar Store and soda fountain, before José Huau purchased it from him several years later.[2]

1883

Gabriel's cigar business, however, took longer to achieve success. At last, the company thrived when wealthy men, Herman Myers, Mayor of Savannah, and his two brothers, purveyors of tobacco and spirits, invested in El Modelo Cigar Manufacturing Company converting it into the largest employer in the state.[3][4][5] Luring Huau's workers to El Modelo was Gato's initial effort as director of the practical manufacturing department of the company.

Halting on the stairs at the second floor of Jose Huau's building, Gato stepped into the expanse of the far-stretching production room. From a dark corner, he studied the quiet, vigorous industry of the craftsmen. Unnoticed, he turned back to the stairway and climbed to the third floor to a room similar to an open market.

Sheaves of tobacco piled against the walls and the heart of pine posts throughout. In the middle of this second great room, men broke open sheaves and spread the leaves on the floor. Other men stripped the leaves from stalks while trashing the stalks. Select leaves for filler and binder were gently transported to tables to be examined and selected for different uses and aromas. Knowing the origin of the leaf and how long it had been cured, the processor created the flavors of various cigar brands as carefully as a vintner chooses a grape. Gato did not stay long in this room. He was a seasoned processor himself. He returned to the second floor, the manufacturing room.

Over the background noise of the room, the Reader, *El Lectore de Tabaqueres*, read aloud to the intent workers in melodic, dramatic tones. He was clearly heard. Sitting on a platform built above the rows of tables, he read from newspapers, magazines, novels and poetry by Marti, Hugo, Marx and Cervantes, among others.[6]

His salary paid by the workers, he dressed in a superior suit and often wore a Panama hat. His black moustache flowed full and long. He educated the workers, men and some women, who learned the politics of America and Cuba, the trouble spots of the world, the outcome of sports events, and the activities of the local Board of Aldermen, including Jose Huau.

Startled, the man ceased reading as Gato ascended headfirst up the stairs. The workers below quickly looked up, almost in unison, to see why the lector quit reading but no one slowed production. Seeing Gato on the platform, they dismissed the interruption as minor.

"Senor," said Gato, leaning forward, "please make this announcement for me."

The Lector, still, holding his newspaper in both hands, did not respond to Gato, who was extending a small note to him.

"Senor," said Gato, "it is all right. You work for them, the cigar workers. This is good for them."

The Lector, confident in his position, maintained his demeanor, straightened his tie with one hand and reached for the note with the other. Without acknowledgement to Gato and without expression, he began to read the note aloud. Gato turned and descended the platform stairs, listening to his words as he left.

The Lector read: *The new El Modelo Cigar Manufacturing Company, recently relocated, will now pay nine dollars per 1,000 for Los Londres cigars. Skilled workers apply at the El Modelo offices.*

All takers will be accepted. Gabriel H. Gato. The Lector balled the paper note in his hand and dropped it to the floor. The workers heard the words but would not discuss them before they talked among themselves.

Gato stepped down to the first floor of his brother-in law's factory, the floor where mostly women banded and boxed cigars for delivery. A buggy waited at the back warehouse door for the boxes. Jose Huau abruptly stepped from his office and stood before Gato. He usually kept shop at *La Favorita* and his appearance, coatless, holding a pen, surprised Gato.

"*Buenos dios*, brother-in-law," said Gato, with a small smile, almost undetectable, running his forefinger down his thick, black sideburn. The marriage of Huau's sister, Enriqueta and Gato, for ten years, had not produced a devoted relationship between the two men.

"I heard the Lector pause," said Huau, "and then, resume with something not as melodious as he usually reads. Now, I find you in the bowels of my factory, without so much as greeting me first. What should I think of all this?" Huau's demeanor stern, his warm smile remained in his office where he had been working.

***

The newspaper announced Gato had outbid other cigar men to hire workers to roll a "laundry" cigar at his new factory.[7] He acquired many new employees, who stayed busy at the new El Modelo, but the "laundry" cigar materials were slow to arrive.

"Men, I would like to announce there is no such thing as a laundry cigar," Gato revealed one morning. The cigar is called *Los Londres*, The London, and the special cargo arrived by ship this morning. We shall disburse materials and begin work tomorrow." A great cheer rose from the workroom rollers without interrupting their labor. Gato continued, "I am sorry to say, you will not be paid our formerly agreed price. Your wage will be eight dollars per 1,000. That is all we can afford."

Pandemonium spread through the workroom as the laborers yelled, banged their fists on their tables, knocking chairs and benches to the floor. Cuban cigar workers were accustomed to waging effective labor strikes against their employers and they were beginning to prove it. Rising as one, as a crowd at a sports arena, they emptied the room in minutes. Gato returned to his offices.

Refusing to work, the men went out on strike. The Cigar Workers Union voted not to make *Los Londres* anywhere in the city for less than nine dollars per thousand.

"That was certainly well-played by him," Huau said to Catalina, in a droll tone, after he heard the news. "Gato just raised the price that all owners must now pay thanks to his expert management." The Huaus strolled home arm-in-arm when Jose left the shop for the evening. Catalina laughed lightly, her head tilting upward. Her brother-in-law never ceased to amaze her.

***

1887

El Modelo Cigar Manufacturing Company relocated four years later to West Bay Street near La Villa, expanding into a new three-story brick building covering a city block.[8] Bay windows on the top two floors looked south over Bay Street and the train tracks stretching along the river. The structure towered south facing the St. Johns and the wharves from the railroad yard. Gabriel Gato held open the front doors of the new El Modelo Cigar Manufacturing Company for his family to tour the premises.

El Modelo Cigar Manufacturing Company, West Bay Street 1884

Inside the factory, Georgia and Willie held the hands of the youngest Gatos as they walked the hall. Elvira Gato, reaching up to hold her mother's fingertips, resembled Marie Louise and Willie, tan like their parents with large dark eyes. Georgia, the oldest sibling was lighter and had a broader face.

Marie Louise marched ahead of the family as they toured, inhaling the rich aroma of stripped tobacco. Although she had never been, Marie Louise imagined herself in Cuba, walking on rich Cuban soil, listening to the expansive tobacco leaves rustling in the breeze. Occasionally, she thought she saw the overseer on the side of the fields puffing a freshly rolled cigar.

Marie wandered first into El Modelo's rolling room, staring at the rows of long tables in two groups with an aisle in the middle, extending across the entire second floor. Dark men sat side by side, heads bent forward, silent and still, but for their whirling fingers. A few men, but not many, used wooden molds to form their cigars. The oldest practice was to construct a cigar using only their hands. A matter of pride, molds were considered new-fashioned, not part of a cherished tradition.

Sometimes Marie stopped beside a table to watch a roller. If the man's fingers did not slow, and he didn't look in her direction, she fluttered her skirts and leaned towards him to get his attention. She made a little clicking sound with her mouth and winked. The man worked on without response. The cigar count at day's end outweighed the importance of *el patron's* daughter anytime.

"Marie, come back over here," Gato called to her. When she turned towards him, she realized Elvira had followed her from the family group. Copying her sister, the little girl, a toddler, also held her skirt in her hands and flounced it like Marie. When Marie spotted her, Elvira looked up and smiled.

"What are you doing?" Marie shrieked and slapped Elvira's shoulder. The girl cried out, teary, and ran back to her mother. Enriqueta reached out to Elvira, and rubbed her shoulder. Leaving the family, she grabbed Marie's arm, yanking her back to the others.

"You are so jealous of a small child, you would hit her?" Enriqueta said. She shook Marie's shoulders and squeezed her hand until she flinched. "You will never touch another of my children in such a manner, do you understand?"

"I do, Mama," Marie whispered, drawing closer to her mother's side, "but I was not jealous."

"What was that? *Santo Infierno!*" Gato called but not a single worker stopped rolling cigars to look at him. "These men have jobs," Gabriel said to Marie. "I am sorry you do not understand that."

"I am not jealous," she said again to her father. Under her breath she muttered, "Why would I ever be?"

***

1888

One night at the evening meal, Gabriel announced to the family that they would be moving to North Springfield, far away beyond Hogans Creek north of town. The younger of the Gatos' five children stared and squirmed. Some tears flowed. Another upheaval, another move. Away from things known and manageable, familiar streets and places, family, friends and neighbors. The family had moved from place to place in Jacksonville for Marie's entire life. For this move, she was eleven years old.

Enriqueta drew a sharp breath. "I'm sure it will be beautiful in the country," she said, her face expressionless, but her voice soothing. "We will have a telephone. The trolley is only a few blocks from the house and the Panama Road crosses in front of it. You will see more people there than you do now."

"Only dairymen and farmers," said Marie.

The Gatos' new house stood approximately two miles north of downtown. Small dwellings and outbuildings spotted the acreage. Gato had built additional small homes for some of his cigar workers on his land.

The Gato family carriage rattled over the plank bridge on Hogans Creek, the tidal creek running off the St. Johns, neatly looping north of the city, lassoing the town's boundaries like a cowboy on a pony. The foul black waters spread into a cypress swamp, connecting acres of ponds and lakes of vast depths. Often a stench hung over the water, oozing with greasy peat and floating creosote waste from sawmills and factories, including a fertilizer plant. Marie Louise peered from the window of the carriage bumping its way across the creek. She felt she was crossing the river Styx.

After bouncing on dirt roads and rough pavement to the new house, the Gatos stepped from the carriage, one by one, looking up, staring, astonished at the formidable dwelling. A Victorian Eastlake design with lathed pegs and balustrades. first and second floors hosted broad wraparound piazzas decorated with catenary arches and decorative pieces like treble clefs.

Gato, in a black suit and holding his hat by the brim, stood on the porch watching his family arrive. His hand draped casually on a railing. He could not conceal the excitement in his eyes. He raised his open palm, presenting the house to his family. All but Marie Louise walked quietly up the steps, turning right and left, hesitating, emitting small assertions of admiration.

Marie Louise wondered who else was nearby to admire the house. Who would she impress in her new residence? There was no one there she cared to interest. Nearly twelve, she thought of her gregarious, beautiful cousin, Katie Huau, living in town. Katie would not tolerate this isolation. Marie resolved not to do so either.

She would wait to inspect the house. Instead, she wandered to the south yard, meandering through the shriveled garden and brittle twigs of an old grape arbor. She reached up and ferociously yanked the shriveled vines from the frame. She tramped through the pine forest. She hated the pungent scent of the pine needles. She crushed them in her hands. She turned to look back at the house, the focal point of all its surroundings, a fancy lace handkerchief dropped into a field. She wished it could lie ignored where it dropped.

Returning to the piazza, she heard Papa speaking of growing oranges and lemons and grapes for wine. A mix of swirling colors. Then he spoke of curing tobacco and fermenting the leaves. Dull brown tones of half-smoked cigars surrounded him. Marie saw the monotony of tobacco fields, mixed with the colorful fruit, an anomalous dream at best.

As Mama had said, the Panama Road stretched across the front of the house. It was known to be a busy byway, but Marie doubted it was true. Tromping through leaves on her way to the house, she saw a boy staring at her from the road over the livestock fence. His red hair glinted in the bright sunlight. In a white shirt with suspenders, he stared at her with grave intent. A peeping Tom in light of day.

Marie Louise knew how to dismiss a man. With an insolent glance in his direction, she turned to a side entrance of the house. She had watched Katie, her caustic cousin, for years. Katie rarely obliged.

The red-headed boy yelled across the expanse between them. "How old are you?"

Marie's head turned abruptly toward him. Her eyelids folded as she squinted at him, her expression blank. She detested his stare, his unannounced creeping on the empty road. Where was his jacket? His hat? She turned away again.

He yelled. "What's your name? I'm Eddie." She continued to the porch without acknowledging him.

"I live down that way," he said, pointing. She pulled open the screen door and stepped into the kitchen.

***

Marie Louise had heard a story, which recurred to her at the moment. A man on the far outskirts of the city, after bolting himself in his shack, had accidentally shot himself in the head. As his body angled forward, his head turned towards the bolted door. A wandering hunter heard a howling dog trapped inside the shack with the dead man. Approaching the cabin, he heard the dog's body slamming against the inside walls. When the hunter broke open the door, the scrawny cur inside, ribs protruding like a rough-woven basket, surged from the cabin and dashed into the scrub surrounding it. Having eaten the head of its dead companion, the dog disappeared in the woods, its sorrowful moan lingering long afterward. Old man Jubal and the trapped animal, both mired in isolation. Marie shuddered, remembering the incident. She found the story foreboding.

Part II – Chapter 5

Edward Pitzer

Edward Pitzer, the red-headed boy who lived down the Panama Road, kneeled beneath the windowsill outside the Gato kitchen. He did it from time to time. He wanted to be close to Marie Louise. When face to face, she ignored him. Familiar but unrecognizable Cuban Spanish floated through the kitchen window. The boy could identify people as they spoke.

"I love her," he said to himself, when he heard Marie's voice.

Occasionally, he popped his head up to peek inside the kitchen. Occasionally, someone inside came out and caught him hiding by the steps, surprising him as he crouched. Depending on who discovered him, the consequences would be different. Enriqueta might gently chase him away or threaten to call his mother. Georgia, the older sister, would scoff at him and deride him.

This day was different, and he knew he would be smart to leave. Katie Huau was in the kitchen. Eddie knew enough about Katie to be nervous. Most people knew her and were happy to be in her company. She was beautiful and smart and a witty flirt, but with a strong will and a strong tongue.

Her father, José, would smile and look down at his midriff, shaking his head, when she flared in his presence. "Oh, Daddy," she would say and laugh, "You know I don't mean a thing I say." Still,

Eddie knew if Katie caught him eavesdropping, she might step outside and poke him with a fork. She might whack him with a ladle.

* * *

By the time they were teenagers, Eddie called on Marie Louise as if he were any young man calling on his sweetheart. The family found him annoying. Georgia did not hesitate to tell him so. Sometimes, Marie opened the door with a huge smile when she saw him. Some days, indifferent, she invited him into the parlor and left the room. Perhaps she would return and perhaps not.

Once, she did not answer his knock. He slammed his fist into the side of the house. "I don't understand," he screamed at the closed door. "I thought you loved me," he yelled. The next night he banged fiercely on the door. When Marie finally cracked it narrowly, her face was dull, her expression blank.

"I have something to show you," Eddie said, pushing open the door. "This is mine," he said. "I'm a pretty good shot." He pushed a pistol through the narrow slit, barrel first, close to her face. "And look at this," he said, shoving his other hand through the space in the door. "Isn't this the biggest butcher knife you've ever seen?"

Marie screamed. He stepped into the foyer and watched her run down the narrow dark hall and up the stairs. "Papa," she shrieked as she headed up to find him. "Come here," she called, her voice gathering tears. Eddie listened to Gabriel's heavy footfalls bang quick-time down the naked stairway. "Look what he's got," Marie said, pointing to the gun and knife Eddie held in his hands.

"What are you doing, Pitzer?" Gabriel's harsh voice filled the house.

The boy backed wholly but carefully away from the man onto the porch, then suddenly changed direction and ran at Gato and the stairwell. He held his blade high above his head, then with great force stabbed his knife as violently as he could ram it into the wooden step. It wobbled upright, stopping straight up.

Eddie paused, glared at Gabriel, still on the stairwell, grabbed his knife and pulling it from the step, broke the metal tip off deep in the timber. Running to the front porch, Gabriel's footsteps pounded close behind him. Then there was a paralyzing grip on his shoulder. He tried to shake off Gabriel's hand while he squatted on the piazza. He reached back and ran the blade across Gabriel's hand, freed himself and paused long enough to sail the broken knife and the pistol over the banister and across the yard. Whirling down the front steps, Pitzer dashed away. The next morning, Gabriel found the broken knife in the yard but not the gun. It had disappeared.

Part II – Chapter 6

Domingo Herrera

May 1895

    Although the struggle between Cuba and Spain had brought the Cuban families, the Huaus, the Gatos and the Fritots, to the United States and to Jacksonville, the federal government remained determinedly neutral in spite of its citizens' enthusiasm for Cuba's insurrection. To deter those suspected of aiding Cuba, Pinkerton detectives lodged in every pothole in Jacksonville's roads, in every crack of its boardwalks.[1] They were to block all activities of Cuban assistance and to be alert for Spanish spies.

    The Pinkertons shadowed Huau and his best hand and nephew, Alphonso Fritot, from their breakfasts to their chambers. Sometimes, the two employed decoys of themselves for the spies to observe while the quarry dined out or sailed a skiff up the St. Johns River.

    On the night of a cotillion at the Florida Yacht Club to honor visiting U.S. naval officers, Catalina Huau looked out her upstairs window. "They're out there now, José," she said, pulling aside the shade to watch the Pinkertons prowl the street. The Huaus would be attending the dance.

    "We are going, Catalina," said Huau, grinning at her. "And we will walk the eight blocks to the river. They cannot cut our throats while we are ambulatory. Besides, you get such pleasure showing off your figure." He winked at his wife. Catalina crimped her lips. She opened her cabinet and retrieved her gloves and purse.

William Astor, Jr. had promoted the Florida Yacht Club which sat eight blocks south on Market Street to the river. Coincidentally, Astor was the only member who owned a yacht. Alphonso Fritot, also a member, possessed a naphtha launch, similar to a small steamboat for those who had no steamboat license. The naptha was bought for revolutionary purposes but Alphonso ran it in Hodges Creek. Huau found the one-yacht yacht club comical. Always a gentleman, only Catalina could detect the amusement in Huau's eyes. One day, Alphonso, with a real boat, would rise to be commodore of the club.[2]

The clubhouse built over the St. Johns River surrounded by broad boardwalks tracked a long wooden dock to shore. Domingo Herrera stood on the club deck waiting for the Huaus to arrive. The young Cuban patriot, a Cuban Army officer on the staff of General Calixto García and friend of Huaus, hoped to join Huau's sophisticated filibustering.[3] [4]

"Your friends are with you, I see," said Herrera, greeting the Huaus while nodding toward the Pinkertons. Alphonso, inside the club, saw them all arriving and went out to escort them to the dance. Holding the hand of his 16-year-old cousin, Marie Louise Gato, to greet her aunt and uncle, José and Catalina and to meet Domingo Herrera.

The luster of the electric lights spread across the room and over the waltzing dancers. A string band played from a corner platform. Alphonso leaned to kiss Aunt Catalina on her unsmiling cheek. Marie Louise, in pink satin and lace, also stepped forward to embrace the Huaus. José smiled lovingly at her and bent to kiss her hand.

"I would like to introduce you to my cousin," Alphonso said to Herrera, standing beside the Huaus. "Marie Louise rode with us in our carriage tonight." Herrera stood straighter and gave Marie a brief bow and a smile. She greeted him with her outstretched hand.

"How do you do?" she said, inclining her head slightly to the young soldier her eyes wide with approval.

When they began to dance, Domingo filled all free slots on Marie's dance card. As they floated by Catalina, Marie knew her aunt was watching. She tried to lose herself amid the swirling couples but at 10:30 p.m., the band retired for a break. In their formal black attire, they crossed to the outside rail to smoke. Crossing the empty floor, Herrera ushered Marie to Alphonso and bowed slightly to his friend.

"I have a question to ask you, my friend." His eyes crinkled when Alphonso looked up. "May I escort Marie to your Uncle Huau's home this evening?" asked Herrera. "It is close by, I know, and I understand she will be staying the night there. I shall take every care for her safety, more than I shall for my own." He smiled at Alphonso, standing especially straight, placing his hand on the hilt of his ceremonial blade.

Standing to greet him eye to eye, Alphonso smiled, too. "Don't tarry, Domingo," he sternly said with a waggish expression. "I told Uncle Huau she would be home by eleven o'clock."

Herrera nodded and snapped his heels as he and Marie Louise, her arm in his, stepped outside to the club's deck. They listened to the river ripple beneath their feet. Reflections from the lights inside danced on the tips of the current. For a few moments, they sat on the porch watching the reflection. They watched illuminated shadows of the warehouses on the south bank. Ferryboats, blasting horns, paddled back and forth across the dark channel. He touched her hand. She looked up and smiled at him.

"We must go," said Herrera, checking his watch. "I promised Alphonso." He raised his eyebrows. In silence, they returned to Bay Street by the wooden dock.

James Pitzer, Eddie's father, owned a small home goods store on West Bay Street, four blocks away from the Yacht Club. Pitzer, who clerked in his father's store, was restocking shelves later than usual. Having emptied the shipping boxes, he stepped out to the street and locked the front door. Voices in the distance and leisurely steps scuffed towards him on the sidewalk. The dim streetlights abandoned the streets as dark and mysterious. Pitzer backed against the store wall further into his shadow.

His heart leaped when he recognized Marie Louise walking toward him with an unknown man from the club. Holding the handle of his bicycle, leaning upright against the wall, Pitzer silently watched them approach.

On occasion, he had seen Marie Louise talking or strolling with other men. He thought they were her brother's friends or an acquaintance from her uncle's shop. This man wore a Cuban army uniform. Marie Louise was smiling. They were laughing. Closer, they approached. Eddie shoved his bicycle, rolling it upright, into the light, into their path. She nearly stumbled. He stepped into the measly light.

"What are you doing out here?" he growled at Marie Louise. She stopped.

No more laughs or smiles.

"We're walking, Eddie," she said, "as you can see. What is it you claim to be doing?"

"And who are you?" Pitzer asked Herrera, demanding. He observed the Cuban's smart uniform. Herrera did not answer. Pitzer turned again to Marie Louise and reached for her hand. She jerked it away. "Why are you not chaperoned?" he asked.

"What's wrong with you, Eddie? Go home," she replied.

"¿*Quién es éste?* Who is this?" said Herrera, his eye on the stranger.

"Eduardo Pitzer, *un amigo*," said Marie Louise. "This is Domingo Herrera," she said to Pitzer. "Now, Eddie, leave us alone. We're walking home."

"I doubt that," Eddie yelled. Jumping forward with a closed fist, he knocked Herrera in the jaw. The man's head jolted back but his hand came up, delivering a punch to Pitzer's rib.

Bent over, throwing an arm across his stomach and gagging, Eddie responded, "This is unacceptable, Marie." He coughed. "We'll discuss it later." He took several deep breaths and straightened. Still coughing, he climbed on his bike and pedaled away, looking back and glaring.

Part II – Chapter 7

MARIE'S SHOPPING

January 14, 1896, 6 p.m.

Marie Louise stepped into the porcelain tub, sturdy on its claw feet. Micaela had braided her hair to keep it dry. Holding the woman's hand for balance, Marie Louise slipped in the high tub, swooping down the slippery surface and bumping onto the bottom.

"*Estúpida! Eso me dolió*—that hurt!" she yelled at Micaela, yanking her hand away. Water splashed across Marie's bronze legs. With her cupped hand, she sprinkled bathwater on Micaela's red-swirled skirt. The woman smiled slightly and turned away.

From her bath, Marie Louise could hear her father's horses trotting along the carriage path. She knew Felix Aberdeen, the gardener, as he liked to be called, was grabbing the reins to drive the horses to the barn.

"And why did you not tell me Father was returning early?" Marie Louise snapped.

"It is not early, señorita. It is the same time as every day."

Marie Louise was nervous. Today was rare, a full day of freedom. As she promised herself years earlier, she strolled away from home alone. Without Mama's counseling. The children shuffling. Or Papa glaring.

Marie envied her Huau cousins who had so much more freedom. They spoke English, attended private schools and several attended college. Even Katie, whose tongue could slice a pineapple, never complained about her father and managed to be mostly courteous to him.

Now, Papa was home. Marie couldn't relax in her bath as she had planned, and she was nervous about encountering him downstairs. She had not yet moved the packages she bought downtown. They still piled high on the back porch.

Micaela returned to the tub and leaned to hand Marie a towel.

"Oh, go away," Marie said, splashing more water.

Micaela pushed a wave of water back at the girl. The tall handsome woman, born in Cuba, had lived in the household of Don Francisco in Bejucal. She had shared the slaughter of the blood-stained wars and the violent loss of the home she had known. Immigrating with Gabriel to the United States, she lived with the family. The children saw her as a visiting aunt, or some other close connection, except for Marie Louise, who mostly saw her as useful.

Marie had begun her free day by clothes shopping on Bay Street.

"Hello, hello, Marie Louise, darling. Always a pleasure to see you. For what are you looking today?" said the store owner, with his prominent stomach and his obnoxious, at least to Marie, toothbrush mustache. Supposedly a friend of her father's, he took her hands and beamed at her. All the merchants on Bay Street sounded like he did, as if they had carefully transported their matching accents from Eastern Europe.

Marie Louise smiled, remembering the story she had heard about his rolling under Uncle Huau's cigar counter while fighting another fat, round merchant. Even Gabriel found that amusing. The man guided her through the aisles of his store, his hand placed on her lower back, stroking up and down. Startled, she turned to him, but afraid to offend him, she allowed him to guide her to the undergarments section.

"Don't you have female clerks?" she asked.

"Oh, I know my own stock better than any of them," he said. He reached to pat her shoulders, sliding his hand to her waist. Marie looked around. The store was empty of customers.

"Goodbye," she said abruptly, backing away. "I'll tell Papa I saw you."

She walked quickly to Cohen Brothers up the street. "I certainly will tell Papa I saw you," she mumbled.

Cohen's, the biggest department store in town was a more current retailer, with big glass windows and high polished counters. They maintained fixed store hours, fixed prices, exact change and did not barter. They were modern. Marie liked that. The Cohen brothers once carted pennies home in bags from New York when Jacksonville suffered a penny shortage.

"It suits you, miss," the Cohen's shop clerk said. Marie chose her merchandise from the glass display cases and long racks of hanging clothes. She charged her father's account. A delivery boy, in a short-billed cap, transported her brown paper bundles by bicycle to the Gatos' lattice-enclosed back porch.

* * *

Marie, still in the tub, started when she remembered the packages.

"It's too late, señorita," Micaela said, understanding. "I'm sure your papá has already seen them. Would you like me to retrieve them for you now?" she asked with a teasing look.

"Of course not," said Marie, grabbing the sides of the tub to lift herself out. Micaela again offered her a towel which Marie refused. Tracking wet footsteps across the floor, Marie glanced out the window at the distant pine trees anchoring the pink and blue washes of the sky. Papa's vast acres would always feel like a walled convent to her.

Dressing for the evening, she wore a tan shirtwaist trimmed with beige lace which she had owned for some time. She descended the stairs to the first floor, heart pounding but chin up. Her father walked towards her from the kitchen. She could see where the packages had been moved to the dining room.

"So, you will join us for dinner?" he asked, observing her dress. "Or are you going out?"

"Yes, of course, I'll be joining you for dinner. As always."

"I was not sure you had finished your shopping," he said.

She paused at the threshold of the dining room. The smells of garlic and roasting pork, the clanking of forks and spoons, and jabbering children annoyed her. Enriqueta, standing by the table, watched her daughter's and husband's eyes meet. Marie Louise's shoulders tightened. Gabriel walked towards her, heavy boots banging on the floorboards.

"I know the needs of this family," Gabriel snapped in her face. "It needs what I say it needs and nothing more. I decide what is bought and delivered here. More important, how dare you wander the streets unescorted, enter mercantile establishments without your mother? That does not reflect well on me, your wandering like a stray dog."

"Yes, Father." she said, then turned and walked to a chair in the parlor. Sitting, she leaned against its plush cushions. After so many years in this country, she thought, he still speaks louder and faster in Spanish than English. She looked up at him.

"I am eighteen years old and a woman. You don't know what I need!" she said. She knew the clothes were hers to keep. Gabriel would never allow her or her mother to carry bundles or return purchases. That, too, would reflect badly on Señor Gabriel Gato. He, himself, would never touch a woman's garment.

"I ran into my friend today on Bay Street," her father said. "We walked a few blocks together. You had a shopping expedition at his place this morning, as well, he said?" She stared at him. "Is this true?" he said. "Answer me. Is it true?"

"I do not think your good friend, would lie to you," she said. "Did he also tell you he touched me, rubbed my back and waist and further?"

Gabriel stopped, his face inflamed. Enriqueta gasped and Willie's face paled. Gabriel moved closer, silent, staring at her. His thick dark beard began to quiver in anger.

Suppressed ticks of silence filled the room. Marie spoke first, looking down at her lap. "There were things I needed," she said absently. "But I didn't get them. I left soon."

Father's and daughter's vision fastened again but both were silent. Then with a dissonant gulp, almost a sob, Gabriel ruptured the quiet. "Never go near that place again." Then more sturdily, "*Nunca más*! Never again!" he said.

Marie stiffened in her chair, watching him. He reached out to her, taking her wrist with one hand and placing the other under her arm. He lifted her up, escorting her to the dining room.

"I will see to him," he said. "Willie, take her bundles upstairs to her room. Marie, you must understand," he spoke softly. "It is not only uncultured for you to wander alone, it is not safe for a beautiful young woman like yourself to be unaccompanied. Any horrible thing could happen to you."

Part II – Chapter 8

Dinner and Duel

January 16, 1896, 7:30 p.m.

Cool winter air flowed through an open dining room window. A young servant, daughter of a cigar worker, carried a large platter of tender chicken pieces in bubbling sauce.

Pungent aromas mixed with fresh country smells from the outdoors. Another servant dished black beans and rice on the plates. The faintest bark of a dog drifted in from a remote field.

The diners passed a plate of yucca, freshly arrived by steamer. Georgia and Enriqueta served the plates of the younger ones.

As they began to eat, Gabriel, who sat the head of the table, heard footsteps crunching on the walkway out front. They continued with the meal until a quiet knock rapped the heavy entry door. No one moved or spoke. A moment's quiet, then the next knock banged with a balled fist.

"Now what? We're just settled. That better not be who I think it is," said Gabriel.

Enriqueta shrugged. Willie glanced at Marie with a knowing smile. Micaela answered the door.

"I know who it is." Marie Louise sighed. "Domingo would never arrive without notice."

"And him, I would not mind to see," Gabriel said. "That would also explain why you are dressed as you are, Marie Louise." With mock irritation, she compressed her lips.

They listened to the voice in the entry. "Eddie Pitzer, of course," Georgia hooted.

"He's earlier than usual," Willie scoffed.

"I'm here to see Marie Louise," they heard him say from the doorway. Gabriel scowled, looked down at his plate. With great force, he impaled a chicken leg with his fork.

Marie Louise snapped her napkin down beside her plate and shoved back her chair. "*Con permiso*, excuse me."

Eddie waited on the piazza, rustling like a nervous bird. His coat hung off one shoulder covering a muslin sling supporting his arm. When Marie Louise arrived, he spoke quickly, breathless, his words impulsive. "You are the girl I love," he said. "I could say that to you forever, Marie. You are the sweetest thing on earth. I mean it."

She stepped backward. "People are listening, for heaven's sake, Eddie. Move away from the window." They walked into the dirt yard, recently raked and tidy.

"I love you now, more than ever," he continued. "I love you more every day."

"Stop, Eddie," she said. "What has happened and what is that?" She pointed to his bandaged arm.[1] "What have you done?" Her voice softened. "Are you all right?"

"Just let me tell you," he blurted. "Quit asking questions." His voice was loud.

The screen door slammed. Gabriel stamped across the piazza holding his napkin, starting down the porch steps, staring at Eddie. "We are waiting for you," he said to Marie Louise.

"I'll be there in a minute, Papa," she said. "Eddie's hurt."

Gabriel turned to go inside. "Finish quickly," he said.

"Marie, it's important," Eddie said more quietly.

* * *

Two days before, January 14, Tuesday afternoon, Eddie had stepped off the trolley at Bay Street and Main by Huau's corner. A dusky boy, about ten, wearing suspenders and a dirty newsboy cap, passed him to board the car Eddie just left. The boy held a letter addressed to Marie Louise. Eddie saw her name as the boy passed.

"Wait up, *chico*," Eddie snapped, following him back on the car, and grabbed for the note. When the boy held it back, Eddie wrenched the boy's arm and snatched the envelope. As he read the note, the boy hollered through the car, "He stole my message. I have to carry that to a lady," and started to cry.

Eddie folded the letter and put it in his pocket as the conductor pushed past him to the youngster. "Shut your mouth, mango head," the conductor growled at the boy. "Sit down or I'll squash you down." The conductor mashed the boy's cap and lowered him into the seat. Sticking out his lower lip, the boy quieted down and sniffed his runny nose.

"Thank you, sir." Eddie tipped his hat to the trainman. "Pardon the confusion."

As he started to leave, Eddie realized the boy might tell Marie about her undelivered letter. He slipped the note back to the youth, who crammed it into his pants.

Eddie left the car and walked to Huau's *La Favorita*, near the trolley stop. Domingo Herrera, exiting the shop, walked directly towards him. Eddie stiffened. Herrera, erect in his smart tailored suit and a flat-brimmed hat, stopped. With an unfriendly gaze, he took a cigar from his pocket and wet his lips. Staring at Eddie, he rolled the cigar between his thumb and forefinger. He bit off the end, spat out tobacco, continuing to gaze at Eddie. He lit a match.

Eddie cleared his throat and stepped back, planning to skirt around him. Certain that Herrera had seen him read the purloined letter, Eddie hurried west on Bay Street towards his father's store. Herrera pivoted, chewing his cigar, and watched him go.

Two hours later, at Pitzer's home goods store, a large colored man in a long coat and a derby approached Eddie's father. "I have a note for Mr. Edward Pitzer," the crinkly-haired darky said. Herrera often used underlings, often Negroes, as messengers for errands or deliveries. Eddie, straightening shelves, heard the exchange and waited for the note to be delivered to him.

It read: *Please give me satisfaction by meeting me on Bridge Street at half past ten or eleven. The weapon of your choice. D. Herrera.*

Eddie's face paled. He pictured the shadows of night and the small space between buildings where such appointments were usually kept. He glanced at the Negro, wondering if he could read. Pitzer called to him. "Get over here." Turning over the note, he wrote on the back of it that he would be present at the designated time and place, and that he chose to duel with pistols. He shoved the paper back at the messenger. "Go on," he said. "Get out of here."

Eddie remained in the store for the afternoon questioning why he'd agreed to the duel. He cleaned and loaded the revolver he sometimes carried. Between customers, he practiced drawing his gun. Holding it at various angles in front of him, he aimed at the cans on the shelves. When his father came near, he pocketed the gun.

"Are you all right, son?" his father asked.

"Couldn't be better," Eddie replied.

At 10:30 p.m., he departed the store and walked west to Bridge Street. He pulled his coat around him. The day had been fair, but the temperature had dropped to the forties, and it was a cold night by the river. Dark clouds formed and showers would fall before dawn.

For three years, arc lights had lit the street. Bay Street stores, some still open, had been electrically lit for even longer. But at Bridge Street, running north to south, the lights disappeared. Only a few stars glowed above him, then slipped behind the clouds.

He turned right on Bridge Street, which divided Jacksonville and LaVilla. A black hansom cab and a fine horse waited for him parked by the sidewalk a half-block away; its door swung open. He took a deep breath, fingering the pistol in his pocket. Stepping up into the cab, he bumped into someone already settled in the back seat. He could barely see his form in the dark.

"Is that you, Herrera?" Pitzer asked, but the person did not answer. The driver's whip cracked overhead and they turned west toward LaVilla. The cab swayed and bumped over untended ruts in the road and stones that knocked the cab awry.

A stench of livestock mixed with burning gas and coal rose from slaughterhouses, animal paddocks and shacks where no one but a Negro would live. Square squalid buildings were marked on maps as colored shacks. The cab plundered its way through the settlement. Only a person who knew the quarter could have driven to the destination.

The cab stopped. The unidentified man at his side grabbed Pitzer's arm, pinning it behind him, pushing him from the cab and forward through shadows and scrub brush. A dim light illumined the frame of an isolated shack that stood behind the ice factory. Two ice wagons parked together between the two buildings. Pitzer stumbled over the protruding root of a rangy tree. Someone he didn't see in the dark pushed him to his knees. He smelled rich black dirt.

A chain clanked nearby surprising him in the blackness. With a guttural growl, what felt like a massive dog shoved hard into Pitzer's leg. He braced, holding his breath for the bite. Its cold nose slid into his hand. He started to pet the nose, when the man behind him pushed him past the dog and into an empty wooden room of the barely lighted shack. Scarcely visible, three men slouched against the inside walls staring at Pitzer in silence. Domingo Herrera was not among them.

Moments passed and no one spoke or moved. Finally Pitzer, his aching arm still pinned behind him, asked if they were still to shoot. If so, who was the principal? One of the men pushed himself off the wall and took the position, hand on a holstered sidearm. "The man you expected couldn't make it," he mumbled.

Another man's lamp reflector shone in Pitzer's face. Pitzer and the stranger drew guns. The other man shot first. His bullet hit close to Pitzer's elbow and straight through his arm. Pitzer's bullet struck the man's left shoulder.

Pitzer fell. The other two turned their guns on him but a third one stopped them. "If we shoot him that way," he said, "someone will kill us next."

Pitzer pulled himself to his feet by leaning on his bent knee. He asked one for help, put on his overcoat and received a barbed scowl in return.

Part II – Chapter 9

Marie's Letters

After Eddie told his tale to Marie, she sat on the front step and stared at the dark yard. She could hear the family inside leaving the table. "Oh, Eddie," she said, leaning her chin on her hand. "What did you do afterwards?"

"I slung my coat over my shoulder and walked home through the mud. The streets were a mess. I splattered muck all over myself. It was raining hard by then. I was afraid of being followed, so I kept turning to watch behind me," he continued, "which was silly in the pitch black. I couldn't see anything, anyway. I walked fast and hid behind trees. You know livestock wander loose down there. And God knows what people do there." He stopped talking and looked around at the yard. "It's different here. It feels safe and comfortable." He sounded vacuous.

"How did you get home?"

"Out of the dark, Police Lieutenant Gruber walked up out of nowhere. He didn't know me. He hunted down a cab to drive me to a doctor. I sneaked into my parents' house at one in the morning."

She stood again hurriedly, hands crossed, with a sober expression. She understood guns and fighting. She'd heard tales often enough.

But this duel, this shootout, was immediate and menacing. She fixed an arm across her torso and plastered the other hand flat against her cheek. Her eyes wide. She glared. "He just did it to scare you, Eddie, and I guess he did."

"Now, Marie, I have told you all about it," he said. "Don't be mad at me," he pleaded. "If I hadn't gone, Herrera would think I was scared." He talked fast. "The man who shot me was a professional shooter. I could tell by how he handled his pistol. He didn't think I could shoot straight and I can't shoot very much, but I can hit someone close, if I have to."

"I am sorry I've caused you such trouble." He hurried on. "I know you can't come down to see me but you can write me some long letters, if you only will. You know about my duel, now. This shows I really love you." He reached for her hand, which she pulled back then allowed him to take it.

"When your father gets over his mad spell, I can come see you again. I want to, awfully bad, but you can write to me, and I can hear from you that way. Write me sweet letters. Write me about you, everything you do."

They stood in the yard looking at each other. They were quiet. The house sounds faded They no longer heard the voices or silver and plates.

"You don't blame me for fighting, do you?" he whispered.

She took back her hand and wrapped her arms around herself, moving a small step towards him. "Eddie, I can't believe you did this. You could have been killed. It isn't right and you know it. All you want is to shoot and fight and Domingo could see right through you. You didn't find him down in La Villa mucking around with bums."

He stepped forward and started to put his arms around her. Holding up a flat hand, she stepped back. "Have you told your mother?"

"No."

She swung around and stomped her shoes up the front steps. "I worry about you, Eddie," she said, her hand on the door. "But if you don't speak to your mother about this soon, ready yourself, for I shall have Mama tell her. You know your mother will blame me for your actions. She thinks I want to make you jealous. I hope you realize that."

She grabbed the door handle, pushing it. "Yes, Eddie, I shall write you. Expect a letter. I only wonder what it may contain." She slammed the door. He ran to the dining room window and tiptoeing to look through it, watched her disappear into the house.

A candle flame in Marie Louise's room, a pinpoint of light in the surrounding night, spread a luminous circle on her desk. The family slumbered in the dark house. Her hair loose, swept around her shoulders. The cool night air caused her to shiver in her long flannel nightdress. Her feet felt like ice.

She had retrieved a pen and paper and a bottle of ink from the parlor downstairs. She began to write the letter she had promised Eddie. She reached for the pen reflected in the convex glass of Domingo Herrera's photo on her desk. Her fiancé for a year and a half; hardly anyone knew. She turned away from his solemn military pose to write. Marie had many boyfriends over the years and on occasion more than one fiancé. Her feelings had always run hot and cold about them. Her father scolded her for it, so she tended to keep her attachments quiet.

Eddie was another matter. He was hard to hide because he was always nearby, but no one took him seriously. Tonight, Marie would handle this shooting business. She would not accept blame from anyone, not her own mother, not Eddie's mother, not Domingo, certainly not Eddie. She began to write. Pitzer had been stupid to steal Domingo's note knowing the occasional fiery nature of Cubans. Eddie should have expected retaliation from Herrera.

Later, some thought Marie Louise's three letters to Pitzer indicated her great love for him. But Marie's emotions regarding men swayed like moss in the trees. Her feelings for Pitzer or any man could change several times before the letters came to light, as they did at his trial.

January 16, 1896
Jacksonville, Fla.

Dearest Friend Eddie:

Hope your arm is better in the morning. Keep in from the damp, please. Papa would not speak to me last night but we will make up. I think he was mad to have supper interrupted.

Eddie, you are mistaken. I am the one that caused you great trouble, not the other way around. Mama is not angry with you but she thinks I am the cause of it all.

I did not care if you stopped Domingo's letter, for it was a fake. I'm sure he didn't mean anything he said. I hate the coward that had to hire a man to shoot for him. Please write me more about it when you get rested. I am uneasy to know. Please don't be afraid to write me. I will not tell anyone. Tell me the truth, please do?

You say I am the sweetest girl on earth but you must hate me. Even though, you say you don't.

Why did you face a man instead of Domingo? I never would have hurt a dog for Domingo. I wish I could come see you and have a long talk, but I can't. And I can't tell you why. I will close because I'm sleepy.

With all my love, I am your friend,
Marie Louise

P.S. Please tear this.

Eddie thought he had never received such an exquisite letter. The ambiguous closing, "With all my love, I am your friend," did not confuse him at all. He was certain she loved him.

On the night of January 17, the day he received her letter, he serenaded Marie Louise at her window. On the second story of the spacious Gato house, a side piazza with an ornamental balustrade extended outside Marie's room. Eddie climbed the back steps of the house to the second balcony to stand at the deep windows of her room. Marie shared a bedroom with her sister Elvira, five years younger, who slept deeply. She had not seen Marie Louise's small candle light or noticed her composing letters the night before. Marie looked over at her younger sister, still asleep.

Lying back in her bed, Marie Louise watched the shadowy figure in the dark and recognized Eddie's voice lifted in song. Dramatic gestures accompanied the "good night" melody he sang to her. It was a lovely scene but she soon forgot it. Concerned others in the house might hear him, she rose, placing her finger to her lips to shush him. She closed the window, blocking his performance from the slumbering household.

The next day, Marie wrote Eddie a second letter. In the bottom left corner, she added, "So romantic at that window." As if she were writing a ditty in an autograph book, at the bottom of the page she drew a heart with an arrow through it. Underneath the sketch, she labeled, "My Heart." At the bottom right of the page, she scribbled she was reading a popular novel. "I am fascinated by A Gentleman of France. It is fine." Her mind wandered as she composed.

January 18, 1896
Jacksonville, Fla.

Dearest Friend Eddie:

I am so glad to have seen you yesterday, as it was a pleasure to me. Eddie, will you grant me a favor? Please be careful and also oblige me by making it known to your dear mother as to how it all was. You know, Eddie, that it is dangerous not to tell. I know it will be hard for you to tell them, but much more so to explain why you didn't tell such a thing to them. It is worse not to tell. If something else would happen to you, then they would be horrified you had more to tell.

I know your mother is perfectly innocent about it all, and she should not be so. She ought to know it from beginning on. If that would cause her to dislike me, you must consider that there are other things to know first. I know it would be more safe for you. Please, I beg you, tell her. I don't, truly, I do not comprehend your way. Do you not tell her because you are afraid she will be unhappy for a while, or are you afraid that she will blame me? Please tell me. Please tell her. No matter for the rest, for if you do not, I will be obliged to do so by Mama; and Eddie, that would be harder for me. I know they will blame me for causing it, but I hope they will not blame you for taking the letter.

I hope you will take this for the best, as I mean you to do. I would write you and make you too sick about it if I did not close. You are sick enough now. Well, I will close. Please answer me. You said you would write today to me, but you did not. I guess you paid me back. That is right; pay your debts. Well, goodbye. You can answer this anytime, if you will be kind enough to do so.

Your always true friend,
Marie Louise Gato

Four days later, she penned a more romantic letter to Eddie again hoping to persuade him to tell his mother about the shooting. At the top left-hand corner of her delicate stationery were the words "Love is a bug that eats the heart," echoing a popular phrase of young women. In the upper right corner, she noted "Love is sweet and bitter." As a final word, she entered at the bottom a last small "Hug."

January 22, 1896
Jacksonville, Fla.

Very Dear Eddie,

    I trust your arm is getting better, and that you will soon be well and strong again. Truly you should not get sick. You are too noble and kind for anything of the sort to happen to you. I hope you will forgive me for the pains you've suffered. I feel ashamed of what happened. I am. I did not intend it so to be.

    I hope this does not put you full of thought, but I will not talk of fighting again. I dislike that so much. I regret to say, I think you did not care how you fought as long as you achieved a fight.

    You say you like me to write to you, then I will write, but Eddie, you know what it has cost me to write to some people. Pray tear these notes, as I would not want anybody to get a hold of them. You can write some loving letters, can't you, but you can't say if you mean them. Domingo sends me enough messengers with letters and gifts. He has many servants. I am told he is not to see me again. I fear that is not true.

    I guess you thought I went to bed early last night, but I desired to be in the dark alone as I felt blue. I saw all you did last night. You did truly look romantic. What was that you were singing in the window? It sounded sweet from here. Believe me, it seems a long time since I played the piano. You ask me what Domingo said of the music he sent me. He does not speak of it in the present. Why is it you want to know?

    Eddie, I wish I could write you longer, but it is quite late now, and I want to send this to you tonight.

    Ever wishing you many happy hours through life, I remain yours truly,

    Marie Louise Gato

    This was most likely Eddie's favorite letter, although he carefully saved all three.[1]

Part II – Chapter 10

Three Friends

March 1896

Half the town was gathered for a special occasion at the river. In his white captain's suit and hat, Sheriff Napoleon Broward greeted the locals gathered on the wharf to watch the cast-off of Broward's new tug, the *Three Friends*.[1] Built locally at New Berlin, a shipbuilding town downriver, the *Three Friends* was making the city's first filibustering mission to aid Cuba's fight for freedom from Spain.[2] Most of the United States stood for Cuba's independence, but not the federal government. Broward's mission of hauling men and arms to Cuba was an open secret from the Federals.

Local curiosity intensified when word spread that the sheriff, soon to be Florida's governor, Napoleon Broward, would captain his boat. The celebrated José Huau, city leader and tobacconist who dispatched the expedition, also garnered attention. Interest in the launch rose as the tug stocked 100 pounds of coal, rations and sealed crates marked "GROCERIES," "BACON," and so on. The boxes, in fact, contained firearms and ammunition. The excited crowds clamored around the wharf to watch.

On the day of the launch, Marie Louise and her cousin Florida, called Flora, her close friend and nearest in age of the Huau progeny, stood in the crowd of onlookers. Marie's brother, Willie, and Flora's younger brother, Hypolito "Polly" Huau, were attempting to sneak aboard Broward's new boat to join the big adventure. Although Uncle Huau had funded nearly the entire trip, Lieutenant William Gruber of the Jacksonville Police Department, stood post and gave the young men no dispensation, blocking them at the gate. He smiled at them as he turned them away. A year later, Gruber would accept Eddie Pitzer's surrender after Marie Gato was shot.

In the months before the Cuban Revolution, the Jacksonville wharves were hazardous places. Spanish spies and saboteurs maimed and killed on the ships and docks; spies replaced boat pilots in the pilot towers and their private cabins.

Huau had pulled the body of John Kennedy, his long-serving store clerk and friend, from the St. Johns River. He had assisted with the smuggled shipments to Cuba. To mislead the Spanish, Kennedy helped address crates to himself at fake sites in Cuba, crates containing food, munitions and medical supplies. Huau kneeled over the drowned man, cradling Kennedy's head. The man had been floating dead in the water, his neck discolored with suspicious bruises. Marie Louise, drifting in the crowd, could see tears swelling in her uncle's eyes.

At the launch of the *Three Friends*, Eddie Pitzer made his way through the throng to Marie Louise, whom he had spotted in the crowd. Presenting himself to her, he removed his hat and bowed. He offered his arm to escort her to a different location, far away from Flora.

"Eddie, please go away," Marie said, marginally smiling. "I see quite enough of you, and today, I'm here to see the launch." She turned and carelessly rolled her eyes at Flora. Eddie saw her do it, but Marie didn't care.

Domingo Herrera, Marie's approved fiancé, would soon join her uncle Huau's filibustering network. As a Cuban Army officer, he was destined to become an adjutant general. From a distance, Herrera watched the red-headed Pitzer approach Marie Louise and saw her give him a sharp dismissal. Herrera decided to join Marie and her cousin. Smiling at him when she saw him approach, Marie Louise lifted an eyebrow with a smoldering look, a singular action for a crowded sunny afternoon.

On the wharf, sprawled on coils of thick dock rope, Stephen Crane, author of the famous novel, *The Red Badge of Courage*, watched the launch festivities. Hoping to cadge his next passage to

Cuba as a war correspondent, he often loitered at the docks and the nearby bars. He would not be aboard the *Three Friends,* but later, his ill-fated expedition to Cuba on the *Commodore* begat "The Open Boat," his famous short story.[3, 4]

United States Coast Guard cutters had stolen south to Savannah, Fernandina, Jacksonville, New Smyrna, and Key West and to Florida's tangled mangrove swamps.

"I heard," José Huau, said to Broward as they stood together on the dock near the *Three Friends,* that the *Boutwell* is no longer hiding in the cove to try and stop you."

Huau flicked his cigar. Broward rolled his own between his fingers, undisturbed by news that the *Boutwell* had been lurking. Broward knew his boat was the fastest boat on the river.

With stoked boilers, and propulsion roaring, the *Three Friends* cut smooth water into the main channel of the St. Johns River. She thrust headlong through the current, spawning a torrential wave. The gathered crowd cheered. The ship swamped the banks of the sea-level town and water skimmed the wooden wharfs. Docking mariners, ending their day, grasped their nets for balance, grabbing their buckets and tackle from floating away on the wake.

Huau and Alphonso had hatched the entire venture in the private room behind Huau's store, "The Filibuster Hatchery," where the local Spanish envoy often dropped by for his favorite cigar and good conversation.[5, 6] "Cast-off was a glorious sight," said Huau, grinning, slinging open the door to the hatchery that afternoon. "Broward will do fine," he exulted to the Spanish envoy.

From a distance, Eddie Pitzer watched Domingo Herrera with Marie and Flora. He knew the important men in town collaborated with Huau's filibustering schemes, men with money. Young men volunteered to sail or fight. Fritot. Herrera. While Pitzer, a shopkeeper, the son of a shopkeeper, languished in his father's store. "I could have gone too," he thought. "I could have died and been a hero."

But*,* he told himself in a moment of clarity, *but here you are, aren't you? And you see no danger lurking. You only see Marie Louise, smiling and talking with Domingo Herrera.* "I am jealous of the Cubans," he shouted into the uproar and commotion. Even those nearby paid him no attention.

Ten days after the launch, the *Three Friends* crossed the St. Johns Bar towards Jacksonville surviving a treacherous voyage.[7] Broward descended his gangplank in his crisp white uniform, denying all knowledge of filibustering. He cut through the assembled crowd, throwing their hats and cheering, and his wife greeted him from an ornate surrey that would escort him to their home. Huau watched with sober attention, thankful for the safe return from a dangerous journey. More ships would launch to Cuba. More secret deaths and fighting would occur. Herrera would join the filibustering and would be stranded on No Name Key. And Eddie Pitzer would continue to clerk in his father's store and fall deeper into despair

Three Friends tugboat circa 1900
Owned and piloted by Sheriff Napoleon Broward

PART III

THE SECOND MURDER

Lt. William Gruber, Jacksonville Police Department, circa 1896

Part III – Chapter 1

Lt. William Gruber, Jacksonville Police Department

April 26, 1897

    Pigniolo's restaurant, the first floor of a three-story building, faced Hogan Street in Jacksonville, with black street numbers outlined in gold painted on a glass transom. Black-and-white one-inch-square tiles lined the floor. At noon, the popular restaurateur Leo Pigniolo, in his white bib apron, labored behind the long counter, shouting food orders to his kitchen staff. Smells of garlic and fresh bread flooded the room. By evening, Pigniolo slipped into a black coat and fresh collar. A remarkable change from *trattoria* to *ristorante*.

    Jacksonville Police lieutenant William Gruber had accepted Pitzer's surrender after the Gato shooting. Blonde and slim, sophisticated as a magazine sketch, Gruber looked completely genteel beside his friend, Joseph Marzyck. Marzyck wore a scruffy beard and an eye patch which he earned fighting a Northern invasion of a South Carolina plantation. The Civil War had not yet been declared. Pigniolo poured a beer for the men. The guileful Temperance League, which deluged Jacksonville, was not the men's concern. They raised their glasses.

Gruber and Marzyck, friends who lived in LaVilla a few blocks west, sat at a table covered by a red-and-white checkered tablecloth and watched street traffic out the nearby window. LaVilla remained a small rural community, rough and untamed and often dangerous. Adjacent to Jacksonville, the town was a mixture of European ethnicities, colored people and early settlers intermixed with slaughterhouses and ice factories. Though slowly refining, LaVilla still allowed wild stock to wander in the yards and roads.

"So, William, you are busy at your work?" said Marzyck, an Austrian immigrant, who had moved to Jacksonville from Charleston.[1] "What's happening with the Gato murder case?"

"Nothing," said Gruber. "Pitzer's in jail. No doubt he'll stay there. The state attorney charged him and the Circuit Court will convene soon. That's it."

"So did he kill Marie Gato?"

"He isn't capable," Gruber responded. "But, he'd like you to think he's tough."

"You are investigating, of course?"

"Of course." Gruber pulled out his watch and stared at it. "I have to get back to work."

"Will you testify for Pitzer?"

"What?" Gruber finished his beer and lowered the glass. "No. All I could say is someone else killed her, because I don't think he could."

Gruber and Marzyck had been friends since the Civil War. Marzyck had rescued Gruber, a virtual orphan, nine-years-old, in Charleston.[2] In November 1860, the Union elected Abraham Lincoln president of the United States and in December 1860, South Carolina delegates signed the Southern states' first Ordinance of Secession in Charleston. Nine-year-old William Gruber perched on a fence watching the celebratory ribbons of colored paper fly in the wind. Bands played. Cannons blasted across the city and sparks flew. The crowd on Meeting Street cheered.

After sundown, William roamed the dark streets listening to the night talk of states' rights and the blameless wonders of slavery. Sometimes, he followed his father searching for renegade slaves. Whites, the minority race in the city, swore Negroes set arson fires most every night. They feared a slave uprising would burst from the fires. Soon, The Great Burn destroyed large swaths of the town and its cherished buildings.

Gruber's father became attached to the proud Charleston Battalion, guarding the harbor and city.³ He would encamp on James Island in the harbor for four years. Because William's mother had already died, William was abandoned and alone. William Marzyck, a street fruit vender who had befriended the wandering boy, soon moved him into the federal arsenal recently seized by the rebels. Marzyck worked in the foundry there and young Gruber lived and worked with him for the duration of the war.

***

Jacksonville 1880

Gruber stood on Joseph Marzyck's front porch sobbing, clutching a rail, his body shaking. He dropped to his knees with a sorrowful moan. He had married Kate Hawkins several years earlier and after years of separation from his friend, had moved with her near Marzyck in LaVilla.

"What's happened, William?" Marzyck put his arm on Gruber's back to steady him.

"The doctor's on his way. My boy is dead," said Gruber, gulping his soggy words.

The son, Marzyck Edwin Gruber, almost five years old, died of bowel congestion. His face had turned a misty grey, his lips were darker, like wood smoke, lined in bluish purple. A beautiful boy in the colors of death.

Joseph bought a half parcel at the City Cemetery to bury the boy for Gruber. It was well used and well appreciated. Five years later, Charles Hawkins Gruber, a second son, died at approximately two-years-old. Edwin Reich Gruber, a two-month-old, died in January 1886. In 1890, Edwin Gruber, the twenty-one-month-old son of William and Kate, died in November.⁴ The Gruber brothers left the world through the portal of Marzyck's cemetery plot. None of their paths had crossed on earth.

***

After fifteen years of painting, contracting, organizing trade unions and watching his children die one by one, Gruber sought change. No one was surprised at his appointment to the police force. He entered the Jacksonville Police Department as a lieutenant. It was a political appointment and he was a congenial man, a popular citizen. His work would consist of ensuring law and order and maintaining peace, not scrambling for labor contracts, organizing workers and attending a dying family as he had been doing too long.

Police officers worked twelve-hour shifts, day or night, but Gruber kept much longer hours. He enjoyed keeping the town safe and homes secure. He chased thieves on horseback, stood alone to settle brawls. He was fond of children, often surprising them with candy and peanuts.

But, coloreds, especially, along with other criminals, feared him. The coloreds lowered their heads when he passed on the street. "You been to Charleston?" Gruber might mutter as they scurried past. "I remember you. You know I do." Intimidation was his specialty. "I saw you in Charleston torching a fire. It was you."

"No, sir. No, sir. It weren't me," the Black would answer. Until accurate forensics was established, the newspapers cited Gruber as a tenacious and skilled detective. He always got his man, especially if he were black.

Part III – Chapter 2

GRUBER NIGHTLIFE

On the night shift, Gruber began rounds at eleven. He liked working the city beats, Brooklyn, LaVilla, Springfield. Sometimes, he logged his rounds on foot, checking the men who stood their posts. Sometimes, he traveled on horseback.

Tracing his nightly route, an exhilarating rhythm washed over him, waves rushing up a beach. The darkness drenched him and he prized the feeling. The night promised him something extraordinary. Spirits of the evening raised him above his usual life. He felt the tingling sense he had as a child with the smoke of war in his nostrils. Something electrifying would happen, something breathtaking lurked around the corner. When he rode his horse, as black as the tip of a burnt match, he imagined things the magical night could bring: a glittering rainstorm, a starburst, an unexpected visitor or even a visitation from one of his dead children.

The white of the officers' summer helmets smoldered like white ash in the dark. Plopped on the head of a stolid patrolman, the helmet drew the savvy horse. It nuzzled the cop who would duck his head and pull away. Gruber seemed not to notice.

The horse, knowing Springfield was next on his beat where he would get extra rations, picked up his pace. A Springfield sentry stood on the timber bridge crossing Hogans Creek. "It's a calm night, sir," the officer reported as Gruber gazed at the soft marshes reflected in the light spreading across the creek from town. The cop saluted.

Gruber saluted and crossed the bridge. He and the horse strolled up Laura. Many blocks north on the Panama Road sat the house of the murdered girl, Marie Louise Gato. Hers was a more pleasant world than where he was riding. Gruber mused about the accused, Pitzer. The defense had asked Gruber to testify for Pritzer. Gruber was unsure of his obligations to the state. Unsure of the defendant's integrity.

Traveling north, the horse's hooves hit the rocks and trash of a wrecked neighborhood, mirroring the bleak lives of its residents. A Negro concert and dance hall opened there every night. Strong beer flowed. Energetic tangle foot whiskey assisted the beer, and all drank as much as they could.

Gruber dismounted. He handed his reins to a man outside the bar, who led the horse to oats and water. The jovial customers ignored Gruber. Usually the only white man there, he was a regular; they paid him no attention.

On a platform at the end of the room, Gruber watched a wide-eyed Negress, black and shiny wet. She danced a spirited hoochie-coochie. Smiling a broad, stage smile, she turned to Gruber in the half-lit room and stared back at him over and between her kicks. He lifted his chin and in one slow move, shifted his eyes down her body, stopped at her breasts, lowered his gaze, stopped again and slowly wandered back up her body. A half-smile crossed his face.

He turned to survey the crowd. The audience, an eclipse of moths hovered around single candles at the tables paid the dancer little attention and barely rustled their wings. One by one they slid from their societies, aimless, fluttering slowly away. For most in the club, midnight came too soon. But the lights extinguished, the place closed down and the moths drifted off to follow the moon. Gruber remounted and headed south towards town.

No longer on duty, stabling his horse, he walked east on familiar dirt roads north of town. From a tall pine, a hoot owl called him. One bright star lit to expose him, then shifted behind a cloud.

He walked to Oakland, past Old City Cemetery, then to East Jacksonville. Neat working-class houses sat near the mills and shipyards on the river. Gruber heard the current where the great bend in the waterway directed the St. Johns to the sea. Close to the banks, music tinkled from an upstairs window. An occasional bottle smashed to the ground. Wanderers offered reserved polite greetings. Others, seeing his uniform, hid their faces and scattered away.

Near a shoddy bordello, craps were played under streetlights. Inside the building, newspapers hung as wallpaper. The first floor, mostly bare, had been arranged with a few dark tables decked with doilies and dusty ginger pot lamps. Bottom-sprung chairs scattered through the parlor. When Gruber entered the front door, the first floor denizens sat up straight, looked down at the boards and studied the dead roaches and cigar butts on the floor. They shifted stealthy gazes from face to face looking for signs as to what they should do. Gruber looked at them when he came in, snorted out loud and grinned as he sprang up the stairs ahead of them.

On the first floor, where men were waiting, a shot of whiskey cost a dollar from a small colored boy toting the bottle. He offered a swallow to all the men lounging there. The boy was barefoot. Dead roaches didn't bother him. His pants dragged. His clothes were torn and patched. Someone else had worn them before.

"You, sir? You, sir?" he offered.

Not a man in the house would let another man cheat the boy, but when a woman floated downstairs, they all watched her. In a silky negligee, a sweeping garment with a long draping train, she drank for free. She grabbed the bottle by the neck and guzzled from it. She also grinned at the men who sat on the floor waiting to come upstairs to her.

Descending the stairs to drink whiskey with her, Gruber's hair was mussed, his shirttail out. He put his arm around her waist and pulled her to him. Placing his fingers on her lips, he grabbed the bottle from the boy, and swallowed from it long and deep. He upended it into her mouth. She wiped her lips, his mustache, with the edge of her gown.

"Here, boy," Gruber handed the young hawker crumpled bills wadded in his hand. "Replenish yourself," he told the boy in a drunk's patois and waved him away.

At other times, he might bend on his knee to the boy's level and place his hand on the small shoulder. With a sad, desperate face, Gruber touched his forehead to the boy's and peered deep into the young eyes. The boy's black pupils jiggled in fear at the policeman's touch.

Gruber's gaze was a yawning bottomless stare, profound in his search for another small face, another little boy in that slight skull, one of his own. Gruber wept.

The evening ended as they all did with someone somewhere playing a piano. Around a corner or up a set of stairs. Perhaps, next door. Always, hard to say about the music, except that it was quick and airy and far away.

Part III – Chapter 3

The Death of Lieutenant Gruber

April 29, 1897

Midmorning, Joseph Marzyck hurried along the Bay Street sidewalk passing familiar stores. Lieutenant Gruber had not returned home after work the night before. Kate, his wife, had sobbed and moaned and called for her husband all night long. Marzyck sat with her as she continually telephoned the station house. It was nine days since Marie Louise Gato had been shot. A shady uneasiness cast on much of the city and the unexplained absence of Gruber intensified the discomfort.

Marzyck stopped mid-step on the wooden sidewalk in front of *La Favorita*, Huau's tobacco shop, long since tidied and swept. The hefty Cuban, Marie Louise Gato's uncle, was stretching his arms in the morning air.

"Good morning, Señor Huau," Marzyck said.

"Good day to you, Mr. Marzyck. Stop for a minute? Have some papaya juice? Time to smoke a cigar? Perhaps you can tell me how to improve it?" Marzyck laughed a little. Both knew Huau's cigars traveled farther and more people smoked them than Marzyck could dream.

"I'd love to smoke your cigar, señor. But I'm in a great hurry to talk to you." Huau stepped in the store to fetch two cigars. He pulled a matchstick from his small, silver pocket box, struck it and lit their cigars. They stood beneath the awning outside the store.

"This comes from Germany," said Huau, showing Marzyck the box.

"Very old," said Marzyck.

"Yes, very."

"I need to find the boy. I need to find Gruber," Marzyck said. "I need to talk quick to the sheriff."

"He's not a boy, Marzyck," said Huau. "Though, he often looks it," he mused.

"I must locate William," said Marzyck, ignoring Huau's remark. "He isn't home last night. We are worried. His wife is crazy over it. He always wanders but it's ten in the morning and he is nowhere." Marzyck cleared his throat. "William goes too fast, too far. He will skid and ruin his life. I am worried for him, Huau. I am much concerned about his wife. I think something happened to him. He was maybe to speak for Pitzer at his trial for murder."

"For murder of my innocent niece, you mean?" Huau asked flatly, his tone changed. "I saw him yesterday," he said, unsmiling. "He was going very fast then, chasing a thief who had stolen some shoes." Huau turned away and drew on his El Esmero, his favorite, his specialty cigar.

"Thank you for the cigar, señor," said Marzyck, holding it down at his side. "I need to hurry on."

At that moment, the body of William Gruber lay undiscovered in a small clearing in an old growth forest on the outskirts of Springfield. Snarled like a jungle and surrounded by ragged dirt roads, the glade where he lay was known to host acts of illicit bustle and sexual congress.

Lt. William Gruber, third ranked of the Jacksonville police, lay stomach down with his face partly mashed in dirt. It was a loss of hope for numerous people regarding the recent Gato murder. Jacksonville had no detectives and the police department regularly fumbled criminal investigations. Many, even most, serious crimes, including murder, hung in perpetual oblivion, unsolved. Gruber stood apart. A popular cop, whom people believed always got his man. He would hunt a colored night and day, they said, to any seedy disreputable place until he bagged his quarry.

***

It was April, the season of growing, and the Pitzer trial would begin in weeks. Henry Gardiner, an elderly Negro, hoed a square of land near the old-growth forest where Gruber lay. Chunking at the dry dirt, he frequently stopped to wipe his hands on his dungarees. An odd-sounding whir orbited the caves of his ears. Searching the sky for the tinny noise, he pounded his head with the heel of his hand trying to clear the drone.

Even fine ladies knew the sound of buzzing flies circling excrement in their barns and stables or in their gardens. When dead livestock began to decay, the ladies heard the flies vibrate like plucked strings of a musical instrument. It never took long for flies to arrive and Gardiner also knew the sound.

Nervously scanning the area, over the end of his hoe, he saw Silcox, the sanitary patrolman, approaching him down Liberty Street. Silcox enforced cleanliness. Morality laws also fell to him as prostitutes were thought to spread disease.

"Yo, Silcox," hollered Gardiner. "Mistuh, I got somethin' for you." The old man dropped his hoe and stepped through the vegetable patch toward Silcox. Silcox thought Gardiner wanted to report sexual activity in the bushes. The sanitary cop stared at Gardiner, who was still swatting his ears.

"Why you beating your head?" he asked. Then, he, too, recognized the tinny hum broadcasting in the woods.

The thicket near the garden sloped to a sandy road. Gardiner and Silcox stared up at the brush and silently began to climb the hill. The tangled growth, dense vines and saplings left bloody scratches.

The deeper the two invaded the glade, the bolder the brassy noise surged. When they arrived, the buzzing stopped. They stopped. The noise swelled again. Then, Gardiner saw it. A patch of dark blue in the woods, unnatural in color, unnatural in texture. He edged closer. The blue patch became a policeman's uniform, chevrons, gold buttons, wreaths. He yelled to Silcox. The men crept towards the recumbent body. They stared in silence at the officer's head wedged in the dirt, his cheek caked in bloody condensation. A six-inch red gash gaped behind his ear. A flap of dried skin curled back from the slash. Bits of brain matter and blood dripped from his ear where a gigantic club had bashed the back of his skull.

The uniform kepi lay upside down on the dirt floor. An angle of sunlight lit wispy debris on the leather brim. A side of his split-tailed frock coat flipped the direction the wallop had sent him sprawling. The newspaper later described his grotesque facial expression and opined the massive blow had caused great agony in his final seconds.

Dried leaves and twigs matted the officer's hair. Flyblow, gooey white larvae and eggs formed pearly hills on the decaying flesh. A small twig stuck on the lieutenant's lip. In spite of the flies, Gardiner thought the cop was sleeping. They waited for movement but none appeared.

One newspaper concluded, due to the proximity of the fingers to his ashen lips, that Gruber had been twirling his mustache when the death blow landed. Anyone who knew the man, and many did, knew his mustache, a neatly trimmed little brush, was not the twirling kind. Gruber shaved clean and kept his mustache short. He liked displaying his handsome face.

Gardiner and Silcox clambered out of the woods, down the hill, to the road. Breathing heavily, they leaned on a broken fence with cut wires for stealing in and out. When the news reached the police station, Officer Frazee, posted in Springfield, took a message at a call box.

"Get over there. Make sure it's Gruber," Police Chief Keefe told him. "No one touches anything. And arrest that nigger who found him. He probably killed Gato, too." For Gardiner's trouble discovering the body, he spent three days in jail.

Part III – Chapter 4

SEARCH OF THE MURDER SCENE

The bulky Keefe whipped his horses north on Main Street, stomping the wagon's mechanical bell. People scrambled to avoid the onrush. When the rig turned east toward Liberty Street, a massive group had already gathered at the scene. The frightened horses reared, scattering the crowd with their towering hooves. Judge Dzialynski, the popular magistrate called the "Big Judge," moved through the throng, attempting to keep intruders from the body.[1] Justice of the Peace A.O. Wright, acting coroner, methodical and decisive, also instructed the crowd.

Deputy Chief Vinzant grabbed Keefe's bridle to steady the horses. "It's horrible, sir," he said. "It's ugly. The golden boy is badly gone." Handing off the bridle, Vinzant followed Keefe up the hillock, talking. "The first officers found a lemon near the lieutenant's mouth with the top sliced off. Sucked, tossed, rolled in the dirt," he said. "They searched his pockets and found his badge, .38 cartridges, a police whistle and nippers. No trace of his gun." Vinzant ticked the items on his fingers.

"Get those people out of there." Keefe watched human magpies flitting on the hill, rooting the murder scene for relics. "Get more officers in place," he shouted.

"They also dug out eyeglasses, a watch stopped at ten," Vinzant continued, "and a chain from his vest pocket, a part of a cigar, a tobacco plug, keys, and a nickel."

Viewing the body, Keefe kicked away a stick leaning against the leg. Keefe had watched Gruber leave the building the previous night after the lieutenant's shift ended. Gruber had caught the northbound trolley to Springfield, the opposite direction from his home in LaVilla. Gruber had seemed cheery and waved to Keefe, a big smile on his face. Keefe wondered where the lieutenant was headed.

"Here's something," someone yelled and Keefe turned. Near the edge of the clearing, a blue serge belt, with two common pins for attaching it to a woman's dress, hung on the bent wire fence. Thirty feet into the clearing, a hanky, marred by a tiny hole, also lay on the ground. Chief Keefe collected the two articles from the men and stuffed them into his pocket.

"That's enough," he shouted. "Let's go. Transfer the body now. It's over. Move out." A local reporter held up half of an addressed envelope he'd found. "Litter," said Keefe and walked away.

Keefe now had three murders to solve, including Marie Louise's and Gruber's.[2] The previous week, east of the Springfield schoolhouse, in the cypress thicket near Hogans Creek, a colored boy had found a newborn white baby girl strangled with her own umbilical cord. The stump still attached. Her lungs still closed, having never taken a breath.

Ignoring Keefe's order to leave, a large group ripe with excitement, continued to search for the dead man's pistol and the club that crushed his skull. "Chief, we haven't really concluded a thorough search," Vinzant said in a low voice. "And some of those articles may be probative."

Keefe wanted the body moved in haste to conceal indelicate facts, but at that moment, Justice Wright convened a coroner's jury and it was necessary they view the body in place, forcing the chief to delay. Wright gathered his jurymen close while the corpse was lifted and turned. Gruber's tongue protruded. At the sight of the ravaged head, the jurymen stepped back. The handsome blonde cop had been transformed. The men circled the body, asking speculative questions while Keefe stood and watched restively.

"Gentlemen," said Wright, finally, "Dr. Stollenwerck will perform an autopsy and present his findings at the hearing. You are dismissed until then. Do not speak of what you have observed." He ordered the stretcher and bearers to remove the deceased.

Men in the crowd removed their hats as the lieutenant's litter passed by. Women crossed their hearts and bowed their heads. When the bearers slipped the body into a waiting hearse, its wheels sank in the sand. The casket jostled and the dead man's blood stained the silk lining.

Three theories for Gruber's murder developed: A jealous lover discovered Gruber in a dalliance. The woman escaped through the wire fence, tearing off her belt. Possibly, a prostitute turned on Gruber when he refused to pay her. Or, Gruber had been killed elsewhere, perhaps in nearby quarters, and his body carried to the woods.[3]

Another possible motive for the murder derived from a rumor that Gruber was one of Edward Pitzer's staunchest supporters and was to be a witness on his behalf. Gruber had bragged he would bring Miss Gato's assassin to justice. Now that Gruber was covered with flies, who would seek Marie's killer? Who would find the perpetrator of Gruber's appalling slaughter?

Chief Keefe soon announced Gruber had died in the line of duty, executed by a killer he'd been tracking. Who was, no doubt, a Negro.

Part III – Chapter 5
Gruber Inquest

April 30, 1897

Justice Wright presided at the Gruber death inquest as deputy coroner the day after Gruber's body was found. No suspects had emerged in the twenty-four hours hence. In full uniform, Sergeant Stephen Brough of the Jacksonville Police Department, another hefty man, approached the witness chair to testify at the inquest. He would soon replace Gruber as lieutenant on the police force. Wright asked the questions.

"After being notified of Lieutenant Gruber's death," Brough said, "I was on the scene at Phelps and Liberty Street, April 29th. I found Officer Frazee guarding the site as he had been directed. I helped manage the investigation.

"Then, you," he said, speaking to Justice Wright, "instructed me later to turn the lieutenant's body upward so the coroner's jury, just convened, could get a complete view of the corpse. When I did so, there was a loud reaction from everyone there. It was a horrible sight. His garments and half his face had been stuck in the dirt." Brough cleared his throat and looked at the floor.

"Tell the jury more about the state of the body."

The sergeant hesitated, staring at Wright, who nodded firmly at him. Brough delayed, brushing at his dark blue uniform.

"When I turned him over," Brough said, looking into empty space above the crowd, "the fly of his pants was unbuttoned all the way down and open. His suspenders were hooked and his vest was closed and in order. The lieutenant's jacket was buttoned proper, but the rest of him was not." The people gasped and began to whisper.

Wright rapped his gavel. "Enough," he said to the audience. "Now, tell us about the site where the body was found," said Wright to Brough.

"It's a small cleared area in a thicket not far from the creek. Leaves were scattered and branches broken from many comings and goings. The spot has a bad reputation for illicit sexual meetings."

"Why was Lieutenant Gruber there? Do you have any thoughts, Sergeant?"

"Well, I suppose he could have been relieving himself, sir, but as it was night, and isolated, there was no real reason to go in the woods. Or, I suppose he could have been chasing a criminal. He wouldn't have said." Brough stopped talking.

"Anything else to add to this?" said Wright.

The witness cleared his throat and covered his mouth with his palm.

"Continue, Sergeant," Wright said again.

"When Gruber worked the day shift, he left at six-thirty for supper. He returned to log the daily reports, then left again about eight." Brough's voice was dry and remote. "He would return finally around eleven. This happened several times a week. I see him because I'm outside for a smoke or I see him through an open window.

"He takes the Newnan Street trolley running north. Several times I followed him and he got off at Union and Washington, walking north over Hogans Creek bridge there. When he left the station at eight-twenty that last night, he said he felt extra good. He shouldered his pistol and belt, and I suppose he rode the car until it turned east at Union to Washington. The line runs the opposite way from his house. He was whistling as he walked out of the station."

"Can you speculate as to his destination?" asked Wright.

"I prefer to keep my speculations to myself, sir," Brough said. The crowd perked up with that remark. "I have an opinion. A lot of the men do. I know Lieutenant Gruber's home is in LaVilla, west of the city. The Newnan Street line runs north near City Cemetery in Oakland. That can be a shady area out there, in many ways."

Justice Wright hesitated, staring at Brough, as if he might have more questions, then finally dismissed him. "You are excused, Sergeant." Curious onlookers watched Brough as he left the building. The newspapers reported Brough had withheld information.

P.J. Stollenwerck, the doctor who performed Gruber's autopsy, testified next. He had refused to share all of his findings with reporters, which had heightened attention.

"I opened the body the afternoon of April 29," Stollenwerck began. "I estimate Lieutenant Gruber died twelve to fifteen hours before, because his internal organs were grayish due to gravitational pull on the blood. There was also dark shade beneath to the downside of the body caused by blood shifting as it lay still for hours. When I cut into the bruise on the base of his head, I found large clots of blood and skull particles pressed into his brain. I slid my fingers under the skin and picked out pieces, as large as one and a half inches across.

"I have to say," he continued, "in spite of the sergeant's testimony regarding Gruber's open fly, no positive evidence exists to believe a woman was involved in this attack. I know that has been widely rumored." On the front row, Chief Keefe gave an open-mouth smile. He had tried to minimize attention to Gruber's open fly and he nodded his approval of the doctor's remark. But Stollenwerck wasn't finished talking.

"The officer's body maintained a terminal, or post-mortem erection, as it is called," the doctor continued as Keefe's lips grew tight. "When a severe blow is struck on a man's cranium, or a man is hanged, certain conditions exist in the male organ," said Stollenwerck. "Some people call it angel lust." Chief Keefe stared bitterly at the doctor and privately willed him to close his testimony, but Stollenwerck continued.

"A particularly odd thing," said Stollenwerck, his voice rising in a puzzling question, "there was an application of yellow mud placed on and around Lieutenant Gruber's sexual organ." Keefe stared more angrily. Stollenwerck was showing no respect for the Police Department.

Then the doctor expanded further on his nagging question. "The mud appeared to be that wet Appalachian rock pavement used on the city's streets. I cannot decide if this was to draw attention to Gruber's exposure or to cover it."

"For God's sake," blurted Keefe. "Would you shut up, man?" Justice Wright rapped his gavel to quiet Keefe, and Stollenwerck carried on undisturbed.

"Perhaps, it was to indicate punishment or revenge, although the blow to the head would singularly suggest those ideas on its own, one would think." As the doctor continued to ponder the situation, the coroner's jurymen, who had also examined the body, looked away or down at their knees, embarrassed to have viewed the tableau.

When the doctor paused, Justice Wright thanked him for his service and called Chief Keefe to the stand. Keefe scowled at Stollenwerck as they passed.

In full uniform, the chief wore his billed cap until he rested it over his large stomach. Stripes bedecked his sleeves. He reported on the murder site and how the crowds saluted and cried when Gruber was removed to the ambulance. "Gruber was very popular and well-respected," Keefe said and stood to leave. When he donned his cap, Justice Wright suggested he sit back down, saying he was not ready to depart.

"Chief, please present to the jury the evidence you have in your possession."

"No, I will not," Keefe answered. "To add these small items to this mystery, that are probably unrelated to the event, anyway, will only confuse justice. We will be wasting time chasing small irrelevant matters." Everyone present knew Justice Wright referred to the serge belt and lady's hanky found near the lieutenant's body. They read it in the newspaper and then also told everyone else they knew.

A heated discussion ensued until Mayor Bill Bostwick, also in attendance, stood at his seat and suggested a week's delay in the proceedings. This postponement would allow the parties to compose themselves, he said.

Justice Wright deferred the hearing to a future date from which he excluded spectators, and news of the belt and hanky was never forthcoming. A so-called detective was hired to investigate the case but was soon fired for drunkenness and that ended the examination.[1]

PART IV

THE PITZER TRIAL

Duval County Courthouse 1866-1901

Hon. Rhydon Mays Call
United States District Judge
Presiding Officer

Alexander St. Clair-Abrams
Defense Attorney for Edward Pitzer

Augustus G. Hartridge
State Attorney

Napoleon Broward
Duval County Sheriff
Governor of Florida

Duncan Upshaw Fletcher
Assistant to State Attorney
United States Senator

Part IV – Chapter 1

TRIAL OPENING

One Month After Marie Louise Gato's Murder

Tuesday, May 25, 1897

    Four great clock faces surrounded the Duval County courthouse spire. Resembling a Gothic church with ornate masonry and lancet windows, the building had front double doors opening onto a crowded entrance.[1] Latecomers bunched together, pushing up the iron stairs to the second-floor courtroom. Rumors had spread. Things looked bad for the defendant, so people were especially excited about the trial's opening day.

    Another crowd massed on the wooden sidewalk to watch Duval County Sheriff and future Florida Governor Napoleon Broward escort George Edward Pitzer to the opening day of his murder trial.[2] The defendant perched on the buckboard beside the sheriff for his three-block journey from the Jacksonville jail to the county courthouse.

    Broward, three times the size of his prisoner, flourished a long mustache swirling up his cheeks. The generously proportioned sheriff bent forward over the reins. The horse hooves knocked rich pops on the brick street. In a well-fitted suit provided by his mother, Pitzer sat upright, his hands manacled behind his back. He whistled.

Pitzer parted his straight red hair in the middle. He had an English mustache, also red, also parted in the middle. He wore a stiff upright collar in white contrast to his black attire. A fine thin nose and small well-cast ears should have made him handsome, an illusory resemblance to his elegant aunt who waited inside. But his features looked pinched and narrow, like a fox or a mouse, but less alert or prepared.

Eddie Pitzer, Times Union sketch

Pitzer, twenty years old, five feet ten inches tall, 135 pounds, nodded to the assembly and smiled to assure everyone all would be well, that he would be well. It was jury selection day.

"I hope you hang, Pitzer," a man called out as Pitzer rode past in the buggy. The crowd stared. Most had never been so close to an accused killer.

"Hello, Eddie. How are things?" A friendly voice. The prisoner cocked his head and grinned, then puckered again for whistling. Arriving at the side entrance of the courthouse, he stepped down, all smiles and good cheer. He continued to warble like an impudent bird.

Broward poked him in the back to stop the inane trilling, but even into the courtroom, Pitzer continued. He and the sheriff passed inside the dark wooden balustrades of the bar where Broward finally unlocked him. Pitzer rubbed his wrists and shook down his coat sleeves.

Beyond the extended oval glass windows in the front of the courtroom, an oak tree spread its crown of thick limbs. Through a side window, catching most of the sun, a raggedy-barked palm tree, a survivor of many years of storms, angled across the glass.

Circuit Judge Rhydon Call's high bench sat beneath the window with his private quarters situated behind him. The witness chair was located to his right.

Pitzer's family and the officers of the court had assembled in the front of the courtroom. Edward Pitzer sat beside his attorney, Alexander St. Clair-Abrams, at the long wooden defense table, the dark surface scarred by years of fingernails digging its grain, carved initials and sustained anxious fidgeting. St. Clair-Abrams' voice, if projected, could be heard in Savannah.

The prosecuting attorneys, led by Augustus Hartridge, the youngest state attorney in the history of Florida, took their place at the table across the room.[3] They were charging Edward Pitzer with the murder of Marie Louise Gato.

Pitzer's father, his mother and his mother's siblings sat at the defense table also. The aunts and uncles had traveled from Pittsburgh to Jacksonville by train, a long slow trip. His most sophisticated aunt, Sarah, his favorite, leaned over to kiss him when he settled. Her rich husband, George Hosack, the one financing Pitzer's defense, closely associated with Andrew Carnegie, owned a coal mining company and other businesses.[4, 5] Across the Monongahela River, where he lived in Carnegie, Pennsylvania, the local school board and public library benefitted from the attention of his wife Sarah.

The men of the family of Marie Louise Gato, the eighteen-year-old murdered girl interred at Old City Cemetery, were wealthy Cubans with large cigar factories in several Florida cities. Near Pitzer's father's small home goods store, El Modelo Cigar Manufacturing Company, owned in part by Marie Louise's father, sat on Bay Street close to the river. The three-story square brick cigar factory covered a block while Pitzer's store, in a string of flat-faced buildings with large display windows, looked no different from any small store on a commercial street in the South.

As the Cuban families entered the courtroom, José Huau, the victim's uncle, rested his hand on the brass handle of the heavy door. As Florida agent for the Cuban junta in New York, working for Cuban independence from Spain, Huau spent great sums to organize filibustering from northeast Florida.[6] With the help of local citizens, he waged secret unauthorized war on Cuba, sending men and arms to help the island free itself from the grip of Spain. Duval Sheriff Napoleon Broward had captained the first boat Huau launched, the *Three Friends*. Alphonso Fritot, Huau's nephew and chief filibustering lieutenant, accompanied them into the courtroom.

"We will behave as reasonable people," Huau whispered to Gabriel Gato. "Some think of Cubans only as fiery rebels, but we are patient. We are not disheartened. We are constant and we follow the law. We definitely do not swing machetes, do we, Gabriel?" Huau said with a wink to his quick-tempered brother-in-law.

Huau's wife, Catalina, and daughter, Katie, also attended the trial, but Huau's admonition was not directed at the women, an unfortunate oversight. Straight as a stick, no bigger than a buttonhook, Catalina wore her white hair swept into a severe knot behind her head. She marched evenly to the front of the room and glared at the Pitzer family. They stared back, unsure how to respond. Huau sighed, placed a hand on his wife's shoulder and turned her away. In Enriqueta's absence, she had appointed herself the dead girl's courtroom guardian. Enriqueta's emotional endurance was understandably low.

Katie Huau Lorraine, a town favorite, also cast a withering look toward the Pitzers, which caused even George Hosack to shudder. When Judge Call saw Katie, his back stiffened and his demeanor momentarily weakened.

Also captivated by the stunning young woman, Eddie Pitzer watched Katie, too. She reminded him of Marie Louise and the Easter Sunday when Marie had allowed him to kiss her. Two days before she was shot. He shook his head. He had to think where he was. It was jury selection day.

In 1897, Jacksonville had fewer than 30,000 inhabitants.[7] The citizens knew, or thought they did, both the accused killer and the victim. Extensive newspaper coverage, with pen-and-ink sketches of the trial principals increased the population's intimacy with them. So, the jury pool constituted men summoned from the countryside, thought to have less knowledge of the murder and less prejudice towards either side.

That late May day was warm and sunny, not yet as blistering hot as it would be in a month. The open windows and large wall fans helped cool the visitors, crowded tightly in the courtroom chairs. The women, wearing deep-crowned broad hats adorned with feathers, birds and fake flowers, blocked the view of those behind. Competition was fierce for a view, but no one dared touch an offending hat. Negroes were allowed in the courtroom if there was extra room. They could sit in empty back row seats or lean against the rear wall.

When the bailiff called the court to order, Judge Call began to interview the venire panel from which the jury would be drawn. When the spirited St. Clair-Abrams immediately requested the court that counsel be allowed to conduct their own voir dire of potential jurors, the judge immediately denied him.

"Take your seat, Mr. St. Clair-Abrams," Call snapped.

Call asked only two questions of the potential jurors, beginning with "Have you talked with anyone purported to know the facts of this case?"

The first man responded, "What is 'purported,' sir?" and was immediately relieved of duty.

The judge's second question, for the remaining candidates, was "How do you stand on capital punishment, sir?"

Another man answered, "I don't know what it is, Judge." He was also excused.

Pitzer followed the proceedings closely. Animated, leaning forward on the defense table, he eyed each potential juror. "I will do that man up, if I ever get out of this scrape," he muttered. "I don't like that one. I don't like those ugly whiskers, on his chin. He's too old. Hartridge is too anxious to have him."

The newspapermen, their pencils flying across their pads, seated in a row behind the defense table, heard Pitzer's comments and reported them in the next day's editions. Their seats in the courtroom were moved the day after that.

James Pitzer, Eddie's father, rose from the defense table and limped out of the courtroom supposedly to search for a pencil. When he returned, Eddie leaned to him and asked if he were nervous.

"Yes," his father answered.

"Well, you needn't be," said Eddie. "It does no good."

The jailers and the few people who had visited Eddie Pitzer in his jail cell had reported he held up well and chatted briskly. The newspapers called him a genial man, who befriended the fellows on his cell block. His father, though, found it odd Eddie showed no signs of mourning Miss Gato, the woman he had always sworn he loved.

Local newspapers *The Florida Times Union* and *The Daily Florida Citizen* billed the Edward Pitzer trial for the murder of Marie Louise Gato as a battle of legal giants.[8] Prosecution attorneys, the accomplished and well-known Messrs. Augustus (Gus) Hartridge, Duncan Fletcher and Augustus Cockrell, matched defense counsel, the older Major St. Clair-Abrams in cunning, recall and eloquence, if not in classic oratory.

Gus Hartridge, twenty-eight, the athletic captain of the Jacksonville Rifles, a home brigade of social prominence, moved quickly. Hartridge was a handsome man with chestnut hair. He and his wife, Birdie, esteemed for her beauty and goodness, shone as social lights of the community. The Huaus and the Fritots, Gato cousins, often moved in the Hartridge set.

The overweight hoary Alexander St. Clair-Abrams, fifty-eight, slammed his full girth on every footfall. A hulking man with a large head and blowsy white hair and mustache, possessed some gentlemanly qualities, adorned with his own modifications. He had personalized his middle name, Sinclair, to St. Clair, creating his melodious tag. With some small basis in historical fact, having perhaps associated with an obscure militia during the Civil War, he promoted himself from Confederate private to Major St. Clair-Abrams.[9, 10]

Judge Rhydon Call was a son of an old and prominent family, including uncles who served as a territorial governor of Florida and as a United States Senator.[11] Call, from Fernandina, a small island town up the coast, held court once a month in Duval County. A dark-haired, stocky man with a flying handlebar mustache, Call loved to fish and he loved a good cigar. He presided over the matter at hand.

In the back of the gallery where the Negroes sat if there was room, Henry Gardiner, the elderly man who had initially found Gruber's body by following the buzz of the blow flies, strained to see the proceedings. He sat erect to view the front of the courtroom over the heads of the white audience and the women's hats. Chief Keefe, on the front row, had scanned the courtroom when he entered and spotted Gardiner in the rear. He stared hard at the old man before he turned to sit. He was certain the colored man was implicated in the lieutenant's death, and had thereby affected the Pitzer trial. But the old man had been cleared. Keefe's hands were tied from holding Gardiner accountable, but Keefe could scrutinize the old darky wherever and whenever he pleased.

Part IV – Chapter 2

NEAL MITCHELL, M.D.

Neal Mitchell, a physician known throughout the East from Florida to Maine, who was the primary attendant of Marie Louise Gato the night she was shot, appeared as the first witness of the trial. He had performed the autopsy and testified for the prosecution on May 26, Wednesday, the second day of the trial. The jury had been seated the day before.

Not one to waste time or to smile without good reason, Dr. Mitchell sat quietly in the witness room waiting to be called. He had presided over the Duval Medical Society and had set up a camp for victims of the yellow fever.[1] With rapid efficient movements, he frequently pulled his watch from his vest pocket to check the time while reading from a small notebook he kept in another pocket. He planned to board a steamer leaving Jacksonville at 1 p.m. that day. It was not a day for dawdling.

"Mr. Hartridge," said Judge Call, "we are ready for your witness."

State Attorney Gus Hartridge rose, his step and manner solemn. With flattened palms, he swiped back his dark hair and straightened his jacket with a quick tug on the front.

The bailiff led Dr. Mitchell across the front of the courtroom. Mitchell had an enviable reputation, having fought several tropical fever epidemics, during which many of the population died, and currently maintaining a brisk practice in the city with his brother and father. Although his father had been a slave owner, he had returned to Maine to fight with the Union Army during the Civil War. He resumed practice in Jacksonville afterwards without his slaves.

Hartridge asked a few initial questions to establish Mitchell as an expert witness.

Defense counsel St. Clair-Abrams, stood, interrupting, and agreed to stipulate to Mitchell's expertise. Hartridge moved to his point.

"Tell us Marie Louise Gato's condition when you arrived at her home on April 20, please, Doctor."

"When I arrived on Tuesday night, she was lying on the parlor sofa. She appeared to be suffering intensely," he said. "One bullet had passed through her hat and scratched her forehead.

"The shooter, not a very good aim, put the second shot in her elbow. It travelled through her arm and exited through her hand, destroying her left thumb. Apparently, she was protecting herself with her raised arm while turning to run away." Mitchell raised his left arm to illustrate. "These two were the most obvious injuries."

"Speculation, Your Honor," said St. Clair-Abrams, "the whole bit of it."

"Your Honor," said Hartridge, abruptly standing. "Seconds ago, Mr. St. Clair-Abrams stipulated Dr. Mitchell is an expert witness."

"The witness should be allowed to speak only what he knows," retorted St. Clair-Abrams. "I didn't agree to his spewing fairytales as to how she was dodging bullets, Your Honor."

"Your objection is denied, St. Clair-Abrams," said Judge Call. "Your stipulation precludes it. He speaks to bullets in her body."

The defense attorney lifted his shoulder slightly in a sardonic manner and with a bored expression resumed his seat. Mitchell continued.

"Another bullet passed through her liver causing a serious wound to the right of the spinal column, six inches under her shoulder blade. I was unable to find the ball after two hours of searching." He paused. "Still another bullet, left of the spinal column, pierced the left lung, and stopped five inches below her left nipple. That ball I was able to cut out. A third bullet rested five inches below the right nipple. Her steel corset had stopped it but caused the corset to dig into her flesh."

He cleared his throat. "When I opened the abdomen," he said, "it was filled with blood from internal hemorrhaging. Either of the first two wounds could have caused her death."

Mitchell sat calmly with his legs crossed and his hands in his lap as he spoke. "Gabriel Gato called me about seven Tuesday evening, April 20, two days after Easter," he began. "I was ill, so at first I told the Gatos I couldn't help. After a while, Señor Gato called again, very upset and explained Miss Gato's injuries. I realized I must attend. He sent his carriage for me. I treated Marie Louise for an hour and a half that night and for approximately an hour the next morning before she died.

"After she died the next day about noon, I performed the autopsy that afternoon to examine the fatal wounds."

"What can you tell us from Miss Gato's autopsy?" said Hartridge, standing close to the witness.

St. Clair-Abrams listened intently to the doctor. Tense and ready to attack the doctor's testimony, he doubted the wisdom of doing it so quickly. That attitude soon changed.

"If I may," said Mitchell, stepping down from the witness stand. "If you would turn around, Mr. Hartridge, I could illustrate more precisely what I am explaining." Pointing to the bullet pattern, three places on Hartridge's back, he demonstrated placement of the entry wounds to the jury.

"Five bullets were shot. Three entered her back," he said. "One stopped below the twelfth dorsal vertebra, ranging from right to left, upward and outward, lodging under the skin in front of the body. One destroyed her thumb."

St. Clair-Abrams shot from his seat and objected on the grounds of speculation and prejudice. "I object. If the doctor saw but three bullet holes and a damaged thumb," said St. Clair-Abrams, "how does he even know five shots were fired?"

"I saw the discharge through the hat, of course." Unaccustomed to interrogation, the doctor countered with disdain.

"Dr. Mitchell, please," said Call, ushering him back to the witness chair. He denied St. Clair-Abrams' objection.

Hartridge returned to his table then approached the doctor with a small white corset stretched between his hands. "Do you recognize this, Doctor?" he asked.

"Inappropriate and prejudicial. I object," said St. Clair-Abrams, staring disgustedly at the garment, as if he had never seen it before.

Dr. Mitchell held the undergarment before him for others to see. "Because of the placement of the bullet holes, I am able to identify it as Marie Louise Gato's corset."

Crossing the room, Hartridge displayed the mutilated garment to St. Clair-Abrams, who rolled his eyes to the ceiling. Hartridge then presented the corset to each juror for closer examination.

"What can you tell us about this corset?" Hartridge asked Mitchell, returning the garment to him to describe its relevance.

"Miss Gato wore this at the time of her attack. As you can see, the bullet holes are visible; they appear very close together, but the wounds were further apart than the corset indicates." He pointed to each hole. "The corset, as it was intended, had compressed Miss Gato's body, but when it is not worn, it shrinks and reshapes itself to its natural size causing the holes, as you see, to be very close to each other, approximately three inches apart. However, the wounds on Miss Gato's body in its natural state were five inches apart. These things are a death trap," Mitchell said, shaking the corset and handing it back to Hartridge. "I mean to say, the way they contort the body."

As the doctor spoke, St. Clair-Abrams hawked something from deep in his gullet. The startled jury panel looked at him. Those who knew St. Clair-Abrams, his apparent cultivated background, his fine-spun sickly wife, recognized this as showmanship, not his regular habit. Nevertheless, he had distracted the jury.

"Do you need to be excused, Mr. St. Clair-Abrams?" Judge Call asked with one eyebrow arched, scowling at the sham.

"No, sir," said St. Clair-Abrams. "Please, forgive my small infirmity. I am fine now."

Mitchell continued. "The trajectories of the wounds indicate the killer knelt and pointed a gun up at Miss Gato's back at point-blank range. Her back was towards the shooter, as she no doubt had turned to run. He must have grabbed her skirt to hold her in place because the three shots blasted diagonally into her back indicated a distance determination that the muzzle of the gun was touching her, or nearly so, for all three shots."

"Your witness," Hartridge said to St. Clair-Abrams, returning to his seat.

St. Clair-Abrams rose, bracing himself on his table and studied Mitchell over the rims of his glasses. Mitchell returned his stare.

"So..." said St. Clair-Abrams, "I understand you're a fine doctor." Mitchell did not respond. "So, Doctor," St. Clair-Abrams continued, "you've decided Miss Gato took four bullets."

"I testified to what I saw," Mitchell said.

St. Clair-Abrams unfurled to his full height. "Do you carry a gun, Dr. Mitchell?"

"Sometimes. Why do you ask?"

"Does that make you an expert on guns?" continued St. Clair-Abrams.

"Of course not."

"But you still tell us with precision what bullets were in Miss Gato's body, where they originated, where they travelled and where they stopped?"

"Yes, I can see as well as anyone."

"Dr. Mitchell, can you also tell us the type of bullet which you found at the autopsy?"

"Of course."

"Is that your expertise, too then? Bullet identification?"

"No, but nonetheless, I can identify a common bullet," said Mitchell, glancing at his pocket watch.

"Can you determine the velocity of a bullet?"

"Only from hearing you crackers talk about it," said Mitchell, who was from Maine.

The audience snickered.

Entering a saloon on a warm afternoon, the sound of St. Clair-Abrams' laughter might be heard punctuating the thrum of the room. His mouth opened wide and his head dropped back for either hilarity or exhortation. He'd likely be buying rounds of drinks for his table or anyone else who raised a hand.

Also likely, in the same saloon, Dr. Mitchell would not be seated at St. Clair-Abrams' table even if invited. His own entrance to the bar would be quick and polite, nods and handshakes. Mitchell's table would also be filled, often lighthearted, discreet. If space was needed on the table for hats, Mitchell's would rest in the center on its crown, the most important hat in the group.

"So, your answer is no, I presume. You cannot tell the velocity of a bullet?" said St. Clair-Abrams.

"Not really," Dr. Mitchell said, "but that is unnecessary in this matter."

"Then on what matters exactly are you an expert?"

"I'm here to tell you that Marie Louise died from internal hemorrhaging caused by bullets shot through her liver from a gun held below her mid-section and angled upwards at her body. If you want me to say the exact course the bullets followed, I cannot. Body tissue can deflect a bullet." Mitchell's trim muscled hands rested calmly in his lap.

"All right, Dr. Mitchell," said St. Clair-Abrams, he lowered his voice. "How did you find Miss Gato's mental condition?" The room grew still with curiosity. "I assume you are not a doctor of the mind."

"She was perfectly rational on both occasions that I saw her," Mitchell responded.

"And how do you come to that conclusion?" said St. Clair-Abrams.

"I know Miss Gato's mind was flawlessly clear because she answered all questions posed to her in a rational manner."

"Do not lunatics answer questions rationally?" said St. Clair-Abrams.

"I'm sure some do," answered the doctor. "In fact, insanity experts say one-half the world's insane."

"So, what is meant by insanity, doctor?" St. Clair-Abrams crossed his arms and approached the witness. "Had you considered Miss Gato might be in a state of hysteria which so many young women suffer these days? Would she then be insane?"

"No, I did not consider that," said Mitchell. "Why are you asking? I repeat that she was perfectly calm."

"Could she have been in shock?"

"Of course, the patient was in shock," said Mitchell. "She had three foreign objects in her body. Her thumb was blown off, her blood pressure low, her heart rate excessively fast. Yes, she was in physical shock. She whispered when she spoke because she was weak, but everything she whispered was completely rational."

St. Clair-Abrams looked out the window, as if pondering, then turned back to the witness. "Did you, Dr. Mitchell," he asked, "offer her medicinal aids for her condition?"

"What do you mean, sir?"

"Did you give her something to boost her system, to alter her mood? An opiate of some sort?"

Mitchell's shoe kicked the witness box as he uncrossed his leg and sat up straight. "Why don't you simply ask if I gave her morphia?"

The gallery hushed.

"And did you?"

"Dr. Dean, who arrived before I did, gave Miss Gato 1/8th grain of morphia, which did not produce drowsiness. And had he not administered it, I would have done so and you know it. It's standard procedure. It's protocol. It's the practice of medicine." Mitchell's decibels increased. St. Clair-Abrams stepped back but maintained a probative stare. "That amount of morphia did not affect her mind in the least. I want to know why you ask."

St. Clair-Abrams looked to Judge Call.

"Dr. Mitchell," said Call. "Please answer the question. It is not for you to question the attorney."

Mitchell did not like that and his expression showed as much. "The shock produced by the wound was sufficient to counteract a considerable higher dosage, more than her normal condition could stand." Mitchell stated affirmatively, "Marie Louise was perfectly sane."

"She was eighteen years old, Doctor," said St. Clair-Abrams loudly. "Morphia was not appropriate."

"She was dying, Abrams, bleeding to death," Mitchell boomed back.

"No further questions," St. Clair-Abrams said abruptly, turning and displaying himself, as though he had won a point.

Part IV – Chapter 3

Trolleys Passing

On the afternoon of the trial's second day, the bright sun no longer shone through the leaded glass window. Those who wished could easily interpret an unpleasant omen from the cloudy overcast sky.

Before the shooting, Pitzer had spent numerous nights calling on Marie at the Gato home. He lived a country block south of her on the Panama Road; so he was handy. Annoyed by his constant attention, one evening she snapped at him that she would be in town with her Huau cousins on the night of April 20, and she told him the rest of the Gatos would prefer he not come to the house that night.

Not trusting Marie Louise, on April 20, Pitzer walked to the Gato place to check on her absence. Telling him the truth for once, she was not there. Still, he would look for Marie in Jacksonville to reassure himself. He walked from 11th Street, where the Gatos lived, to the trolley terminus at 8th Street. He boarded the southbound trolley to town. It was a crucial decision.

The State next called Mr. E.T. Smith of the trolley company that owned the car on which Miss Gato rode. The man was round, as were his glasses, and bald and very serious. Clearly from his demeanor, he would not have his company blamed for the tragedy.

"I am foreman of the Main Street Railway Company." Smith cleared his throat and said, "I can tell you right now this organization has never suffered a single accident or injury. We outfit Jacksonville with fifteen miles of electric railway lines, including the Main Street line, which runs into North Springfield."[1]

Hartridge nodded. "Please describe the Main Street trolley system in the Springfield area," he said.

"It's still rustic out in Springfield, on the other side of Hogans Creek, with open fields and pine forests," said Smith. "Until five years ago, we ran the bobtailed cars with mules and horses. Our electric trolleys now have smoother rides and starts than the old hay-burners. There are streets out there now crossing east-west but most are still dirt. It's a developing area."

Hartridge leaned toward him to interrupt with another question, but Smith continued to talk. "The car shed at West 8th Street and Main, the terminus of this line, was the livestock stable."

"He's giving a lecture," whispered Pitzer to St. Clair-Abrams and elbowed him. St. Clair-Abrams ignored the young man and batted away his protruding elbow.

As Smith continued, Hartridge interrupted him. "Do you, sir, recognize the defendant in this case?"

"Of course. Yes. He's Eddie Pitzer." Smith looked befuddled when Hartridge changed the course of the questions.

"When was the last time you saw Edward Pitzer?"

"On the 20th of April this year, the night of the shooting of Marie Louise Gato. I did. Yes," Smith said. "I saw Eddie that night."

"By 'Eddie,'" Hartridge interrupted again, "are you referring to the defendant, Edward Pitzer?"

"Yes. I am. Of course, I am."

"And where did you see him that day?"

"I saw Eddie, Edward," Smith said, "at the trolley stop at West 8th and Main Streets near the car shed I mentioned. He was walking toward me to board the trolley."

Pitzer, who stretched his legs beneath the defense table, glanced around with a casual attitude. So casual that it puzzled his supporters.

Hartridge displayed a large plat of Springfield, already accepted into evidence. The city engineer had drawn the plat based on surveys and his own inspection of the Gato property, marking the Gato house and houses in the vicinity. The map purported to reflect all pertinent areas, including fences.

Hartridge said, "Could you point to the place where you saw the defendant the evening of April 20?"

"Here. Right here," Smith indicated a spot on the plat. "Where I'm pointing. That's where he came from." He touched the spot on the map. "Edward walked right up to the trolley pulling out a pocket watch on a chain. I figured it belonged to his grandfather or someone important to him. Why else would he be constantly grabbing it from his vest and rubbing it and polishing it, gazing at it. Each time he glanced at the watch, he walked faster as if he were matching his steps to the second hand as it circled the face of the watch. And there's where he landed," said Smith, "at West 8th Street and Main." The man dragged his finger on the map along the platted road.

"From which direction did he come?" asked Hartridge.

"From the north. From the direction of the Gato house."

Hartridge stepped back, covering his mouth to hide his satisfied expression at Smith's answer.

"Objection," St. Clair-Abrams barked. "He could not see from where Mr. Pitzer arrived. The most he could see was his approach from the west." Through his white walrus mustache and short goatee, he glowered at Hartridge. Surprise at his bombast stirred through the room.

"The objection is sustained," said Judge Call. "Mr. Smith, you have no idea where the defendant had been before boarding the trolley and you will refrain from further conjecture in your remarks. Jurymen, ignore this specific reference. Proceed, Mr. Hartridge." With a look, he warned Hartridge to control his witness.

"What was Mr. Pitzer wearing that night, Mr. Smith?"

"He was dressed in a black suit and wore a black derby hat."

"Did you speak with the defendant at the time?"

"Yes, I did."

"What about?"

"Nothing significant that I can remember. We talked for a minute and a half and then Edward boarded the south train at six-thirty sharp. The trolley is always on time."

"What happened next?"

"Nothing."

"Did he tell you where he was going or where he had been?"

"Objection. The state attorney is leading the witness," interjected St. Clair-Abrams.

"Sustained," rendered Judge Call.

"No," said Smith.

"Your witness," Hartridge said to St. Clair-Abrams with a charming smile. The older man curled his lip in response.

St. Clair-Abrams began his cross-examination. "Mr. Smith, you remember the exact time and place Mr. Pitzer boarded the train."

"Yes," Smith said.

"You remember Edward Pitzer's every movement in your presence that evening. You know what he wore. You remember how long you conversed, but you have no memory regarding any aspect of the conversation. And why might that be, Mr. Smith, this particular failure of memory?"

Smith, startled, paused before answering. "Sir, I am a very precise man. A trainman," he said. "If I don't recall a conversation, it must have been of no consequence, or it did not happen." His head steadied with his importance.

"Indeed," said St. Clair-Abrams, pleased the trolley man felt the exchange was unimportant or nonexistent. "Your Honor, I reserve the right to recall this witness if he remembers something we should know."

Smith left the witness chair, his expression tight and his lips drawn.

Hartridge next examined George Durrance, the conductor on the same southbound car that Smith had ridden. Durrance said he, too, had seen Pitzer at the car shed that day. "Pitzer boarded the six-thirty southbound train at 8th Street," said Durrance. "As the car traveled toward the city, he rode with me on the rear platform outside. We conversed in a general nature, but nothing was said that I can remember."

"How would you characterize Mr. Pitzer's behavior?"

"Actually, he acted a bit odd. He was talkative as always, but that day, he seemed stiff, staring at both sides of the tracks in the direction of the oncoming northbound, although it hadn't yet approached. He stared speculatively, as if waiting for something or someone, especially when we stopped at the 2nd Street switch for the northbound train to pass us."

"At the switch?" asked Hartridge, puzzled. "Explain, please?"

"Since Main Street only has a single track from Bay Street to 8th Street when the north and southbound trains pass, the southbound trolley pulls off on an alternate set of tracks which swerve away from the main track. We call it the switch. A man pulls a lever which starts a mechanism to operate a moveable track. Sometimes known as frog legs. The tracks swing out and the trolley rolls off onto the alternate track. Only the southbound car goes into the switch. In our case the northbound passes us on the main line and takes eight minutes to get to the terminus at 8th Street. We on the switch, going south, wait two or three minutes for the track to clear.

"While we were at the switch waiting, Pitzer ogled the opposite passengers one by one. I wondered if that was why he rode on the platform in the first place. Then as a total surprise, at least on my part, Marie Louise came clattering along on the northbound car, placidly gazing into the distance. Pitzer's head jerked forward. His eyes got big. We were as close to her as I am to you right now. About two feet apart. Pitzer had time for a nice long look. We could have touched each other from car to car.

"When the trolleys passed, a peculiar sensation descended on me and on him and probably her, too. In the afternoon sun, it seemed a thick fog suddenly seized us all, immersed us in a mist. It scared me and I think it scared Pitzer. I felt we had listed into a sloping tunnel, totally black, with a single headlight roaring towards us, and with the loudest screaming steam whistle I ever heard. The whole thing lasted only a moment. A brief phenomenon but my heart shook. It may have been Pitzer screaming."

St. Clair-Abrams rose slowly with an incredulous face. "You seem to be a regular fellow," he said to Durrance. "I object to this silliness."

"Your honor," Durrance continued, almost pleading, "the smell of friction floated from the wheels as if they were tearing metal. It made us cough. All I could think was a menace had been provoked in this fatal switch. Pitzer felt it, too. I know he did and that's why he jumped and flew away. He threw himself off the car, his knees hitting the ground. Then scrambling to his feet, he darted up 2nd Street.

"Everyone knew he loved Marie Louise, but at that moment something struck him. He realized she might not love him. I can't tell you why I know that's true but it is what I believe."

"Prejudicial," St. Clair-Abrams blared. With all his thunderous might, goatee vibrating, he roared his objection at the conductor's characterization of the switch.

"I withdraw the question," Hartridge replied quickly. "I have finished my examination of this witness."

St. Clair-Abrams' first question was whether other people dismounted the train by hopping off between stops.

"Yes, it happens," Durrance replied. "The distance from the rails to the ground is only about twelve feet. It's not the way most people exit a trolley, but Pitzer was not the first."

Hartridge watched Durrance answer St. Clair-Abrams' questions. Was Pitzer an obsessional stalker? Had he boarded the trolley to confirm Marie's location? Pitzer knew Marie was out and about and he would find her. He knew everything about her. He called on her everyday. He followed her everywhere. He sent her presents. He spied on her. He begged for her attention.

He now saw she had lied to him and the two were traveling to opposite poles. When he spotted her traveling alone, he threw himself into the air. He would race her to her home. He would battle past her to her yard.

Part IV – Chapter 4

Serena Field and Drucilla Bryant

The State's next witness, Serena Field, was a colored girl of sixteen, but she had no birth certificate and never did. She followed two long strides behind the bailiff to the witness chair. She knew to follow him. He would not escort her. Straight as a pine sapling, head erect, but her eyes cast down as she walked. A cleaning woman had given her the crisp white blouse she wore, as well as her long dark skirt. All previously owned by the cleaning woman's white lady.

When Pitzer saw Serena settle in the witness chair, his eyes narrowed to scrutinize her. She hadn't testified at the coroner's inquest, and so he thought he'd never met her, but in fact, he had.

As Serena faced the gallery and swore on a Bible she wouldn't lie, she had never seen so many white people together at one time. She felt her hand shake on the book. But her voice was strong. She sat back in the wooden witness chair, her eyes anchored and steady on the state attorney's face. The audience leaned forward, chuckling quietly at the sight of the young Negress sitting in front of the court. Most were sure she'd lie in spite of her oath. Especially the ladies would never trust a colored woman.

"Where do you live, Serena?" asked Hartridge.

"I lives near the new cut of Laura Street, way above town. Above the railroad track."

"That's even further out in North Springfield than the Gato place, yes?" Hartridge asked with a smile. He meant Gabriel Gato's 170 acres.

She nodded yes.

"Serena, you will need to answer my questions out loud for the court transcriber to hear and record them. Would you do that, please?" asked Hartridge. She bobbed her head she would.

"Serena," Hartridge said, gently, "you must speak aloud to me. A nod won't do." Her eyes looked desperate, still clinging to his face. Some spectators continued to smirk, but others grew more interested, hearing she lived near the Gatos.

"Yes, suh. I lives way over the tracks, in the direction of the Trout Creek."

"Do you ever fish in Trout Creek?" he asked mildly, turning away before she answered to look at a paper he held. "So you live beyond the 12th Street railroad track. That must be pretty remote out there."

"No, suh," she said. "I don't fish much. And it ain't so remote. Lots us lives out there."

Pitzer, shifting his gaze from the judge to the witness and back, scowled at the black face in the witness chair. He didn't know her. He knew damn well he didn't know her and he wanted to make that clear to someone. He touched St. Clair-Abram's arm again but St. Clair-Abrams sloughed him off, concentrating on the testimony.

"You know of the Panama Road?" The state attorney cupped his hand to his ear as a cue for her to speak out.

"Oh, yeah. It run near my house."

"Indeed. And it runs by the Gato place as well, correct?"

"Uh huh," she nodded.

"Do you use the Panama Road?"

"Yes, suh," Serena said. "Most times goin' to town. It can be dangerous for us, though."

"Yes, why is that?"

"You know, somebody might go after us out there."

Pitzer's face began to tighten and his eyes grew sharper as he watched her.

The Panama Road, known as an old but important byway, began out east running north to Panama Mills on Trout Creek which merged west into the St. Johns River. The road returned south to the city through dense woods and underbrush near Serena's home, crossed the Florida Central and Peninsular tracks at 12th Street, ran south in front of Gato's, returned to Main Street and to the city. Drays loaded with logs, carriages, horses, walkers and cyclists ranged it day and night.

Hartridge paused for a moment staring at Serena, then moved on with his questions. "Have you seen this man before?" He pointed at Pitzer.

"Yes, suh."

Barometric pressure in the courtroom plummeted. Pitzer's open mouth froze that way. Spectators craned to see the girl more closely. Catalina Huau, near the front, hands crossed on her knee, stiffened her back and straightened her shoulders, attempting to appear restrained.

"What's his name?" Hartridge asked.

No one moved or breathed.

"Eddie Pitzer," she sang out lightly.

"She's lying. She's never seen me," Pitzer yelled. The audience fluttered.

Judge Call hammered his gavel. "Mr. St. Clair-Abrams, would you like to apologize for your client?" he asked.

St. Clair-Abrams stood. "Yes, sir, I am sorry. It won't happen again." He leaned and whispered to Pitzer, his heavy hand tightly gripping the defendant's shoulder. Many thought St. Clair-Abrams chastised his client, but he actually loved the courtroom drama.

"Where did you see Mr. Pitzer, Serena?" Hartridge asked.

"In the jail, suh. I pointed my finger at him when I go in. He whistlin', walkin' round with his hands in his pockets."

"Oh," murmured some of the observers, understanding. She had lost their serious attention.

Hartridge continued. "Directing your thoughts to Tuesday, April 20th, Serena, did you see the defendant that day, also?"

"Yes."

"Where did you see him?"

"I seen him near the Panama Road. I seen him that night, the night of the murder. He the man I followed on the murder night."

Pitzer jerked forward, hands on his table, elbows jutting. "You never saw me anywhere," he mumbled. Behind him, Pitzer's mother cried out. The stunned gallery now stared hard at Serena. Who was this girl, black as tar? Where did she come from?

The men of the jury listened, unresponsive. Catalina Huau watched the jury more than she did Serena. In truth, these farmers and other men from the country, employed good colored help of both sexes. The men knew how to appraise horses and the people they employed.

"Continue, Serena," said Hartridge, "Why were you on the Panama Road that evening?"

"I walks every evening down Laura and Hogan, to Mr. Arthur McDaniel's at West 4th. I meet my sister and walks her home. Drucilla Bryant her name.

"It be more dangerous to walk alone but I never scared," she said. "I's bigger than Drucilla. I can run fast if somebody get after me. I can run faster than Drucilla. She wear shoes. That slow her down. But I would never leave her."

"Where exactly is this McDaniel house?" Hartridge interrupted.

"Corner of 4th Street and Hogan Street. It all right. It keep Drucilla busy. She make a dollar fifty a week." Hartridge raised his eyebrows. He paid his Negro help $3.50 a week.

Serena's confidence expanded. She filled more of the chair with more to say. "Drucilla's stockings always mended," she said. "She clean. Her hair in loopin' braids, one over each shoulder. She pretty, that girl." The listeners laughed at the notion.

"Tell us about seeing the defendant on April 20," said Hartridge.

"We just walking home, Hogan Street to 8th, then turns right a block to Laura Street. We likes the wooden sidewalk on Laura 'cause Hogan still dirt. Mostly Drucilla like it cause her shoes stays more clean."

Gabriel Gato owned most of the land surrounding their walk, roads, trees and houses. In April, evening shade still spread over the sisters' journey home.

"When we walkin' all a sudden," said Serena, "a man behind us and we didn't hear nothin' til he just beside us."

"Did you recognize him?"

"Shore, I did. I say, 'That Ed Pitzer,' to Drucilla, when he pushed by us."

"Exactly where was this?" asked Hartridge.

"Between 10th and 11th on Laura. He wiggled past like he runnin' and walkin' at the same time."

"What did Mr. Pitzer do?"

"He heard me say it, and turn around. He still movin', and threw a 'shut yo' mouth' kinda move with both his hands."

"Did you see him again that night?"

"Yes, suh. We seen him a little further up the road, still walkin' real quick ahead of us."

"Did you see him after that?"

"Yes, suh, then we seen him from Laura. He on the Panama Road near Gato's where it cross at 11th Street. He a block to our left. We seen him plain as day. At 11th Street everything between them roads clear and flat. A little south of Gato house. That's how we see him so good."

Hartridge stepped aside, his forefinger to his chin.

"What was Mr. Pitzer doing? Had he stopped?"

"He was hiked up on a fence rollin' up his pants leg."

"What does that mean, hiked up?"

"You know. He leg hiked up on the wood fence."

"You mean he had his foot resting on the fence? Describe that," said Hartridge.

"His leg on the low board of the old cow fence where the gate is broke and hangs. He didn't see us, 'cause he was lookin' at the house."

"And you're absolutely certain it was Edward Pitzer you saw that night?"

"Oh yes, suh. I know Eddie real well by sight. I seen him lots before. I seen him all the time round there. I sometimes see him sorta hidin' in Gato yard at night. He ain't really hid'n." She closed her eyes, crossed her arms and gave two deep purposeful nods.

"Could you demonstrate—" Hartridge began.

Serena, suddenly inspired, leaned over in the chair and reached to her ankles. "See, this here what he's doin'." She lifted her leg, bent at the knee beneath her skirt.

"What?" expressed Abrams at full volume.

Using her fingers at her ankles, she rolled cuffs on her legs as if she were wearing pants. She looked up at him.

"What are you doing?" said Hartridge in a fraught voice.

"I don't know neither, suh. I seen boys unroll their pantses when they had sand in them but not roll them up for no reason. Maybe he didn't want no sand getting' in 'em. He didn't put nothin' in them pant legs, neither."

The jurymen sat perfectly still, except one chomped the tip of his finger.

Straightening himself and taking a step forward, the state attorney offered a fresh beginning. "I believe we understand, Serena. Now, where exactly did this trouser and fence business occur? Where exactly was he hiked up?"

"I say, he standin' a half-block off from us. We seen him and the fence and the Gato house good." She rocked a little, looking around the room. "We looked, but we kept going."

"What happened after you saw Edward Pitzer rolling his trousers?"

"We walked on a little more, then we heard shots."

Everyone listening perked up more.

"What did you do?"

"What did we do? We runs cross them railroad tracks is what we did. Like rabbits." Serena's voice got louder. "Five shots." She held out her hand to show all five fingers.

"Then what happened?"

"We running and looking back at Gato's. Ed Pitzer done moved from the fence and we afraid he shootin' at us. We runs like the devil on our tail, over the tracks, 'til we gets to the woods."

"Thank you, Serena," said Hartridge, turning and nodding to St. Clair-Abrams.

The defense attorney rose for cross-examination. Making a show of thumping loudly to the witness stand, then glowered down into the young woman's face. Best to counter undisciplined force with martial restraint. She stared up at him, questioning.

"This man you saw with his foot on the wooden fence, can you describe him?" St. Clair-Abrams asked roughly.

"Him," she said, pointing. "Him. Eddie Pitzer," tipping her forehead towards the defendant.

"What time of night did you see him on Laura Street?" asked St. Clair-Abrams.

"First time, say five to ten minutes after we start from Mr. McDaniel's. We leave out there 'bout six-thirty."

"And when did you see the defendant the last time, at the fence, hiked up?" St. Clair-Abrams asked in a wry tone.

"We usually passes Gato's 'bout seven. So, I say two, three minutes before that."

"So, you are saying you saw the defendant close to the Gato yard a little before or a little past seven?"

"Yessuh, probly."

"Do you own a watch, Serena, or does your sister?"

"Nah, we just tell time by where we is. We walk it so much we knows where we is based on stopping and starting places."

"There are no streetlights out that far, are there?" asked St. Clair-Abrams.

"No, suh."

"Was the man you saw near the Gato fence tall and dark?"

"What? No suh, I didn't see no tall and dark man. All I see is Eddie Pitzer. A colored man pass me, further down, goin' slow, but that be all. He weren't no Ed Pitzer, neither."

"Does it surprise you to know," asked St. Clair-Abrams, "there was no way Mr. Pitzer could have been where you say at that time, because he had fifteen blocks to walk and you had six?"

"Objection," Hartridge bounded up. "That is incorrect calculation."

"Withdraw the whole question," said St. Clair-Abrams.

"That ain't right, sir," said Serena. "Not if he come from East 2nd Street, like what I heard. That ain't no fifteen nothins'. That is some wrong numbers."

"I withdrew the question, young woman," said St. Clair-Abrams. "You obviously have added inaccurately, if you disagree."

"Nuh-uh," she said.

St. Clair-Abrams ignored her. He turned to the judge.

"That's all I have, your Honor." He shot a warning look at Serena as if challenging her to speak out again. After a moment, she stood and walked stridently from the courtroom, no further questions being presented her.

Next, the bailiff led Drucilla Bryant, Serena's sister, to the stand. The sisters did not acknowledge each other as they passed before the bench.

Drucilla glided behind the bailiff in a black dress with puff sleeves and high-necked collar, similar to the Gatos' mourning dresses but without lace or fancy work. Her dress was also a hand-me-down. She was half the size of Serena and a head shorter.

The spectators' mood changed. Their hands danced through little chores, straightening ties, folding gloves. Drucilla disquieted them. She made them nervous with her comfortable air, light skin, and elfin nose. Colored women did not appear prominently in public places, not with authority, not in court, and if they did, they acted shy and scared as Serena had first done.

"I know it was six-thirty when we started home because I generally leave work then and always look at the clock before I do," Drucilla testified. Her big brown eyes looked with confidence at Hartridge over the tip of her nose. She seemed aware that she might have a certain aptitude with men, even white men.

"Are you acquainted with the defendant?" Hartridge asked.

"No, suh. I didn't know him but when he came behind us, my sister said, 'That's Ed Pitzer. He always hangin' round the Gato place.' He ran by us and for awhile, we could see him on the road ahead."

Hartridge nodded and began again. "Do you see the man in the courtroom who ran by you on the night of the murder?"

"Over there," she pointed. "I chose him before at the police station."

"Only answer questions you're asked," Judge Call said before St. Clair-Abrams had a chance to object. "What did you observe about him?"

"When he stopped, we caught up with him at the old Gato fence, the livestock fence along the Panama Road. He had his leg on the bottom plank, rolling his trousers over his ankle. Half that fence had already fallen."

"Was he rolling his trousers as if to have them pinned for hemming?"

She smiled, then continued. "No, suh, he was rolling them like he planned to wade." People chuckled. Then, she added, "Gatos have a fountain in their front yard—"

"Objection. Speculation."

"Yes, St. Clair-Abrams. All right. Sustained." Call was tapping his fingers, staring at Hartridge.

"What was he doing, Drucilla, besides rolling up his pants?" asked the state attorney.

"He was starin' around the house and yard, lookin' real close at everything."

"Could he have been checking to see if someone was in the yard, to make sure it was empty?" asked Hartridge. The spectators were quiet. The testimony had taken a suspenseful turn.

"Objection, leading the witness," St. Clair-Abrams stood.

"Sustained. Do not answer that," said the judge to Drucilla.

The room quieted and Hartridge continued. "What did Mr. Pitzer wear?"

"A dark suit and a derby hat."

"What time did you see him?"

"We usually cross in front of Gatos' round seven. So it was a little before that."

"Anything else unusual happen on your walk home that night?"

Drucilla straightened in her chair. "I heard pistol shots after we passed the Gato place while we were crossing the tracks."

"What did you do when you heard the shots?"

"We turned to look, but didn't see nothing. Then we ran home."

"Were you frightened?"

"Sure, we was. We thought the shooter was after us. It's not that odd, you know."

Because they were Negroes, Drucilla's and Serena's testimony of encountering Edward Pitzer on the Panama Road created uncertainty in the courtroom. A heavy quiet suppressed the audience, who believed coloreds were often liars.

St. Clair-Abrams was anxious to begin his cross-examination, although even the intrepid defense attorney seemed thoughtful, almost hesitant, about how to question this colored girl. He could not sense the jury's leanings.

"Drucilla," he began, "as I understand it, you did not know Edward Pitzer until your sister recognized him and yet you are here testifying to place him near a murder scene."

"Not knowing the man," she replied, "does not prevent me from recognizing him as the man we saw on Laura Street and saw again at the Gato fence." Some in the audience stiffened at the spirit of the Negress, admittedly handsomer than most, who dared speak with such temerity to the white man.

St. Clair-Abrams, from his vantage point, appeared unbothered. "That is simply coincidence, my dear, since neither you nor your sister witnessed Edward Pitzer shooting at all. In fact you saw no one shooting anyone. You simply heard random shots on a country road. Not unusual. You have not, in the slightest, assisted the state prosecutor in his cause."

Hartridge bounded from his chair to object.

Part IV – Chapter 5
Mrs. Eliza Huau

Mrs. Eliza Huau hesitated at the courtroom door, nervous about entering the yawning room full of middle-aged paunchy men. With unplumbed expressions, they stared back at her over worn leather books with foxed pages. The weight of heat and humidity of the room bore down upon her. She heard the disembodied clicks which sneak into the vacuums of quiet rooms. She felt the tricky legalities.

"The bailiff will escort you, madam," Judge Call said.

She placed her arm on the bailiff's and with small steps crossed beside him to the witness stand. Her black dress fitted the spheres of her body. A black kick-ruffle flared at the hem. Her long white hair, coiled into a chignon, curled beside her ears.

Because of extensive gossip and publicity regarding the Gato murder, the courtroom crowd greatly anticipated the testimony of Eliza Huau. If it had been theatre, some might have stomped and whistled. But the gallery remained quiet as Mrs. Huau entered, round as a snowball, an appealing fairy godmother. She took the witness stand knowing she couldn't grant a wish, also knowing she carried, tucked inside her, the darkest knowledge of all. At the defense table, Pitzer froze when he saw her, as did his mother, his two uncles and an aunt. How could the jury not believe whatever she said?

When Eliza turned to the audience to sit back, her youngest grandchild, four-year-old José Gato, attending the trial with his Aunt Catalina, squealed to see Eliza. *"Abuelita,"* he cried. She smiled and gave a quick, serious nod for him to be a good boy. But in reply, he shook his blond curls. The onlookers laughed. Judge Call smiled and Eliza Huau swallowed hard. Catalina settled the boy, then handed him to a relative to carry him from the room.

Eliza Huau's family called her the English woman, the second wife of the French Cuban, Dr. Joseph Cadorette de Huau, father of José, Enriqueta Huau Gato and Matilda Huau Fritot.[1]

State Attorney Hartridge straightened his lapels and strode toward the witness. "Mrs. Huau, were you present at the Gato house the night of April 20?"

"Yes."

"Tell us about the evening, please, madam."

She took a breath before she spoke. In her stiff corset, she found it hard to breathe deeply. Perspiration gathered on her forehead. "I ate supper at the Gato house that night." Her English accent, its particular phrasing, was a notable contrast to the Cuban and Southern dialects filling the room.

"Marie Louise and Gabriel hadn't come home yet," she said, "so we began without them. We all sat at the dining room table."

"Where were they?" asked the state attorney.

"I didn't know. I suspected Gabriel was still at work. I sat at the table end nearest the door, looking a bit out the window for them. Suddenly, we heard shots so loud, it was as if they flew across the table. They didn't, of course, but we all started and looked at each other and out the windows. Then, we heard screams and more shots. Georgia and I flew to the door, Georgia yanked it open."

"And who is Georgia, Mrs. Huau?" interrupted Hartridge.

Eliza smoothed the back of her hand across her moist forehead. Her face was flushed.

"Why, Georgia, Mr. Hartridge, is Marie Louise's older sister, of course." She seemed surprised at his question. "At the door, we saw Marie bent over about to fall, facing the yard gate, don't you know. I ran past Georgia. I don't know why, but I passed her. Georgia was stunned, I think, and I must have been, too. I rushed down the piazza steps to Marie Louise.

"When I reached her, I wrapped my arm under her shoulders and helped her limp to the house. She was moaning and buckled over. Then, Fritz, the gardener, raced up and helped us. Her legs dragged, poor little thing, but we finally made it to the house." Mrs. Huau began to cry. Quiet tears seeped down her cheeks. Her head tilted forward.

"Your Honor," said St. Clair-Abrams, respectfully, so as not to prejudice the jury against him, "perhaps Mrs. Huau would be better able to give her remarks after a brief respite, when she is steadier."

Hartridge offered Eliza his handkerchief. Pitzer's gaze fixed relentlessly on Eliza's face.

The room sank further into silence. The grandmother's testimony had shifted the tragedy closer to the observers, into their own front yards and living rooms.

"I'm fine," the witness said, lifting her face and dabbing at her cheeks with the cloth. With a deep breath, she began, "As Marie stumbled towards the house, her voice was labored, but I could understand her—"

St. Clair-Abrams, jumped to his feet and yelled, "Objection," so loudly that no one could hear Eliza's next words. Shocked, Mrs. Huau's face reddened and she began to dab at her cheeks again. She placed a hand on her chest.

"Your Honor, may counsel approach?" St. Clair-Abrams asked, still in a booming voice, standing. Hartridge and St. Clair-Abrams met at the judge's bench. "Your Honor," St. Clair-Abrams said, softly. "I object to this woman's testimony as to any words the poor girl may or may not have said. If Miss Gato did speak, her words are hearsay and inadmissible."

"We'll consider the matter in chambers," said Call. To the jury, he announced, "Gentlemen, we will recess until 3:00. Have a nice long lunch. You are reminded not to discuss the case. Mrs. Huau, you are not to discuss your testimony with anyone during this break."

Pitzer loved Pigniolo's restaurant. As he watched the jurors leave, he wondered if they were going there to eat. He wanted their lunch and a loaf of Pigniolo's good bread. He had asked several times for some but was denied each time, being reminded he was on trial for murder and marched back to his cell and his prison fare.

During the break, counsel met with the court reporter in Judge Call's chamber. Seated at his desk, surrounded by book-lined walls, overlooking the rooftops and the bay trees and oaks that grew along the city roads, the judge listened to the lawyers' arguments.

"Your Honor," Hartridge contended, "the decedent's words repeated by Mrs. Huau are admissible evidence by excellent authority." He tapped his forefinger on a large, canvas volume and handed the judge a long list of cases, scripted in the flourishing hand of his assistant.

"Mrs. Huau's testimony will be proper," argued Hartridge. "*Res gestae*, a long-established hearsay exception includes the admission of Marie Louise's words after her deadly ambush. The words she cried out were a natural and spontaneous utterance, part of the entire action. The victim had no time neither to concoct a lie nor calculate her remarks. Mrs. Huau's testimony as to what she heard her granddaughter say should be allowed."

Call looked at St. Clair-Abrams, imparting permission to speak. St. Clair-Abrams delivered in full voice a black-letter definition of hearsay and its exceptions. In addition to the impossibility of cross-examining the speaker, the victim, he argued against the exception in this case, saying it was not likely to get an unbiased report from her grandmother.

Returning from lunch, banded in formation, the members of the jury shuffled to their seats. Those in the gallery, who had left at the break, snaked up the metal stairs to the second floor in a wriggling mass.

Judge Call announced, after all court officers had resumed their positions, that the spontaneous utterance question had been argued and discussed and, having heard all, he had decided Mrs. Huau was entitled to testify as to Marie Louise's words at the time of her attack.

Mrs. Huau returned to the witness chair and the interview continued as if there had been no interruption. "Madam," Judge Call said, "please remember you are still under oath."

Hartridge, returning to his position beside the witness, asked, "On the night of April 20, did Marie Louise say anything when you reached her and put your arms about her?"

Pitzer's hands gripped the arms of his chair. His breath hastened. His heart rushed.

"Marie Louise was moaning when I reached her," said Mrs. Huau. The woman curled her hand before her mouth and looked as if she would cry again. "Then she said, 'Eddie Pitzer has shot me and killed me.'" A sound like a bleating goat swelled out of her throat, then dissipated. She flattened her fingers on her lips. The audience muttered unintelligibly, louder than their usual rumble.

"Are you absolutely sure those were Marie Louise's words?"

"Of course, I am," she mumbled, words swollen and thick.

Pitzer smacked his fist on the table. "Marie would never say that." He lowered his head to the desk for several seconds. Call looked over at him, deciding not to speak. At the same moment, Tillie Pitzer also began to weep into a hankie.

Hartridge began again. "How far were you from the Gato house when you reached Marie Louise?" he asked Mrs. Huau.

"About thirty to thirty-five feet." Eliza pointed. "From here to that gentleman at the end of the row."

"Was anyone else in the Gato front yard?"

"Yes. Eddie Pitzer at the gate when I first ran out. Then Fritz dashed up."

"What was the defendant at the gate doing?"

"Fiddling with the latch. I was told later Fritz had attached a new one that day."

"Did you recognize the man at the gate?"

"Of course, I recognized Eddie Pitzer, six or seven feet away from me. I couldn't help but do."

Eliza's eyes began to droop, her words almost indistinguishable. She struggled to say, "The family ran out the front door and flocked around us as we headed inside." Her head dropped slowly forward. Her body slumped. She slid from the chair.

"Mrs. Huau? Are you unwell?" Hartridge exclaimed, springing forward to catch her as she slipped. He lowered her to the floor.

The judge called for the bailiff to bring water. Ladies from the gallery hurried toward her, past the bar, holding their broad hats steady and moving as fast as their corseted frames would allow. One waved smelling salts beneath Eliza's nose until she coughed. They helped her into the judge's chambers to rest on a cot until she could be driven home. St. Clair-Abrams' cross-examination was delayed as well as anything additional of Marie's spontaneous utterance.

Part IV – Chapter 6

Georgia Gato

While the bailiff secured the next witness for the prosecution, Tillie Pitzer began to weep more loudly. She flung her head vigorously into her hands. St. Clair-Abrams had mentioned to her that if she felt overcome by distress in the courtroom, there was no shame in crying or leaving. In fact, sympathy for her grief would do her son no harm.

Tillie had chosen an inopportune time for her breakdown. It was Mrs. Huau who had engaged the crowd's attention, not Tillie Pitzer. Now, as Georgia Gato entered the courtroom to testify, Tillie chose to exit. She slammed against the spectators' chairs as she stumbled out. Shielding her face with her hand, the crowd focused on the next highly anticipated witness. Tillie did not attend the trial regularly thereafter.

Georgia Gato's high-laced black shoes knocked against the oak floor as she strode to the witness chair. Marie Louise had always walked as if she were floating. Her older sister was more robust. Shorter and stockier than Marie, Georgia wore her golden hair tightly pinned at the back of her head. Her complexion was lighter than her sister's. She dressed in black mourning clothes, as did the rest of the family.

"Yes, I have known Eddie Pitzer for the last five or six years," she answered Hartridge in a straightforward manner, but with a slight

Cuban accent. The family spoke Spanish in their home. "He grew up in the area. We attended school at the same time."

"Tell us what you remember about the events of the night of April 20th," said Hartridge.

"The facts are these, sir," said Georgia in a blunt tone. "On the evening of April 20th, I sat at supper with Mama and the family. When Papa works late, he cannot join us. We thought Marie was at the Huaus' visiting our cousins. As we ate, I heard two gunshots from the front yard and then a scream. The dining room window was open. I heard Sister yelling, 'Oh, Mama, I am shot.' I know her voice very well, of course. I ran to the foyer door and as I turned the knob, I heard three more shots.

"I looked out the door and saw Marie bent forward, clutching her middle. My *abuelita*, grandmother, pushed past me from the dining room, and reached Marie first. She had her arms under Marie's shoulder trying to lift her and help her walk. Sister was bent nearly prone. I think I shouted, 'It's Marie Louise.'

"I could hear *Abuelita* begging her, 'Come on, Marie. Come on.' In a low groan, Sister said, 'Eddie has shot me. I'm dying,' or something like that."

"Objection," said St. Clair-Abrams. Georgia looked startled.

"Overruled," said Call, looking at St. Clair-Abrams. "And you know, I base my ruling on the earlier discussion of the same hearsay exception. You may register your protest on the record."

Continuing, Hartridge asked Georgia. "What happened after you observed your sister?"

"She was almost at the yard gate, bending to the ground—then I saw him there, too." Georgia pointed her arm straight at Edward Pitzer.

"Let the record reflect the witness is pointing to the defendant," Call said.

"Eddie Pitzer was at the gate," Georgia continued. "I saw him most clearly, shoving his pistol into his back pocket. I saw the silver flash in the light from the piazza. I saw the gun's reflection." The gallery groaned. "I think it was a thirty-eight. It looked that size and that's what the boys carry.

"I was on the piazza at first," she pointed at Pitzer again, "while he tried to unfasten the bolt at the gate. A new gate latch had been attached that day and he had difficulty with it. He was accustomed to the old one. He opened the old one often enough."

"And how far from you was this gate you describe?" asked Hartridge.

"I don't know. I was running towards it through the yard." She pointed at the hall door. "At first, as far as that door, I'm guessing about thirty feet."

"And you are sure Pitzer was the man at the gate?" Hartridge continued.

"Yes, I am sure he was the man at the gate. I am positive." She punched her words with emphasis.

"Had you ever seen Mr. Pitzer in your yard at night before this time?" asked Hartridge.

"Oh my, yes," she said. "I often saw Eddie Pitzer in my yard at night. He liked to loiter at our house and grounds, to watch us, to spy on Marie Louise. It was funny to see him in a bush or his head sticking out from behind a tree when he thought he was invisible. Sometimes, though, it frightened us. Papa would go out and yell at him to vamoose. Eddie always says he was never there. That he never hid in the bushes. And he didn't, really, because he was never hidden to us."

"When did Marie Louise meet Edward Pitzer?" the prosecutor asked.

"They met about seven years ago when we moved to the Panama Road. He lived nearby. He came to our yard. He had no brothers and sisters. He climbed trees and kicked stones with my brother, Willie. When he grew older, he grew sweet on Marie Louise. She sometimes liked him, too, but never the same and not as much. I think she just humored him."

"Objection. She can't know what Marie Louise felt or thought," said St. Clair-Abrams.

"Sustained."

"For more than two weeks prior to the shooting he called every evening and stayed until 10:00 to 11:30," Georgia continued. "He couldn't see Marie was bored with his visits. It wasn't normal."

Catalina Huau cocked her head, angling her flat-brimmed hat. Marie should have known better than to entertain such an odd man. Marie Louise could have had her choice of men. Certainly, Enriqueta, her mother, should not have allowed it. While Enriqueta withdrew in her house instead of attending the trial, Catalina resolved to support the girl now by her own consistent presence.

"Thank you, Miss Gato," said the state attorney. Judge Call signaled to St. Clair-Abrams he could begin. St. Clair-Abrams could smell a tough opponent across the St. Johns River and would row the width to confront one. Georgia's eyes narrowed as he lumbered toward her.

"That evening," he began, "would it not have served you better to investigate what you thought you saw, than to haphazardly shout my client's name? Do you not realize screeching across the yard influenced your sister to name him as the shooter?"

"Marie had already spoken Eddie's name. I certainly did not influence her," Georgia said. "She knew Eddie too well. Her identification was accurate. I did exactly as I should have done." Georgia spoke evenly at first, but her volume increased. "When would you prefer I had told my family? Should I have let them finish their meal first?"

The judge said, "Miss Gato, please maintain civility."

"Your testimony in this matter," St. Clair-Abrams said, "is different from your statements at the coroner's hearing. What version do you choose today? Will you continue to change what you say, Miss Georgia?"

"Sir, you are completely inaccurate and very offensive," she retorted.

St. Clair-Abrams' ironic smile showed through his white mustache. "I believe your exact words at the inquest, Miss Georgia," he said, looking at the transcript of the hearing, "were that you recognized Edward Pitzer by his clothes, his hat and his build. I am reading it right here."

"Should I have described his nose hairs?" she snapped.

"This is not a joking matter, Miss Gato," said Judge Call.

"Indeed not, Your Honor," she replied, more subdued.

"Previously, you described the killer's coat and hat, Miss Gato?" said St. Clair-Abrams.

"I'm sure I did because he was wearing them. I also described his head and body."

"But not his face."

"Of course, his face. I'd know that face anywhere."

"You did not have enough light from the porch to identify Edward Pitzer's face."

"You must be joking. It was a bright evening. There was a bulb on the piazza and light from the hall. I know Ed Pitzer when I see him as well as I would my brother. Believe me, there was plenty of light to recognize Eddie."

"Your sister's scream convinced you it was he, because you have known him to be there in the past, or at least, that's what you say," St. Clair-Abrams said.

"Major St. Clair-Abrams, you are not confusing me and you, as I recall, remained silent at the hearing, perhaps because you knew nothing about the matter."

"With whom did you discuss your testimony after testifying at the inquest?" asked St. Clair-Abrams.

"Many, many people."

"A police officer?"

"I spoke with several of the officers who were there that night."

"One explained to you, I believe," St. Clair-Abrams said, making a slow reel toward the jury, "that Edward Pitzer was not in your front yard, as you so stated, but instead downtown, two miles' distance, and could not have been in your front yard at your gate?"

Georgia's face flared. She took a deep breath and composed herself before she spoke. "No, sir, no one ever proved anything like that. It's ridiculous to say that when he was in my front yard at that time."

"Are your remarks today inspired by a pre-existing prejudice toward Mr. Pitzer?" St. Clair-Abrams continued.

"Not at all," she said. "And furthermore, my remarks are not conflicting. What I say today is correct. My testimony has always been consistent and what I have always said from the beginning." She emphasized each word. "Eddie Pitzer was in my yard. I saw him," she said, her voice rising again. "He had a gun. He ran away."

St. Clair-Abrams turned and walked back to his desk before he continued. "You and my client, Eddie Pitzer, have a history, don't you, Miss Gato?" said St. Clair-Abrams. "You haven't liked each other for some time, is that correct?"

"Our relationship is unpleasant. That's not news," said Georgia. "We attended school together and that was unpleasant, too. It's always been unpleasant with him. Every time he came to the house, something untoward occurred. To be honest, Mr. St. Clair-Abrams, I've always thought him a simpleton. When we attended school, every time he saw me he would stick his tongue out."

"I assume he does not do that now as an adult." The audience laughed.

"No, he's obviously much worse, now," she said, though few people heard her.

"And how would you characterize his relationship with Marie Louise?"

"He pestered her," Georgia snapped. "Sister found him a nuisance. I found him a nuisance as well. But we all treated him politely."

"I can well imagine," St. Clair-Abrams mumbled into his cuffs, drawing a hand across his face.

Pitzer leaned forward, sneering at the witness. His father, sitting beside him at the defendant's table, patted his son's shoulder to interrupt him and cause him to straighten in his chair.

"Are you aware, Miss Georgia," St. Clair-Abrams asked, "that Eddie and Marie were in love?"

She laughed. "No, Major St. Clair-Abrams, that is quite untrue. Sister did not favor him at all."

St. Clair-Abrams hesitated slightly. The fullness of his jowls seemed to stretch. "They have been seen together often, have they not?"

"And what young man at some time or another has not been seen in the company of my sister? She had many admirers."

"But your sister and Edward Pitzer were sweethearts."

"Sir, you are deluded. Do you not know Domingo Herrera, to whom she was engaged, who is out of the country fighting for Cuba's freedom? Marie Louise was in love with Domingo. Edward Pitzer never stood a chance with her. There were others, also, like José Carbonne, now traveling from Cuba to avenge Sister's death. Only two days ago, we heard that some poor young man coming from Detroit, was mourning his love, Marie Louise Gato, murdered in Jacksonville, Florida.[1] No, Major St. Clair-Abrams, you are confused about Marie Louise and poor Edward Pitzer."

"Apparently Miss Gato, you will soon be much surprised to learn of their relationship," said the defense attorney.

"Do not testify, Mr. St. Clair-Abrams," said Judge Call. "Do not record that comment," he spoke to the transcriber.

Edward Pitzer grabbed the edge of the desk and inhaled a short breath, registering his surprise at Georgia's list of Marie Louise's boyfriends. She looked at Pitzer with disgust as she rose to leave.

Part IV – Chapter 7

Fritz Aberdeen

State Attorney Hartridge continued to build his case, dealing his cards in organized fashion beginning with the death of Marie Louise. Following Dr. Mitchell's testimony, he presented witnesses to the events of the evening in chronological order.

The Gato gardener and handyman, Fritz Aberdeen, stepped through the courtroom door in a dusty waistcoat and a soft collarless cotton shirt. Accompanied by the bailiff, Aberdeen strode stiffly to the witness chair. A large German with a confusing Scottish surname, he had hulking shoulders and broad features but his eyes were bright blue details on his weathered skin. His spoken words were short and brisk with guttural R's hoisted from the back of his throat. His lips and jaw tight, he emphasized points with louder speech, rather than a change of pitch.

"Do you know this man, Mr. Aberdeen?" asked Hartridge.

Aberdeen looked toward Pitzer. The hopeful defendant gazed at the gardener with pleading eyes and a weak smile. "That man be Eddie Pitzer, rarely out of my sight for a year and a half," said Aberdeen without expression. Pitzer ducked down, after being ignored.

"And where do you know him, sir?"

"At the Gato place. Night and day. All the time, hiding in the bushes, his head growing like a damn cabbage in the ground."

"Objection," raised St. Clair-Abrams. "Condescending slander."

"The jury will disregard the witness's last metaphor," said Call, "and his unnecessary profanity."

"Mr. Aberdeen," said Hartridge. "You say that you have seen Edward Pitzer at the Gato place often. Where in particular have you seen him?"

"I seen his red head there, near every night and day, sneaking and dodging about the house, in the shrubs, peering in windows. I run him off several times and so did Señor Gato, but nothing kept him away from spying on Miss Marie Louise. He'd be there now but for the bars on his jail."

St. Clair-Abrams mumbled, "God save us from this fool," under his breath, which Judge Call could hear.

"Mr. Aberdeen, were you on the Gato premises the night Marie Louise Gato was murdered?" said Hartridge.

"*Ya.*"

"Please describe that night to us."

"I ate a supper in the kitchen. I heard two shots." His volume increased and he leaned toward Hartridge. "I jumped from the table. I heard three shots more. I ran across the side porch into the yard. I passed the grape arbor on the south side of the house, then I saw that one in the front yard." Aberdeen's thick arm and index finger pointed like a gun at Pitzer's head as if he might pull a trigger.

The spectators exclaimed. Tillie's sister gave a high polite shriek of surprise. Pitzer cocked his head to avoid the loaded finger.

"Order!" Call banged his gavel. "This court will come to order!"

To the witness, Call said, "Mr. Aberdeen, one more trick like that and you will be held in contempt of this court."

Aberdeen glared at Pitzer, crossing his immense forearms across his chest. The defendant, having survived the makeshift gun, straightened himself and sneered back at the hired man.

"What happened next, Mr. Aberdeen?" continued Hartridge.

"The man was trying the front gate latch I fixed just that morning." Aberdeen wiped his leathery hand across his cheek.

"Do you mean, sir," said Hartridge quickly, "that you saw the defendant at the Gatos' front gate that night?"

"Aye, I do. Trying to pry the lock. Also shoving a small revolver into his pocket."

Catalina Huau threw her open palm across her mouth, elated someone besides Georgia had seen the gun.

Aberdeen described helping Mrs. Eliza Huau assist Miss Marie Louise to the Gato house.

"No further questions," Hartridge said, heading back to his seat.

St. Clair-Abrams rose to cross-examine the witness. He looked wryly at Hartridge who peered back but made no verbal exchange.

"Mr. Aberdeen, you strike me as a man who knows things and controls situations. Am I right?" said St. Clair-Abrams.

"You say so." Aberdeen shrugged his shoulders.

"Yet, it was a dark night, without stars, when Marie Louise was murdered and you still say you saw Edward Pitzer at the Gatos' gate?"

Aberdeen leaned against the back of his chair. "It was the gloaming, Mr. St. Clair-Abrams," he replied. "That's not night. There was radiant light from the sinking sun. I wouldn't say about stars. I have no idea about stars. There was light from the porch. I would say I'd know that carrot head if it were black as pitch and no lights or stars. I was six feet from the man, eight feet, tops. I could see Ed Pitzer fleeing out the gate, stuffing a gun in his pocket. And that's it, period."

St. Clair-Abrams wheeled about, to face the witness again. "So your eyesight's good is it, Mr. Aberdeen? You couldn't make a mistake?"

"I could not," Aberdeen said flatly. "I'll read the date on a penny now. Just hand me one."

"You have perfect sight and you do not wear glasses, is that correct?" he asked

"*Nein*. Never. Hope to God I never do."

"Thank you then, sir. That is all," said St. Clair-Abrams.

Aberdeen looked startled but fetched himself up to his feet. He hesitated, looking at Abrams as if wanting to speak before leaving. Hartridge noticed the abrupt conclusion of questions, as well. Unsure what to make of it, he envisioned St. Clair-Abrams administering a vision test to Fritz.

Part IV – Chapter 8

Lulu and Malvina

The opal-stained windows of the courthouse glowed in the afternoon sun. The palm tree fronds breezed slowly across them. Hartridge called Lulu Lee, his next witness. Lulu, a little darky, he called her, the size of a coffee bean, sat in the witness chair, a faultless pickaninny. Her black hair was skewered in stubby spikes, each tied in a strip of rag.

Only twelve years old, she may have been the most important witness of the trial. Her feet did not touch the floor. The bailiff lifted her into the witness chair, the blackest child he'd ever seen. He positioned her with her feet straight out, the tips of her shoes pointed up.

She had shrunk against the entryway as Fritz Aberdeen passed through to leave. More than once, Fritz had threatened to shoot her dog, Sam, when he ran onto Gato property. Sam was the reason Lulu knew what she knew and the reason she was called to trial.

Sam, fluffy and black, licked her when she stroked his ears and loved to chase the birds in Gato fields. The birds soared in madcap escape when Sam, a barking fool, leapt at them through the air. Legs outstretched and ears swept back, he never quite made lift-off. Once more, many in the audience huffed with disgust at the colored moppet on the stand. Pitzer ran his finger against his smooth red mustache. He concentrated on Lulu, with particular attentiveness. He wasn't sure he remembered her.

"Who is this child?" St. Clair-Abrams asked the judge, plodding toward the small witness, pulling his shaggy eyebrows, appearing amazed and indignant. "May I approach the bench?"

The judge motioned for both attorneys to come close. "That is Lulu Lee. You know it," said Call.

St. Clair-Abrams whispered loudly, "Your Honor, this child is not competent to testify. I strongly object to her presence here, and to anything she may have to say, if that is the point of her company."

"Judge Call," said Hartridge, also approaching the bench, "this witness has important information to share. She is small but she is twelve years old and competent."

St. Clair-Abrams argued, "Sir, this child should be thoroughly evaluated before being allowed to speak. What can she possibly know of our procedures? What does she know of an oath? What can she know, period?"

"Naturally, Mr. St. Clair-Abrams, I will examine the witness's comprehension. Please be seated, both of you."

"Lulu," said Judge Call, "please, turn toward me in your chair. There, that's good. Now, do you know who I am?"

"Yessuh, you the judge." Her face angled towards the man. Her eyebrows lifted and her eyes enlarged. She smiled at Call.

"Tell me, Lulu, do you know who it is who made you?"

"Gawd made me," she said, quickly.

"Very good, Lulu," said Call. "Do you know what it is to swear an oath, Lulu? Suppose you took an oath to tell the truth and you told a story instead, what would become of you?"

"I'd go to the bad land, I guess." Her shoulders and arms shivered noticeably.

"That's right, Lulu. That's very good. Now, these gentlemen also have some questions for you. I know you will tell the complete and total truth because you don't want to go to the bad place. I rule the witness competent….. Your witness, Mr. Hartridge."

St. Clair-Abrams looked sour as Hartridge stepped forward. Some in the gallery cooed about how cute little coloreds were; others ruffled their lips in contempt.

"Thank you, Your Honor." Hartridge approached the witness chair. "Where do you live, Lulu?"

"I stays most time right cross Panama Road from Mr. Gato's at Mr. Caballero's. My sister work there and I help."

Hartridge nodded. "I'm going to ask you, Lulu, about the shooting at Mr. Gato's," he said. "Do you remember that night?"

"Yessuh."

"How do you remember it?"

"I thought that old man, that Fritz, that stays at Mr. Gato's place, shot Sam. Sam, my dog."

"And what does that have to do with that night?"

"Cause that Fritz always sayin' he gonna shoot Sam, if Sam go through their fence."

"Did Sam go through their fence that night?"

"I don't know. I didn't see no Sam that night, but I heard shots and I thought maybe he shot Sam."

"Where were you when you heard shots?"

Lulu said she'd been at Mr. Miguel Caballero's that evening with her sister, Malvina Lockett, who cleaned his house. They were diagonal across the Panama Road south from the Gato place. Mr. Caballero worked as a cigar packer for El Modelo, but she didn't know what that was. Lulu also said she had known Ed Pitzer for more than a year.

"That's him," she said, "that's him," correctly pointing him out.

"When I heard them bullet shots, I run cross the Panama Road and through a broken place in the wood fence which got lots of torn-up spots. I run real fast between that fence and their yard fence lookin' to see Sam. It like a path in front of they house. Right then, Ed Pitzer come bustin' out pass me. I heard his pants legs swishin' as he come close. He pushed me outta his way."

"Where exactly did Edward Pitzer pass you?"

"Almost to the front yard gate. I stepped over, but he too fast and he bumped me against that old fence. It hurt."

"How close was Edward Pitzer to you when he passed?"

She held her small hands up to measure. "He right there. We touchin'. Path between fences two foot. Besides, he be lookin' back and puttin' up his pistol, too. That's why he run into me, he lookin' somewhere else."

"You saw Edward Pitzer with a pistol?"

"Stuffin' it in his pocket when he shoved me." She yipped and wiggled her head up and down.

"Lulu, was it a dark night," said Hartridge, "the night Mr. Pitzer ran into you?"

"No, suh. Uh-uh."

"Could you see stars?"

"Uh-huh. They was plenty of stars and they was lots of lights at the house."

"Thank you, Lulu," said Hartridge, returning to the prosecution table. "Your witness," he said to St. Clair-Abrams.

St. Clair-Abrams rose and sauntered over to the little girl.

"Lulu," he said, "but are you certain you are telling the truth about running into Ed Pitzer the night of Miss Marie's death?"

"Yes, suh. Uh-huh," she squinted at him and drew her bottom lip over the top one.

"Is this story something Mr. Gato or Attorney Hartridge told you to say?"

"Ain't nobody told me to say nothin'." She returned her lip to its odd position.

"Isn't it true that you and Mr. Gato walked on the Panama Road in front of his house, practicing what to say today?"

"No, suh. Uh-uh. I didn't need no help." She slapped her hands on her thighs.

"Didn't Mr. Gato tell you to say Eddie Pitzer ran into you that night so we would think Eddie shot Miss Marie Louise?"

"No, suh. Uh-uh." She jerked her head back and forth.

"He never said anything like that to you?"

"No, suh. Uh-uh." Her eyes narrowed. Her childish voice grew louder. She leaned forward, more determined.

"Lulu, why are you so sure it was Edward Pitzer who brushed you?"

"I seen him! He practically on me!" Lulu said, balling her hand to wallop the seat of her chair.

"Objection," Hartridge got to his feet. "Mr. St. Clair-Abrams is harassing the child," said Hartridge.

"I agree," said Call. "Mr. St. Clair-Abrams, you've tried to make a point. It's time to relinquish the attempt."

"Your Honor, if I may state for the record…" Call nodded his acquiescence. "Although our distinguished judge has ruled this young girl competent to testify, I disagree with that decision and think it is an error. I object to this child's testimony. She does not act or look like a twelve-year-old and it is difficult to believe she fully comprehends this trial or its meaning. Lulu seems much younger. Furthermore, I don't think her responding she would go to the bad place if she lied under oath indicates an understanding of the crime of perjury or jail time if she were held in contempt of court." There was miscellaneous clapping from the audience.

When St.Clair-Abrams was finished, directed by the judge, the bailiff called the next witness, Malvina Lockett, Lulu's older sister by three years, who tended house for the Caballeros. She testified she was working when she heard shots on the Panama Road and ran to the window to look toward the sound. She pulled the blind, but only one side rose so the blinds hung cockeyed. She tried to shove the window open but the sash was broken, too, and the window froze in place. Releasing the blind to bang against the glass, Malvina chased outside after Lulu, running through the dirt of the Panama Road at the 11th Street cut into the Gato yard. Beneath a chinaberry tree, she collided with Edward Pitzer running south from the Gato front gate.

"Is there any way you could have mistaken the man's identity?" Hartridge asked Malvina.

"No, suh," she answered with emphasis. "I watched him run over 11th Street, then south on Laura Street. He turned to see if anyone followed him."

Malvina testified like Lulu, when asked by St. Clair-Abrams on cross-examination, if she was absolutely sure it was Pitzer. Yes, it was Pitzer. It was not too dark to see, and Mr. Gato had not told her what to say.

St. Clair-Abrams left her and walked past Hartridge to the defense table. A quick unstated glance passed between them. They hastily looked away. What really was the probative value of any of these colored witnesses?

Part IV – Chapter 9

Mr. and Mrs. Sanchez

The state attorney continued to call his witnesses in the order they'd seen Pitzer the evening of the attack. Having reviewed the murder scene, Hartridge began to question Gato's neighbors, who saw Pitzer running south on Laura Street from Gato's yard.

Edward Sanchez lived on 11th Street near the corner of Laura, facing town. He was a block east of Caballero's, where Lulu Lee and Malvina encountered Pitzer at the livestock fence. Sanchez, a small brownish man with shiny black hair slicked into a pompadour, radiated energy walking to the witness chair. As did many skilled cigar workers, he dressed in fine style, a pin-striped jacket, a watch chain on his vest, and shiny pointed shoes.

"Where do you live, Mr. Sanchez?" asked Hartridge.

"My wife and I live on 11th on the east side of Laura Street in Springfield."

"Do a lot of El Modelo cigar workers live out your way?"

"Yeah, Mr. Gato has lot of rental houses around. I heard he planned a cigar town out there. Like Ybor City. But it fell through. He is growing tobacco, though."

"Tell us what you know about the night of the shooting."

"I was finishing supper in the kitchen when I heard two pistol shots. I said to my wife, 'Someone is shooting dogs.' Then I heard another shot, then another. It was strange there were so many. I pushed back from the table and ran out to my front fence. I untwisted the wire that fastens the gate and when I looked up, Ed Pitzer was running by as fast as a man could run."

"What happened next?"

"I yelled at him, 'Eddie Pitzer, you are afraid. You are afraid of gunshots. Come back, *cobarde,* you coward.' He was a friend at Gato's. Shocking to see him rush from sounds of trouble at their house."

"Did he answer you?" asked Hartridge.

"No."

"How are you sure it was the defendant?"

"Oh, sir, I could see him so close. He ran on my side of Laura where there's a wooden sidewalk. I could have reached out and touched him. I could hear him panting. I been seeing that man for years, you know." Sanchez lifted his hands to indicate a short distance. "I could have touched him," he said to himself and shook his head.

"What was the defendant wearing that evening, Mr. Sanchez?"

"A black suit and a black derby which balanced real good on his head as he ran. I noticed that."

"What did you do after Edward Pitzer passed you?"

"I ran toward the Gato house. My wife came outside. I told her go back in so she wouldn't get shot but she wouldn't. I heard her speak to Pitzer, as I ran to Gato's. I couldn't hear what she said, but I know she said something. She definitely would."

Hartridge next called Sanchez's wife, Marie, also Cuban, larger than her husband. She wore a full-length day dress, multi-colored, which barely cleared the floor. Kicking her skirt when she walked revealed black shoes, trimmed in red, with concave curved heels.

"As I was eating supper, I heard two shots," she said. "My husband ran outside. I followed him. As I got to the lattice door on the porch, I heard three more shots. My husband was already at the street. 'For God's sake, come back in,' I said. 'Something has happened. You should not be out here.' He said I should go in the house and keep my mouth shut. Someone would shoot me. At that moment, Eddie Pitzer came running by."

"And this is when you first saw the defendant that night?"

"Yes, racing by the gate, his coat collar turned up around his neck."

"But you were still able to recognize him?"

"Oh yes," she said. "I said, 'What's the matter, Eddie?' But he didn't answer." She lifted her shoulders with indifference.

"Thank you, Mrs. Sanchez," said Hartridge.

St. Clair-Abrams strode slowly toward her.

"Mrs. Sanchez," he began, "did you not say, in a conversation with the man who drew the site map of your area—the map right over there—that you did not intend to testify to anything for Mr. Gato which would swear a man's life away?"

"Yes, I did say that. He was picking me for information."

"Did Mr. Gato, in fact, ask you to testify to certain things?"

"No, he did not."

"Did Mr. Gato encourage you to say you recognized Pitzer?"

"No, sir, he did not."

"Did you leave the city and go to Tampa because you understood you would be summoned for the defense?" asked St. Clair-Abrams.

"No. How would I know that? I went to Tampa because my mother was sick and I am here, ready to answer questions."

"How did you recognize Edward Pitzer?"

"I knew him. I recognized him."

"You recognized him by his shadow?"

"Don't be ridiculous. A woman is obliged to notice a young man she sees frequently," she said. "It is natural for her to do so. I was close enough to see Eddie Pitzer and I'm absolutely sure he passed me that night." She swung the heavy gold hoops that dangled from her ears and smiled big at Abrams.

Part IV – Chapter 10

Henry Guinard

"At exactly ten minutes before seven on the evening of April 20th, I heard five shots," Henry Guinard reported on the witness stand. "I know the precise time because I was in my living room lighting a cigar. The matches are on the mantle beside the fireplace clock. I was looking at the clock when I heard the shots. I saw the exact time." Guinard, the prosecution's witness, lived on 11th Street between Main and Laura, a block and a half east of the Gatos.

The crowd murmured, impressed someone knew the time by actually looking at a clock. The jurymen, as usual, betrayed no thoughts.

"What did you do after hearing the shots, Mr. Guinard?" asked Hartridge.

"I ran outside toward Gato's and met a man rushing toward me at the corner of Laura and 11th. He turned right, going south on Laura. I had seen him before but couldn't recall his name. The next morning I went to the county jail to pick him out. I chose Pitzer. No question he was the man I saw the night before."

"What happened when you arrived at the Gatos' that night?" Hartridge asked.

"They were carrying the wounded girl in the house when I got there. I waited as a crowd gathered. Later, the police brought Pitzer back to the house to see her, but it didn't work out. A fight almost broke out, so I left."

St. Clair-Abrams rose at his desk to take his turn. "For whom do you work, Mr. Guinard, or do you prefer *señor*?"

"I work for Gabriel Gato," Guinard said, ignoring the question.

"Do you rent one of the Gato houses?" St. Clair-Abrams pulled out a handkerchief and wiped his forehead.

"I do. Why?"

"I am implying, sir, that you have very close ties to Gabriel Gato, father of the deceased."

"I do not lie for anyone."

"Well, good for you. And how it always should be. Just one more thing, sir," said St. Clair-Abrams. "When do you wind your clock, this clock that sits on the mantle?"

"Sunday mornings and I never forget."

"It is not one you wind once a year?"

"I would notice a clock not working for fifty-one weeks of the year. I would throw it out the window or maybe, I would stick in the key and give it an annual twist."

"Ah, so," said St. Clair-Abrams. "I suppose that's true." He turned to the gallery and lifted his open hands. "A very bright man," he said.

Part IV – Chapter 11

ERNEST BENTON

As the afternoon had worn away, the prosecution team called Ernest Benton to the stand to continue narrating Pitzer's activities after the deadly shooting. Spending most of the day listening to the line of prosecution witnesses identifying him in Springfield on the evening of April 20, Edward Pitzer appeared less breezy than he had earlier.

Benton, a young deliveryman, drove for Altree, Son and Nephew, bottlers and bakers located on East Bay Street. At 6:30 p.m., April 20, he had stabled his horses for the night between Main and Laura Streets on Church Street. After settling the horses, instead of returning to his boardinghouse, Benton trekked eight blocks north to an industrial area near Hogans Creek. He was heading toward a bawdy house on Orange Street; when he arrived, the house was dark.

Ordinarily, Benton wore a soft-billed driver's cap and his collarless shirt, but for his court appearance, he dressed in a short-collared shirt and a ribbon tie dangling at his neck. While vigorously rubbing his scalp, he carried a narrow-rimmed bowler as he walked into the courtroom.

"What were you doing in that area?" Hartridge asked. "Wouldn't it be deserted at that time?"

"It was. I was just turning to walk home. I walked on Orange over to Laura Street," he drawled. The witness dropped his hat in his lap and gingerly drummed two fingers on it. With the other hand, he swiped the side of his head.

"After walking up to Orange Street that night, did you see anyone on the street?" asked Hartridge.

"Not then. I passed Guy Pride's Natatorium and his Ice Works in the first block but nobody was there. I stopped at the corner of Laura and looked toward the Exposition building."

"That would be Waterworks Park and the Sub-Tropical Exposition building where you were looking, correct?"[1]

"Yes, sir," Benton said, "on 1st Street."

"Did you see anyone near the creek or the swamps?"

"Yes, sir. I saw someone coming from Springfield over the bridge at Laura on the other side of the street. The south end of the bridge is close to where I was standing."

"Was it a man or woman?"

"It was a man. I could see his hat."

"Did you recognize him?"

The witness stared down at his hat, rubbing the brim softly. "When he got opposite me at Laura Street and 1st Street, I recognized Ed Pitzer walking, almost running, real fast. He had his coat collar turned up."

"How can you be so sure it was Pitzer?"

"Because I know him. I know Ed Pitzer real well for about two years. We're on good terms. We always stop and talk. Besides, he was under an incandescent light."

"Did Pitzer speak to you?"

"No, sir, he didn't. I said, 'Hello, Ed. You're in a hurry tonight.' But he didn't reply. Just kept rushing." Benton's hand brushed his head again. He rubbed his nose with the other.

"Mr. Benton, what time did you see the defendant at Laura and Orange Streets? Please, be specific."

"Yes, sir. It was five to ten minutes after seven. Maybe six minutes after for specific. I know the time by where I'd been and where I went after seeing him. I also heard one of the city clocks chime at seven. That also helps me know specific."

"Thank you, Mr. Benton." He turned to St. Clair-Abrams. "Your witness, sir."

St. Clair-Abrams smiled pleasantly at the witness on the stand, who now gripped his hat with both hands, anxious to put it on and leave.

St. Clair-Abrams smiled at the young man. "So, Mr. Benton," said St. Clair-Abrams, observing the witness fidgeting, "are you nervous?"

"No, sir."

"Maybe you have reason to be. Is it true you were offered a job in Savannah by Gabriel Gato if you testified you saw Edward Pitzer at the Laura Street Bridge at seven, April 20. I understand Señor Gato has business connections in Savannah."

"No, that sure ain't true. I never spoke to Mr. Gato."

"Did anyone else speak to you about this possibility of employment in exchange for your testimony?"

"No one offered me nothing!" Benton declared.

"Were you aware Mr. Gato's business partners are primarily located in Savannah?"

"No, I'm not. I know nothing about them. Whoever told you that's a liar."

"Your friend, John Thrasher, said it."

"He's not my friend and he's known to be a liar."

"Mr. Benton, if you were at the corner of Laura and Orange that night, as you say you were, why were you looking in the direction of the Exposition Hall? It seems you would be looking the other direction if you were heading home, as you also say."

"What?" said Benton.

St. Clair-Abrams asked again. "What was of particular interest to you in the waterworks park that night, Mr. Benton, or should I say whom?"

"What was I looking at? I don't know." He squinted at the attorney and shrugged.

"I said," St. Clair-Abrams bent down to eye level, "for whom were you looking in the parks and on the banks of the creek? Anyone in particular? We both know that's an excellent place to seek unescorted females after the sun goes down. Were you looking to find one who needed an escort, Mr. Benton? Or were you establishing a reason for your presence there."

"Objection. Outside the scope of the direct examination." It was the state attorney who spoke."

"You raised the issue as to where the defendant was looking, Mr. Hartridge," said Call to the prosecutor. Hartridge detected a smirk of merriment on the judge's face. "Sustained."

The whites of Benton's eyes swelled like hard-boiled eggs. "What?" he tried to say but mashed the word.

"Oh, I think you understand?" said St. Clair-Abrams. "Did you see anyone interesting out that way?"

"Eddie Pitzer," Benton mumbled.

"Ah yes." St. Clair-Abrams whirled and approached him again. "I guess this aimless staring into the park explains the extended time lapse for you to walk to the park from the stable. You were able to say you saw my client rushing across the Laura Street Bridge. I submit after all your wanderings, you have no idea what time you supposedly saw Edward Pitzer that night. I submit, in fact, Mr. Benton, you did not see him at all."

"That ain't true," hollered Benton, bumping his hat to the floor and watching it roll away. Hartridge glared at them, yearning to squash the tumbling hat as it rotated by him.

Part IV – Chapter 12

Mrs. Eliza Huau Recalled

On May 27, Thursday, the third day of the trial, Pitzer's uncles and father were faithful in attendance. Sarah Hosack, his mother's elegant sister from Carnegie, Pennsylvania, inherited his mother's courtroom duties after Tillie's crying jag the day before. The State still had an estimable number of witnesses left to testify, but first St. Clair-Abrams recalled Mrs. Eliza Huau, Marie Louise's silver-haired grandmother, for further questioning. She fainted during her testimony the day before.

"Good morning, Mrs. Huau," he said and she smiled in return. The lady, now composed, remained an endearing presence to the audience. Many in the gallery, softly cooing, were pleased to see her return. Even Judge Call gave a subdued but welcoming smile.

"Mrs. Huau, please describe the condition of Marie's clothing when you reached her that night in the yard," said St. Clair-Abrams. She looked a bit surprised at what she considered a delicate question.

"Her skirt was falling off her, sir," she said and averted her eyes to her knees.

"Was there blood, madam?"

"Oh," she whimpered.

An angry Hartridge rose. "Objection," he said. "She has previously explained the incident in detail, as has Dr. Neal Mitchell with his description of the young woman's autopsy. Perhaps, the distinguished defense counsel fails to recall."

"Watch the sarcasm, Hartridge," snapped Call.

"I withdraw the question," said St. Clair-Abrams blandly. He looked at the top of the lady's bowed head and asked quietly, "Mrs. Huau, did you recognize the man at the gate?"

She sighed, "Yes."

"Did you see his face straight on?"

"I have known Eddie for years. I see him frequently. I know his walk. I know his figure. I know his general appearance. I swear to you, I saw Edward Pitzer leaving the gate that night."

"So you cannot identify him singularly," St. Clair-Abrams said. "Mrs. Huau, is that why you did not identify Edward Pitzer at the coroner's hearing?"

"I did identify him!" she said with emphasis. "If I did not say this at the coroner's hearing, which I am sure I did, I was exhausted. I had been nursing Marie Louise all the night before."

"I'm sure you were exhausted," said St. Clair-Abrams, rising in stature, looking over her head toward the jury, "but the fact remains that you did not actually see the man at the gate. You did not look upon his face," he thundered to the panel of jurors.

The English woman looked weary. She tried to reply, but the attorney, completing his sentence, drowned her voice.

"One last question," St. Clair-Abrams said, "do you consider yourself Cuban?" In a dismissive way, he rolled his hand towards the Cuban families in the room and cocked his head at her. Her eyebrows rose in a query.

"Never mind," he said before she could answer. "There seems to be a deep plot by the Cubans to frame my client. I was going to ask what you knew about it." He turned from her with an amiable smile, as Hartridge jumped to his feet.

"Objection," Hartridge yelled too late. The pot had boiled.

"Sustained," said the judge. "That's far beyond your boundaries, Mr. St. Clair-Abrams. Don't slip your quaint opinions into the mix again."

Part IV – Chapter 13

GABRIEL H. GATO

Gabriel Gato, father of the dead girl, and other witnesses had been excluded from the trial by Judge Call. He wanted no witness to hear the others' evidence. Their own testimonies must be fresh and independent. Gato sat on a bench outside the courtroom, dressed in a fine black suit, his excellent black homburg resting beside him with a black mourning band around its crown. When he tired of sitting, he walked the hall, but never far from the courtroom door. His hard stares and contemptuous manner scared all who passed him. Passersby took wide circuits around the angry Cuban. Even St. Clair-Abrams, if in the hall, deliberately shifted his gaze to avoid Señor Gato, who glared at St. Clair-Abrams' every step.

José Huau, also excluded from the trial, met Gato, by chance, outside the courtroom. "Gabriel," he said, touching his brother-in-law's arm. "We must go. We are of no use to Marie Louise now. We should return and attend to work." Gato jerked his arm away from Huau's hand. "They will never allow us to hear the others' testimony," Huau continued. "They fear it might affect our memories."

"From where comes this *esta maldita,* exclusion, to keep me from the trial of my daughter's assassin? In Bejucal, a wave of my father's hand brought justice. There was no dickering of who was where and how and when and what they remembered."

"And that's exactly the point they fear," said Huau. "If something is said to betray you, you will wave your hand in a summons to arms." Huau smiled. "Come, we should leave."

"Go if you like." Gato said, lighting his cigar again.

After Eliza Huau was dismissed, Gabriel Gato was called to appear. He tossed his cigar to the brass spittoon on the floor already damp with expectorant, and grabbed his hat from the bench. Striding to the witness chair a brisk two feet ahead of the bailiff, Gato, a surly combatant, banged his boot heels on the timber floor. When he sat, finger by finger, he removed his leather gloves, and laid them in his lap. His black walking stick, topped by an amber knob, leaned against his knee. He looked up at Hartridge, who had waited to begin questioning him.

"Marie Louise Gato was my daughter. I own a cigar factory. I grow tobacco," Gato rumbled. The strong curl of his Latin dialect rang through the room. "Only the finest Cuban seed. Much of my property is forests and pasture." He pressed his shoulders back in the chair. "I own houses on my land. Some near my own home. Most I rent to my cigar workers."

A small compact man, he hardly moved when he spoke. Thick ebony hair waved and curled on the witness's forehead, around his ears. Heavy facial hair covered his chin, joining his sideburns and mustache. Catalina glanced down to brush her knee. With plenty of reason for anger, his voice was a growl. He would not be a popular witness. Of course, he would not; he was Gato.

"What time did you leave work the day of the murder?" asked Hartridge.

"I left the factory about 6:30. I often do."

"About the same time on that day, Marie Louise boarded the northbound trolley at Bay Street. Why did she not ride home with you?"

"Objection. The man could not possibly know the answer to that," said St. Clair-Abrams.

"I'll allow it," said Judge Call.

"I am now told she was having a day of adventure, a day of freedom. She liked to wander on her own," Gato answered. Although Gato had not looked at the defendant, Pitzer had begun to shift and wriggle when Gabriel entered the room.

"How did you learn of the murder at your home that day?" asked the state attorney.

"When I was almost home, nearing the corner of Laura Street, someone called out to me," Gato said. "Two neighborhood boys banged the side of the carriage and grabbed my horse's bridle, surprising both me and the animal. The horse shied. The boys said to me, 'Hurry home. There's been a shooting at your house.'"

"Did you know the boys, sir?"

Gato crossed his legs, his boots glistening in the sunlight from the window. Chairs creaked as people leaned forward to listen. Though the papers had covered his story, this was the father of the dead girl. A star witness. Everyone focused.

"Neighborhood boys. I had passed one of their houses, Mrs. Allen's. Her husband works for me. One was her son."

"Did you know the boys' names?" Hartridge repeated a second time.

"I recognized them." Gato paused, bringing the boys to mind. "I don't know their names," he grunted.

"What did you do when they told you of the shooting?"

"I snapped the horse's reins," he growled, "and drove to my back yard as fast as I could. I left the reins hanging and jumped out of the carriage. My man was nowhere about."

"How did you find the situation when you arrived inside?"

"I ran through the kitchen. Marie Louise lay under a blanket in the parlor; the family was nursing her, wiping her face and that sort of thing. A doctor was there.

"Her brothers and sisters were all in the room, most weeping. *Abuelita* Huau, Fritz, also present. José, the Fritots."

"What did you do, Señor Gato?"

"I put my arms around her shoulder. I said, 'Marie Louise, my darling, what is the trouble?' 'Eddie Pitzer shot me from behind the bush,' she said."

"Objection," interceded St. Clair-Abrams.

"Overruled," said the judge, stretching a former ruling. "We've covered this exception."

"Do you know the defendant, Señor Gato?"

Gato straightened his shoulders again and laughed, two loud blasts. He crossed his arms in front of his chest, his forefingers tapping his arms in deliberation.

"I suppose one could say I know him. Since he was twelve or thirteen."

"Do you see him often?"

"Pitzer comes constantly to the house. He brought Marie Louise gifts. He was a *parasito*, a pest," Gato's voice flashed.

St. Clair-Abrams objected.

"Answer the questions only, señor," said the judge with a harsh look.

"If she would not accept the gifts, he became enraged, noisy and loud," said Gato. "If he brought candy and she refused it, he threw it into the trees or into the fountain." Gato flung his hand as if he were tossing candy.

Pitzer picked at his sleeve, pretending to ignore the witness.

"He frightened my daughter."

"In what way did he frighten her?" asked Hartridge.

Pitzer looked up, shyly watching Gabriel's face. Catalina Huau shifted in her chair. She remembered the story.

"Once, two or three months ago, Marie Louise came running upstairs, upset that Pitzer had brought a revolver and a large knife with him when he came to the house. When he pulled the knife from his pocket, showing off, it cut his finger and he bled."

The defendant's face colored. Gato stared menacingly at him. The defendant's face became a darker red. "I heard him yell at her from downstairs, 'I am not a coward.' As I walked down, Pitzer jammed the knife into the stairs. The blade broke in one of the steps. Before he left, he threw it and the revolver into the yard. I found the knife in the grass the next morning but the gun was gone."

Without warning, Gato banged his heavy gold ring on the arm of the witness chair and grabbed his cane. He hit his cane against the floor with a resounding crack, and pointed it at the defendant. Pitzer slapped his palms on his table and ducked.

The judge quickened and St. Clair-Abrams looked up abruptly. The crowd scuffled. Cubans could be tricky with their Latin flair, St. Clair-Abrams thought.

"Stop that," said Judge Call, banging his gavel with full force.

"I have no further questions of this witness," said Hartridge.

"So, Señor Gato," said St. Clair-Abrams next. Quiet, cautious. "On your ride home after work between six and seven on April 20th, did you see Edward Pitzer in the vicinity?"

"No."

"Did you see Edward Pitzer anywhere that evening other than later at your home under police supervision?"

"No."

St. Clair-Abrams did one of his half twirls, ending by facing Gato again. "And, Señor Gato, when the boys on 11th Street stopped your horse and carriage as you traveled home on that night, did either of them mention Edward Pitzer to you for any reason?"

"No."

"Thank you, sir. That is all I have."

St. Clair-Abrams gave a slight bow toward Gato and finished his spin toward his table. Gato sneered at St. Clair-Abrams' pirouette, his front teeth white through thin pulled lips.

Part IV – Chapter 14

Dying Declaration

After Gato had retired from the witness stand, State Attorney Hartridge announced he would offer Marie Louise Gato's dying declaration into evidence, her last words on earth. "I will call Justice Wright to authenticate the document, which I hope the august defense attorney will not attempt to thwart—"

"The august defense attorney certainly will thwart," boomed St. Clair-Abrams, already on his feet. "I have much to say on the subject."

"Step forward, gentlemen," Judge Call said to the attorneys. "What do you intend?" Call asked Hartridge, his voice low so the jury could not hear.

"The dying declaration should be presented to the jury as a matter of law, Your Honor. A settled exception to the hearsay rule. I fear Mr. St. Clair-Abrams will attempt to sully its clear intent before the jury."

St. Clair-Abrams countered straightaway. "The document is inadmissible as a dying declaration. There is no unblemished evidence she thought she was dying, a fact I intend to illustrate fully." He spoke with such force, his jowls shook.

"This evidentiary matter must be reviewed," said Call. He immediately turned to the jury and excused them from the courtroom. Facing his associates, Hartridge rolled his eyes before continuing.

"The State calls Justice A. O. Wright," said Hartridge and Wright was summoned to the courtroom.

"Justice Wright, state your full name and official title, please," began Hartridge.

*A. O. Wright, Justice of the Peace
10th Justice's District*

"Justice of the Peace A. O. Wright, 10th Justice's District."

"Tell us, your particular duties as justice of the peace that related to the Gato case, please."

"One of my duties is to confirm and investigate deaths in my jurisdiction. I did so in the case of Miss Gato. As assistant coroner, I also presided over the coroner's inquest or trial."

"Justice Wright, are you familiar with the document I present to you now?" Hartridge handed Wright a piece of paper, which he had retrieved and Wright inspected with a glance.

"It is Marie Louise Gato's dying declaration." He handed it back to Hartridge. "I recorded it for her." He threaded his fingers together and crossed his hands across his waistcoat.

"For what purpose did you draw this document, sir?" asked Hartridge.

"On April 20th, the night Miss Gato was attacked at her front gate, she thought she was dying and she wished to make a statement before she died."

"Please, describe for us Miss Gato's situation when you arrived at her house that night."

Wright took a breath and shifted in his chair. Absolute silence stretched from wall to wall to hear every word he uttered.

"An officer rang me from the Gato house at ten-fifteen on the night of April 20th and ushered me in to see her at ten-thirty. I had already heard someone had shot Miss Gato. A doctor present informed me she would probably die from her wounds due to internal hemorrhaging. I found her lying on the parlor couch."

"Justice Wright, would you recall for us your communication with Marie Louise Gato, sir?"

"I introduced myself. I spoke softly, adjusting my voice to the stillness of the room. I told her someone called me because of the attack. Then I asked her if she would like to make a statement. She said she would.

"I explained to her that if she lived, of course, she would testify in court. If she believed she would die soon, she could make a dying statement admissible in court. It would be good in court only if she truly thought her death was impending. I asked if she understood. She nodded yes. She spoke with difficulty due to her weakness.

"I asked her how she felt," Wright continued, "and she moved her head side to side to indicate she felt bad. Her face was white and, if I were to guess, her expression seemed a mixture of sadness and great pain."

"Other than suffering from her physical condition, did her mind seemed affected by her injuries?" asked Hartridge.

"She answered all questions intelligently and appeared to be completely rational," answered Wright. "When I asked her if she believed she was going to die, she said she understood her dying condition. Miss Gato never said, at any time, that she had hope of recovery. She lay very still and quiet, but spoke in audible whispers. Then, I assisted her in writing this document."

"How exactly did you do that, Justice Wright?"

"I asked her a question, and she dictated her answer. Then I framed the question and her answer together as a declaratory sentence. After writing the entire statement this way, I read it to her line by line. She indicated each line was correct. I asked her if she wished to sign the statement and she made a slight side motion with her head to indicate she couldn't. Her weakness prevented it."

St. Clair-Abrams looked down at his desk and shook his head in vigorous opposition.

"How did you proceed since she could not sign the document?" asked Hartridge.

"I asked her if I should sign her name and she make her mark beneath it. She nodded yes. I signed her name to the document, held it within her reach, and placed her hand on the pen. I guided the pen for her to make her cross beneath the signature."

Sad stifled cries and moans erupted throughout the gallery. Call's gavel slammed. "I know this testimony is hard to hear, but you must maintain silence or I will be forced to clear the room," he said to the audience.

"Is this the paper you described?" Hartridge showed Wright the document again. "Marie Louise Gato's dying declaration?"

"Yes, it is."

After examining the witness, State Attorney Hartridge offered the declaration into evidence.

Pitzer had sat unusually quiet that morning. He breathed with effort and dark circles hung beneath his eyes, but he watched the proceedings with strong intent.

"I object, Your Honor," said St. Clair-Abrams, rising quickly. "This is no more the dying declaration of Miss Gato than it is my own. This document is clearly the language of Justice Wright and not Marie Louise Gato," he said. "Miss Gato could not have accurately concluded her killer's identity in this, her so-called last statement.

"She didn't see the killer's face. The coward who shot her hid behind the shrubbery. The first shot tore her hat and scratched her face. She threw her left arm across her eyes and turned from her shooter. Running away, pulling against him, she could never have seen the killer. The attacker, on his knees, grabbed her skirts, and held her, shooting upward into her back. She fell forward, away from him.

"Moreover, Miss Gato in her final hours, in a highly weakened state, was influenced by those around her shouting Eddie Pitzer's name. In addition, under the influence of opium, she was in no mental state to make this declaration, which was not even in her own Spanish language."

"Counsel is mischaracterizing the evidence," Hartridge said.

"No, Your Honor," said St. Clair-Abrams, maintaining that too many assumptions and unanswered questions prevented substantive weight being attributed to the document.

He continued to examine Justice Wright in minute detail for hours. Where was the proof Marie Louise had seen the shooter while she was protecting herself? How did Wright know her mental faculties were sound? With what certainty did he interpret the movement of the girl's head? Why did Wright assume she wanted to scratch two crossed lines to accuse the man she loved? The two attorneys argued the issues for additional hours.

"This document is not what it asserts to be," St. Clair-Abrams said of the proffered evidence, at last, "and it is being unfairly exploited against my client."

"And, I will stop you there, Mr. St. Clair-Abrams," said Judge Call. "You've made many attempts to make your point. You have exhausted everyone in the courtroom. The only matter I need satisfied at this point is whether Marie Louise Gato was aware she was dying when she signed her dying declaration. I rule it is proper to investigate Miss Gato's mental abilities when she declared herself to be in such a condition. That will be the entire scope of further inquiry."

Both attorneys nodded in assent. St. Clair-Abrams declared, "I wish to call Alphonso Fritot, the deceased's cousin, who was among those present when Justice Wright wrote this statement." Wright descended the witness chair and left through the halls for the witness room to wait until recalled.

The tall slender young man, an older living cousin of the Cuban families, stepped forward. Socially connected to several of the court officers, his fiancée had been a bridesmaid in State Attorney Gus Hartridge's wedding. He nodded briefly to several of the court officers as he entered.

"Mr. Fritot," asked St. Clair-Abrams, "did you visit with Marie Gato on April 20th before her death?"

"Yes, I did. She lay on the couch. They had loosed her hair so it spread over her pillow. Her eyes were closed most of the time. She looked like a beautiful angel."

"Did you have any conversation with her that night?"

"Marie requested a drink of water," Fritot's hands lay crossed in his lap, "and she asked her father to raise her pillow."

"What did she say to you the night of April 20th?" asked St. Clair-Abrams.

"I remember. I always will. I asked her how she felt. We all asked her that, I suppose, and she said, 'Oh, I feel pretty bad. How do you feel, Alphonso?'

"I feel bad because of what happened to you,' I told her. Then she said, 'I can't stand this pain any longer.'"

"Is that all she said?"

"She said, 'I can't stand this pain any longer. I can't live. I am going to die.' I told her not to say that because the doctors were trying to save her."

"Did Marie ever say anything to indicate she had hopes of recovery?"

"No, sir."

"Did Miss Gato ask you if she were going to die?"

"No, she did not."

"Are you absolutely certain of that?"

"I am certain."

"Is it your impression from observing Miss Gato the night of April 20th and from what she said before signing her dying declaration, that she believed she was dying and intended to sign the document?"

"Yes, it is," said Fritot.

"Were Marie's eyes open or closed when she spoke to you, Mr. Fritot?" he asked.

"They were open as she spoke," said Fritot.

"Were you sitting or standing by Marie when she asked if she were dying?"

"Neither. She did not ask me that question."

"Did she ask anyone else if she were dying?"

"Marie Louise did not ask me nor did I hear her ask anyone such a question."

"Were you always in the room, Mr. Fritot?" asked St. Clair-Abrams.

"I was."

"And you heard her every conversation?"

"I did. There were not many."

St. Clair-Abrams had worked himself into a frenzy trying to force Fritot to say Marie Louise expressed a wish to live. A spot of spittle appeared on his mustache. He wiped it with his handkerchief and turned away.

Call excused Fritot, subject to recall. Fritot frowned at a recall and strode quickly down the aisle.

"I have another witness to examine," said St. Clair-Abrams. "I have two questions to ask Dr. R.H. Dean as to Miss Gato's mental condition when she spoke her last words. He was present with Dr. Mitchell soon after Marie Louise was shot."

After the doctor was seated, St. Clair-Abrams asked him if he had administered an opiate to Miss Gato on the night of April 20.

"Yes, I did, Counselor," said Dean. "One-eighth grain of morphia, a very small amount."

"Did the medication affect Miss Gato's mental condition?"

"The shock produced by her wounds was sufficient to counteract a considerably higher dosage. That amount is the weight of a seed of barley. Perhaps of wheat without the husk. It did not affect her in the least, except to reduce some of her pain and stop her heart from racing. In fractional terms, it equals nothing, no weight at all."

"The agony Miss Gato suffered was mind-numbing, was it not?" asked St. Clair-Abrams. "And adding a dose of morphia to that condition rendered her incapable of rational thought or profound statements, don't you agree, Doctor?" said St. Clair-Abrams standing close to the witness's chair, while facing the jury.

"Of course, that's not true. Her mind was not altered. That amount of morphia could not do that." The crowd rustled. Some shook their heads.

After another hour of argument, the court was dismissed for the noonday meal. Willie Gato, sitting beside Catalina, remembering Marie's anguish the night of the attack, squeezed his aunt's hand.

***

In the witness room, Justice of the Peace Wright sat quietly alone while the trial proceeded. He had presided over Marie Louise Gato's coroner's inquest about a month before, as well as Lt. William Gruber's inquest ten days later. As he waited for the Pitzer verdict, he mused on the death of Gruber, who had arrested Pitzer in the aftermath of Marie Louise Gato's killing. He pondered the odd thing Stollenwerck mentioned about Gruber's privates being covered in Appalachian rock mud used to pave city streets. What had Gruber really been doing and what had he done to deserve that symbolic gesture? And from whom?

Wright also wondered, as did many, if Gruber's abrupt removal by brutal bloodshed would affect the resolution of the Gato murder. If Pitzer were cleared by the jury's decision, who then would hunt the Springfield killer or killers?

When court resumed at 3:00 p.m., the jury was readmitted to the courtroom and Justice Wright returned to the witness chair to repeat his testimony regarding the dying declaration before the panel members. St. Clair-Abrams objected to the dying declaration and Judge Call overruled him. Wright identified the declaration, then read it aloud as the room fell quiet.

"I know I am about to die and that I am in a dying condition. It was Eddie Pitzer who shot me. He shot me five or six times. I looked right at him and know that it was he. I saw him shoot me. He shot me this evening as I was coming in and without provocation from behind the bush.

Marie Louise H. Gato,
Her (X) Mark."

Pitzer dug his nails in the cracks of the defendant's table and rocked in his seat. Two of the Cuban girls dabbed tears from their sad faces. Willie gazed up through the stained glass behind the judge. Catalina stared straight at the defendant and the jury looked straight ahead.

Part IV – Chapter 15

AN ADDITIONAL ANTE MORTEM STATEMENT

After the declaration was read, after Wright departed the chair, State Attorney Hartridge immediately rose again. "The State calls Señor José Huau to give testimony to an additional ante mortem statement given to him by Miss Gato."

Judge Call excused the jury for the second time that day.

José Alejandro Huau, a portly but elegant man, whose midriff extended from his chest to beneath his belly, wore tailored clothes fit to perfection. His manicured nails were trimmed and neat and, unlike all the other trial participants, he was clean shaven. His facial features defined his European lineage, his skin only slightly tan.

Huau had been the one who thanked each neighbor in the Gato living room on the night of the shooting and escorted each person back outside. He and Georgia had spoken to the assembled crowd from the porch. Although mostly reared in Cuba, he had been schooled in the United States. His physician father, of French descent, had been born in Maryland during a French legation mission.[1] José Huau had little pronounced Cuban accent.

"Were you present at the Gato house the evening of Miss Gato's attack, Señor Huau?" asked Hartridge.

"Yes. I believe I was one of the first to arrive." Huau had been at his store when Willie called him to come out to the Gato place. He was a subscribing witness to the dying declaration.

"Please describe how you found Marie Louise that evening, sir," said Hartridge.

"She lay on a couch in the parlor, very weak, her eyes mostly closed. She spoke little and when she did, she whispered. Her mother, my sister Enriqueta, sat on a chair beside her, holding her hand. I saw her the next morning, also."

"Did you speak to Miss Gato?" Hartridge asked.

"I did. I said something in the nature of 'I want to ask you one question, darling. Are you sure Eddie Pitzer shot you?' 'Yes, Uncle,' she said, 'it was he and no one else.'

"Then, I said to her, 'Marie, my darling, how are you feeling now?' She responded, 'I feel very bad.' 'Well, you are dangerously hurt,' I said. 'Yes, I am afraid I am going to die,' she told me."

Quick to see Huau's misstated evidence, Hartridge sprinted to the witness stand. "Mr. Huau, you previously stated Miss Gato knew herself to be in a dying condition. That is what you testify now also, correct?"

"Yes, sir." Huau stared at the prosecutor in confusion, questioning the man's implication.

"Objection." St. Clair-Abrams also jumped on the error at once. "Mr. Huau reports Marie said she was afraid she might die. Therefore, she entertained a hope of recovery."

"Mr. Huau," said Judge Call, raising his palms to calm the attorneys, "when did you say this last conversation took place?"

"The morning of the day she died, April 21st."

"At what time?"

"Between nine and ten o'clock."

"Señor Huau," Call said, "You are a man of integrity. I ask you again. Did Miss Gato's statement indicate certainty of her imminent death?"

"Yes, that is correct," Huau answered in a low voice, still not completely understanding the effect of what he had said.

The judge sat in silence for a moment, staring at Huau. He lowered his voice. "That is not what you said, sir, and what you said is not proper testimony for the admission of a dying declaration." said Call. Addressing the court, he continued, "I cannot allow this testimony to be admitted. It also requires that I rule against admitting her written declaration.

"Miss Gato's words the following morning, as Señor Huau testifies, 'afraid' she will die, indicate she had a change of heart and mind in the intervening hours after signing the written statement of the night before."

Judge Call ordered the jurymen back to the room and informed them the dying declaration they earlier heard was inadmissible as evidence for legal reasons. They were not to consider it as Miss Gato's last words. The members of the tribunal looked askance at each other. A few shrugged slightly. They could not unhear the information they had heard.

St. Clair-Abrams rustled papers, pretending nothing unusual had occurred. Pitzer flashed a toothy grin, regaining his natural pinkish hue. Animated now, he peered about the courtroom in a fresh interested manner.

He suddenly noticed some young ladies, late to the courtroom and unable to secure seats. Sitting on the floor, they had crowded themselves before the witness chair, near the judicial bench. In a sweep of gallantry, Pitzer rose from his own chair and pushed it toward one of the women, holding it for her to sit.

Someone replaced Pitzer's chair at the defense table. When he saw his newly placed chair, he immediately pushed that one towards another woman to surrender it also. He sat himself at the foot of the judge's desk and smiled broadly. People in the gallery reacted to the spectacle with both frowns and smiles. Catalina bristled.

One more time, as a last attempt to include a dying declaration into evidence, Hartridge called Alphonso Fritot back to the witness chair to describe another of Marie's last utterances. Once more, Call dismissed the jury from the room. Out they trooped, trying to maintain fair-minded faces with only partial success. Their trips were an aggravation. Fritot repeated his conversation with Marie Louise on the morning of April 21, a half-hour before she expired.

"'I am going to die,' Marie said. 'I can't take this pain any longer.' And that is all I know," Fritot concluded.

On cross-examination, St. Clair-Abrams repeated his questions to Fritot multiple times. "Tell us about Miss Gato's mental clarity on April 21, Mr. Fritot. Did she speak with a clear mind, Mr. Fritot?"

"Of course," answered Fritot.

"In what language did she converse?" St. Clair-Abrams asked.

"If she was addressed in English, she answered in English. If addressed in Spanish, she spoke Spanish."

"Are you certain, sir, she said the words, 'any longer?'" Judge Call intervened "I thought you said earlier she said she couldn't stand the pain much longer. That's a very important distinction, Mr. Fritot. 'Much' implies she plans to live."

"I said it this morning and I say now, Marie Louise thought she was dying. She never asked anyone if she were going to live." But Fritot was injured. He was worn and weary. Enduring the unceasing fire of questions, he had become confused at last. He had swapped any for much. And he knew he had done it. "She said," he repeated, staring, still and unyielding, into the space above the gallery, "'I am going to die. I cannot take this pain.'"

"Thank you, Mr. Fritot. You are dismissed," Judge Call said. "Miss Gato's words, according to you, are not a dying declaration. The victim had to be utterly convinced of her imminent demise. Marie Louise Gato did not think she was dying. None of the proposed dying declarations will be admitted into evidence." Fritot stared into the crowded hall. "Please return the jury," the judge said to a bailiff. "I will instruct them of the developments."

Bouncing from his chair, moving fast on his long legs, Fritot, somewhat restored, frowning in fury, exited the building in silence. Except for the fading sound of his boots in the hall.

Part IV – Chapter 16

DEFENSE DIRECT REBUTTAL WITNESSES

In the late afternoon of Thursday, May 27, the state attorney stood before the judge seemingly undisturbed in the face of the exclusion of Marie Louise's dying declarations. He leaned to reassure the Gato family that nothing of great note had occurred. The jury had heard it all. When the State rested its case, Hartridge returned to his table, and St. Clair-Abrams stood before the judge.

"Your honor," said St. Clair-Abrams, fresh and uplifted, ready to begin the defense case, "this may be an appropriate time for these good gentlemen of the jury to inspect the cheerless scene of the attack." The jury looked slightly expectant at the request for a change of scene, a breath of fresh air.

Without hesitation, Call said, "Your motion is granted, Mr. St. Clair-Abrams." He ordered the jury to be transported to the Gato place to inspect the murder scene in Springfield. He instructed the jurymen to speak only to one another, and reminded them again not to discuss the case.

In an omnibus with leather seats, pulled by two brown horses, Sheriff Broward conducted them out Laura Street to the Panama Road and the Gato homestead. Pitzer, escorted by a police officer, traveled in a separate carriage with his attorney. Smells of kitchen cook fires, horses and unpaved dirt roads hung across the countryside.

In the still country afternoon, the jurymen moved mutely about the Gato yard. At first, they clumped together on the shell path, estimating the distance from the piazza to the fence where Marie Louise was shot. The men observed the silent landscape in the twilight. They examined the rose bush where the killer had hidden, the fountain where Marie's candy fell. They inspected the space between the two Gato fences, remembering the testimony of face-to-face encounters with Pitzer there that night.

The jury tested their eyesight under the incandescent light of the piazza and noted the placement of trees and bushes. One man walked to the gate to test if another could identify him. Some strolled to the back of the house to see where Fritz Aberdeen had emerged, and to see his running path toward the sounds of shots.

Then they climbed back into the omnibus to return in silence to the city.

***

The next day, Friday morning, beginning the 4th day of the trial, a flock of young women filled the building corridors, storming the courtroom long before the session opened. They seized empty chairs in the front, leaving even the bailiffs to stand for a while. St. Clair-Abrams steamed into the courtroom, eager to present the defense of Edward Pitzer. With coy nods, the girls glanced at him and waited for the celebrity defendant to be escorted from the jail.

Outside, clouds like mounds of misshapen drop biscuits hoarded unspilled rain. Yet, the sky was blue and the air still. Motionless trees, blurry through leaded-glass windows, resembled an English watercolor. A bright morning hailed an encouraging beginning for St. Clair-Abrams.

The girls in attendance were members of the Young Woman's Christian Temperance Union, promoted by the Congregational Church.[1] Tillie Pitzer, a temperance leader in the church, sponsored the eager group; they attended weekly meetings, presented programs to the public, and distributed leaflets castigating the consumption of alcohol.

"Girls, it's your choice whom you choose as club mascot," Tillie had said when the girls were voting their choice, "but I believe that's a solid twenty-five hands raised for Eddie Pitzer. Congratulations, son." She bobbed her head. Thereafter, Pitzer often joined them at their meetings.

Loyal in their efforts to cheer their accused mascot, the girls had brought him treats throughout his incarceration and flowers to brighten his cell. Solid in his defense, they had spurned the prosecution's case and rushed to court only to observe the defense case when it began. Tillie returned to court then, also.

"Thank goodness, it's not August," one girl said loudly to another, both in clothes draped from collar to hem to wrist. Their corset stays, squeezing their lungs beneath layers of fabric, promoted the likelihood of their fainting. "I'll fan you, if you like," the girl said to the other, reaching for the paper fan each had found on her chair. The young crusaders were convinced a nice white boy would never trouble to shoot a Cuban girl, even one as pretty as Marie Louise. They twittered as much that morning.

* * *

When the judge and jury were seated, St. Clair-Abrams began his direct defense by calling Zeph Harrison, the civil engineer who had drawn the map illustrating the murder scene. "I wish to introduce this map into evidence," St. Clair-Abrams attempted, but Hartridge rose immediately.

"Sir, I cannot accept this map due to its obvious errors," the state attorney objected. "That tree, for instance, is not planted in the correct spot."

So began what one newspaper called a "Battle of the Titans" as the state attorney and defense counsel reached deep within themselves for the primal and legal skills to parry in the courtroom war. Their clash resounded beyond the walls.

Hartridge spent fifteen minutes viciously attacking the map, especially when Harrison indicated there were no clear lines of vision from porch to the gate from which Pitzer was said to depart. "There was no way," the engineer swore, referring to the map, "that Georgia Gato, Eliza Huau, and Fritz Aberdeen could possibly have identified Edward Pitzer." According to Harrison, because of the placement of electric lighting and the night shadows, it was "simply too dark a night to distinguish a running man. Not to mention the banana tree leaves blocking the view of someone from the corner of the Gatos' piazza."

When the witness admitted he had included on the map only the things he felt necessary, Hartridge asked him to describe those objects in detail.

"That was six weeks ago," the engineer replied. "I can't recall what that stuff was, much less the exact size." At that, Hartridge began to criticize not only the map but the man's credentials.

One daily newspaper recounted that Hartridge made the map and its maker appear decidedly ridiculous. Nevertheless, after discussion, Judge Call decided the map was adequate. Enough had been depicted on the rendering for him to admit the map into evidence. The jury did not appear confused by this decision, but some onlookers wore baffled expressions.

St. Clair-Abrams called as the second defense witness a member of the coroner's jury which Justice Wright had appointed to examine the premises the night after the murder. He, too, spoke to the clarity of the scene. The man testified their focus was on the ability to distinguish a person in limited light at the Gato yard gate from the Gato front piazza. Some could identify people correctly. Some could not. The exhaustive cross-examination revealed all but one of the jury always wore glasses or at least wore them to read.

After challenging the visibility of the crime scene as described by prosecution witnesses, St. Clair-Abrams began a systematic challenge to the state's witnesses' individual observations. First, he called J. Hugh Stephens, an editor of a morning paper, who had attended school two years ahead of Pitzer.

"I stood beside Georgia Gato at the house shortly after the shooting," Stephens said. "She recognized him by his collar and dark clothes. When Pitzer was escorted to the porch and she saw his attire, she said, 'I knew it was him. I just knew it.'" On cross-examination, Stephens conceded he was a member of the Jacksonville Rifles, a local militia of which Pitzer was also a member.[2] The man asserted the membership did not affect his testimony.

Next, St. Clair-Abrams called the court stenographer to read the transcript of the coroner's hearing in order to compare it with the trial testimony of Georgia Gato, Eliza Huau and Fritz Aberdeen. After thirty minutes of reading the transcript into the record, he recalled Georgia to the stand. She strode forward, defiant as ever.

"What I am saying now is what I have said twice before," Georgia said. "I saw Edward Pitzer standing near Marie Louise the night of her murder. As Sister was dying, he fumbled at the gate. He stuck his gun in his back pocket, then darted into the Panama Road like a *conejo asustado*, a frightened rabbit."

St. Clair-Abrams also recalled Eliza Huau. Again, he accused her of altering her testimony, and she once more declared, "If details of my testimony as to what I observed a month before, vary from a month ago, blame my exhaustion at the time. I nursed Marie Louise eighteen hours until she died. Sweet Enriqueta, so distraught, could not do much as the night went on. The next day after Marie died, I also helped Georgia sort out the funeral plans. The hearing you speak of, by the way, you scheduled the very afternoon of the funeral."

"Not me, madam," responded St. Clair-Abrams, stepping back, surprised.

* * *

Next, there followed a series of witnesses who challenged the eyesight of Fritz Aberdeen, the gardener who had seen Pitzer struggling with the new gate latch.

"Of course, I know Mr. Aberdeen," said Mabel Shad, a newly wedded milliner dressed in a shirtwaist and skirt. She wore no hat herself. "Fritz is a darling man. He boarded with my mother on West Adams Street at the same time I did, several years ago. He read at the table every night and he wore glasses."

Hartridge rose to cross-examine. "Mrs. Shad," he said. "You are a young woman, so I must ask. Do you know the difference between farsightedness and nearsightedness?"

"No, sir," she said, hesitating, "I don't think I've heard those terms."

"When a man uses glasses to read his newspaper, are you aware it has nothing to do with what he can see in the distance? When he can see distance, he is farsighted and can see perfectly at a long range, even if he wears glasses to read a newspaper."

"Oh," she said and glanced at the bailiff. Neither side had further questions. Judge Call quickly dismissed her.

Mabel Shad's mother, Sarah Reed, testified next. She was a saleslady at the establishment where her daughter worked as a milliner. She agreed with Mabel that Aberdeen needed glasses. He often read papers and magazines in German. This remark drew chuckles from the crowd as if the foreign language needed stronger spectacles.

Mr. Hartridge walked brusquely forward again. "Mrs. Reed," he said, "do you think Mr. Aberdeen's use of reading glasses benefits his understanding of the German language?"

"Of course not," she answered.

"Do you think not wearing his reading glasses prevented him from seeing the defendant at the Gatos' gate?"

"Perhaps, Mr. Hartridge. That and the fact he could not identify a person across a table from where he sat." She smiled sweetly. The crowd thought her reply was amusing and laughed accordingly.

"Indeed, Mrs. Reed, are you an oculist?"

"If you mean an optometrist, I am not, but I know he has bad eyesight."

"Are you an expert on that subject? We have not qualified you as such," said Hartridge.

"You know I am not."

Then, Hartridge took a different tack. He backed a few steps away, paused and looked at her. "How many times have you visited Mr. Pitzer in jail?"

Mrs. Reed's pleasant expression, usually part of her trade as a saleslady, turned stony. "I don't recall."

"Isn't it true you have visited Mr. Pitzer in the jail several times?" he continued.

"Yes, several times. As have many," she said.

"Not so many," answered Hartridge. "Do you know that Pitzer is usually visited by girls and young women, protégés of his mother, members of the Young Woman's Christian Temperance Union? Why would a mature woman such as you have so much interest in him?" At his reference to her age, a general gasp floated from the ladies through the courtroom. Mrs. Reed began to tremble; her face reddening.

"Sir, I visit those in prison because it is my Christian duty."

"Is it not true, Mrs. Reed," Hartridge's voice was razor-sharp, "several years ago, you were a resident of tiny Pittman, Florida, where the defendant and his parents lived for ten years?"

"Yes." Her voice quivered in reply.

"And that you and your daughter, Mrs. Shad, were neighbors of the Pitzers, were you not?

"We didn't live all that close," she responded, regaining her strength. "It's like a jungle down there. Not always easy to get around."

"And weren't you a proud member of the freshly minted Pittman Presbyterian Church, where Mrs. Pitzer rose so prominently?"[3]

Hartridge had discovered minutes and a membership roll of the nascent Presbyterian congregation near Altoona and Pittman, Florida. Catalina Huau jerked forward, her dark-brimmed hat slipping precariously, her mouth open in surprise. She knew Mrs. Reed. She had even bought a hat from her, but she hadn't known of this connection.

"Yes, but I didn't think it was important to mention," said Mrs. Reed.

"Were you close friends?" said Hartridge.

"We were acquainted. It was a small town." At last, members of the jury stirred and watched the witness more closely.

"Are you aware Mr. Pitzer owned a hardware store nearby?"

"Of course," she answered, "in Altoona."

"Did you shop there often?"

"On occasion. Of course, I did."

"I think it is possible this lengthy relationship could influence your testimony here today, Mrs. Reed. I think it could also account for your multiple visits to your young friend in his cell."

"Are you calling me a liar?" The woman bristled.

"Of course not," Hartridge responded, appearing shocked at the same moment St. Clair-Abrams rose to object.

* * *

St. Clair-Abrams continued with his theory that none of the State's witnesses could see to identify the escaping shooter at the Gato gate. He called Mrs. T.F. Allen, mother of Charlie Flynn and neighbor of the Gatos, who lived on West 11th Street near Main. She testified she and her husband both worked at El Modelo and lived in one of Gato's houses.

"I saw Fritz wearing glasses as he rode in a buggy recently," she blurted immediately, as she took her seat. "I also saw Mr. Gato talking to Lulu Lee." The woman appeared to the attorneys at least to be overly coached for her testimony. Even St. Clair-Abrams attempted to tamp down her enthusiasm.

"Yes, yes, I see," he uttered quietly. "Please wait for my questions, Mrs. Allen, before you speak. That's the way this works."

She also said she had seen Aberdeen hammering a nail while wearing glasses, and she saw Lulu Lee and Mr. Gato walking in front of his house as he pointed things out to her on a Friday afternoon. But when Hartridge approached the witness for cross-examination, and addressed the subjects she had been so eager to discuss, she became agitated.

"Mrs. Allen, did you not also see me with Lulu Lee and Mr. Gato the same Friday afternoon you mentioned?" he asked.

"Yes, I suppose I did," she snapped, staring at him harshly.

"And did you also remember I came to your house that day, too? Were you inside the whole time I was at your door?" Hartridge said.

"Yes."

"And how long had you been inside?"

"Fully half an hour."

"Why did you not come to the door when I knocked?"

"I thought you wanted to take my son, Charlie. I thought you were going to arrest him."

"Did you tell people I was hunting your son with handcuffs?"

"Yes, I did."

"Were you afraid your son would identify the defendant?" Hartridge asked. She was silent. "So, you refused to let me see him?" She glared more harshly at him. "You hid your son with neighbors, then sent him upriver so I couldn't talk to him. Yet, you allowed him to talk to defense counsel?"

"Mr. Bigger and Mr. Pitzer told me to do it," she returned.

"In that case," he snapped back, "it's all perfectly fine, I suppose?"

Rising from his seat, St. Clair-Abrams said in stentorian tones, "I advised them to do so."

"I object, Your Honor, to this woman's entire testimony. Her behavior has been highly prejudicial, if not a contemptible or criminal offense," said Hartridge. After a brief sidebar with counsel, the objection was overruled.

Hartridge asked for its specific inclusion in the transcript. As in the case of the dying declaration, he knew the jury had heard it all.

Part IV – Chapter 17

William Arpen

St. Clair-Abrams, known for his guile in the state legislature, the circuit court, and the local tavern, next called William Arpen to testify.[1] The witness, a tall lumbering dairyman, interjected a new issue to the defense attorney's strategy. No one had yet mentioned the straw man of the murder evening, the red herring by which Abrams and Arpen upturned the State's orderly presentation. It transformed the Gato murder into a befogging whodunit.

William Arpen lived north of the Gatos on the Panama Road, on West 12th Street over the railroad tracks. He testified that near seven o'clock on April 20th, as he was driving his wagon north on Main between 10th and 11th Streets, he recognized Marie Louise Gato's voice.

"She was walking with the Bigger boy, then she looked up at me and gave me the sweetest smile. My old cart rattled past them two, as I turned off the Panama Road in the front of Gato's land." Actually, Gato owned all the woods and pastures through which the man had been driving.

"Did you notice anything peculiar as you passed Gato's that night?" asked St. Clair-Abrams, smiling pleasantly at the man as if they had long been friends.

"Yeah, I did, as a matter of fact. Between the yard gate and the livestock fence, a large fella walking real slow passed me going south.

Now, I'm not absolutely sure he was colored, but I'm pretty sure he was. I can't absolutely say he was colored or white, but I know one thing, he shuffled along like Blacks does."

"How was this man dressed?" asked St. Clair-Abrams.

"His coat was long and his clothes was dark. That's one reason it was hard to tell about him."

"How would you describe his body shape, his physical bearing?"

"There again, he was wearing that long coat, also a hat, which makes the answer hard. I will say I know for sure, I think he was large and dark."

"What was this gentleman doing when you saw him?" asked St. Clair-Abrams.

"That's just it. That's what made me notice him. He wasn't doin' nothin'. Like I said, he was just walking slow. Sometimes, he stopped, looked around."

Hartridge stared motionless at Arpen dropping this unexamined news. Many did not react, not recognizing the implications. Some, like Hartridge although quiet, saw an altered playing field ahead.

"What time did you see this man at the Gato's fence?" asked St. Clair-Abrams.

"Ah, a little before seven that night, I'd say."

Hartridge could hardly contain himself to begin his cross-examination. When he did, he was quick and steadfast and soon elicited from Arpen that the horse he drove clipped along so fast, that he, Arpen, hadn't seen much at all.

"Are you certain it was not Edward Pitzer lingering at the fence as has already been reported?" Hartridge asked.

"He ain't colored and he ain't big. This man was both of those."

Hartridge also brought out by examination that Arpen's timing was slightly off. Still, what the man said could potentially undermine the prosecution's case.

Part IV – Chapter 18

Lycurgus Bigger

Lycurgus Bigger took the witness stand for the defense, a plain middle-aged man with a solid frame and a head full of thinning light brown hair. "Mr. Bigger, are you related by any bloodline to the Pitzer family?" asked St. Clair-Abrams.

"No," replied Bigger.

"Do you have any other connection to the Pitzer family?"

"We are friends and James Pitzer and I were once partners in the dry goods store that Mr. Pitzer now owns as sole proprietor.[1] That commercial relationship is not ongoing. It was dissolved and settled five years ago."

"How would you describe your current relationship with Mr. Pitzer?"

"I would say we're friends."

"Are your children also friends?"

"They know each other, certainly, but my oldest son is in Kansas and the others here are younger than Eddie."

"You also have a son named Edward Pitzer Bigger, is that right?"[2]

"I do, but he's only three. I meant the name as a tribute to James Pitzer and his family."

"You obviously think a great deal of them."

"I do."

"Mr. Bigger, do you know the Gato family?"

"Of course, I believe everyone knows the Gatos."

"So you knew Miss Marie Louise Gato, is that correct?"

"It is correct."

"Is there anything you can tell us about the evening of April 20th, when Miss Gato was shot?"

"Yes, Marie and I rode the Main Street trolley home together," Bigger said, "meaning we were on the same car. We left Bay Street at six-thirty in the evening and rode to the end of the line at 8th Street. It takes fifteen to twenty minutes. Marie got off on the left side of the rear platform and walked through the car shed on the corner to West 8th Street. She started across the street to a cut that ran northwest through the woods to her house."

"Did anyone else depart the train at this stop?"

"Yes. A male passenger boarded, a Negro I think, between 2nd and 4th streets. That's where the conductor rang up the fare, at any rate. At the end of the line, West 8th Street, the man also departed to the left of the car. Walking ahead of Marie, he stopped at the cut where she was headed, then turned and looked back at her. I saw it because I had circled the train to speak to her on the opposite side from me."

St. Clair-Abrams showed Bigger the map previously entered into evidence. Bigger traced the map's surface with his finger to indicate the location of the shed and the cut through the woods. "Did you get a good look at the man?"

"He was a tall man, and dark, a large man. He might have been a mulatto or a Cuban but he probably came from Africa. He wore a long-tailed coat and carried a stick. Just as I approached Marie to ask her to join me, she walked toward me wanting me to walk with her. She said the dark man made her nervous. That she had never known a colored to pay a nickel for such a short ride."

"So, did you walk with her?" St. Clair-Abrams asked.

"I had a great many bundles," Bigger said, stretching his arms to illustrate. "I couldn't carry them and walk her all the way home, too. So I told her, 'If you come to my house, I'll send one of my boys with you.' We walked to 10th and Hubbard where I live. I called Johnny, the oldest at home, to accompany her and off they went. That's the last I saw of her."

"Thank you," said St. Clair-Abrams. "Your witness, gentlemen," he said to the prosecutors.

Attorney, Augustus W. Cockrell, Jr. walked slowly towards Bigger for cross-examination. Mid-thirties, a graceful man who spoke with flowing gentle syllables, he wore a mustache and goatee. The scion of a well-respected local law firm headed by his father, he had just that day returned to Jacksonville from Alabama ready to assist the state attorney.[3]

"Mr. Bigger," Cockrell began. "I am going to read the transcript of the coroner's inquest at which you testified about a man who departed the trolley at West 8th Street, where Miss Gato also disembarked."

"I didn't say I didn't notice him," Bigger replied, sounding less friendly. "I said I didn't notice him particularly. I recalled later he was a colored man." He leaned back in his chair.

"At the time of the coroner's hearing," continued Cockrell, "you swore you could not say the man on the trolley to be colored, Cuban or white—is that accurate?"

"I thought he was Cuban," said Bigger. "But later I realized he was colored, like I told you. It could have been a white man with charcoal on his face, I suppose." He grinned. It was an odd idea since the man wasn't performing minstrel, but Bigger got a few laughs.

"Nonetheless, you swore, less than twenty-four hours after the incident, that you did not particularly notice this man, isn't that correct?"

"Apparently, it is. Even though I've changed my mind, as I said."

"Also, according to this transcript, Miss Gato made no reference to a black man being unwilling to pay for a short trolley ride."

"If I didn't say it," said Bigger, "I must have forgotten."

"Do you see this signature, Mr. Bigger?" said Cockrell, showing him the report from the coroner's inquest.

"I do. That's mine, but I signed under protest." The man shifted his torso forward, elbows on the arms of his chair. He stared at Cockrell with a leaden face.

"To whom did you protest?" asked Cockrell.

"Judge Wright."

"He would not allow you to amend your statement about this unknown dark man?"

"He said I could correct it in court. That's what I'm doing."

"So you swore to and signed an incorrect report of your statement at the coroner's inquest?"

"I told Judge Wright it was mostly correct," said Bigger, straightening.

"And what did you tell him was incorrect?" asked Cockrell.

"Where it says, according to me, the man wore a military coat."

"What did you actually say?"

"I said he wore a long coat."

"Are you sure that's what you said?"

"Of course, I'm sure. I protested, didn't I?"

"Hmm," said Cockrell, "that's an odd mistake. The words don't even sound alike, do they?"

"No."

"Did you tell anyone at any time prior to this trial that your memory changed about the dark man on the car and now you remember him clearly?"

"No," said Bigger.

"Is the coat statement the only incorrect thing you said in the report?"

"Yes and that I wasn't sure he was colored."

"And that Miss Gato didn't remark about the man not wanting to pay a fare."

"Yes."

Cockrell paused for a moment with his folded fingers to his lips. He changed the subject. "Did you say you were at one time in business with Mr. James Pitzer?"

"Yes, and I am still in the mercantile trade."

"A clerk?"

"Yes."

"Do you come from a family of shopkeepers," asked Cockrell, "as does Mr. Pitzer?"

"I come from a family of soldiers and statesmen. I have an uncle who was governor of Indiana," replied Bigger evenly. "I'm sure there were merchants in both families, as well."

"How long have you known the Pitzers, Mr. Bigger?" Bigger flinched slightly, surprised at the question. He had to think a minute.

"I have known James Pitzer since around 1876. That's when he and Tillie got married."

"So you have known them more than twenty years?"

"I've known Tillie and her family, the Cubbages, much longer than that," he said.

"You knew Tillie before you knew James Pitzer?"

"Yes. The Cubbages settled across the river from Pittsburgh, in a little town called Carnegie. I was from Warren County, Ohio, not too far away. We were all Presbyterians and convened often in Pittsburgh. We had a mutual friend in the church, Rev. McCaughan. His family and the Cubbages intermarried."

"And you continued your friendship with the Pitzers over the years?"

"Not so much. We all moved West near the same time. We all married people in the church and we met through the church. When we moved to Florida, we saw the Pitzers more."

"Were you in Lake County with the Pitzers?" asked Cockrell.

"No, closer to Tampa. I farmed at the time."

"Did you also know Major St. Clair-Abrams, who then lived in Central Florida?" Cockrell turned and motioned to the big man.

"Certainly I knew him by reputation." St. Clair-Abrams' head rose as he acknowledged the mention.

"So, it seems you have a mind for detail, Mr. Bigger?"

"I like to think so."

Cockrell nodded and paused again. Then, he said, changing the subject, "I understand you have been trying to gather evidence for this trial, is that correct?"

"Yes."

"Mr. Bigger," said Cockrell, "you said you and Mr. James Pitzer advised Mrs. Allen to send her son, Charlie Flynn, away. Did you know at the time, he was a material witness in this case?"

"I don't know what Pitzer did, and I don't know that I can say I did that."

"Why are you so interested in this case, Mr. Bigger?"

"Nothing more than to see justice done."

"Do you know a case where justice required preventing a witness from testifying?"

"You heard his own mother say you folks were dogging him with handcuffs," Bigger replied, "and she was afraid you were going to carry him to jail. Since he had already been subpoenaed by St. Clair-Abrams, I told her I didn't see what right you had to take him early. I said I thought the boy should leave, and he did."

"So you felt it your business to encourage a subpoenaed witness to flee rather than testify at this trial?"

"Yes, as a friend, I did."

"And Mr. St. Clair-Abrams didn't mind?"

"Apparently not."

"Did you know your own son had been subpoenaed by the State?" asked Cockrell.

Bigger lifted his eyebrows. "I didn't know that."

"You didn't know he was subpoenaed three times by the State?"

"I knew he was summoned by the defense."

"They are two different things."

"I know that." The witness soured.

"Was he not subpoenaed for the coroner's jury?"

"Yes."

"That's the State, too. And a preliminary hearing."

Hartridge stepped up to take Cockrell's place. "You know it was absolutely false I was chasing Charlie Flynn with handcuffs, don't you?" asserted Hartridge.

At Hartridge's question, Major St. Clair-Abrams jumped up so rapidly, he startled everyone, shouting, "I object to having this witness, any witness, denounced as a liar by a man even as great as the state attorney."

The young females of the YWCTU cheered and twisted in their chairs. Some stood and clapped. Judge Call banged his gavel and called for order, which did not deter them. They continued to applaud and loudly wished the startled Pitzer good luck.

"Stop this right now," Call said in full voice. "And sit down. If another such outburst occurs, I'll have the sheriff clear the room." Some people tugged at the girls' skirts until they reluctantly sat.

Cockrell, rising, back at the prosecution's table, said, "This is an outrage, Your Honor. Those with no sense of propriety have no place here."

"It's those women who are doing this," said Hartridge, turning to stare at the group.

Call overruled St. Clair-Abrams' objection regarding Charlie Flynn being chased with handcuffs. Lycurgus Bigger then responded he didn't know what happened with the handcuffs.

This brought another supportive demonstration from the girls. Cockrell rose again. "Your Honor, I insist. Such proceedings are improper and must be stopped."

"I agree, Mr. Cockrell," the judge said, annoyed, looking at the sheriff who had risen from his appointed chair. "Sheriff Broward, maintain order," insisted Call. "If you cannot do it alone, put more officers throughout the room."

Two bailiffs moved to the aisle where the girls were seated. In the midst, Cockrell announced he had another question for the witness. The judge looked annoyed again. His full brown mustache puffed out with air he exhaled, but he signed for Cockrell to proceed.

"Mr. Bigger, where did you sleep last night?" Lycurgus Bigger, taken off guard again, flashed another surprised look. Before he could answer, Cockrell modified the question. "Did you spend last night at the Duval Hotel?"

"Yes, I did," said Bigger.

"Why did you do that, sir?" Cockrell persisted.

"I was afraid of the Cubans, of course. They can be very hot-headed. Johnny stayed with me, too. I have to protect my family."

Part IV – Chapter **19**
JOHN BIGGER

Saturday, May 29, 1897

John Bigger walked into the witness room. His father had finished testifying and returned to the witness room.

"I'm glad to see you, boy," said Lycurgus. "Something important has come up."

"I'm early. I'll leave," John said. "We're not supposed to talk."

"Did you hear me, John?"

"Yessir," said the boy.

"Stop moving and listen. Our side will call a new witness. You don't know her but she's from close to home, Ohio, Miami County. You may have heard of her family. Some of us remember her. Now she owns the River View Hotel here. She says Pitzer was at the hotel the exact time Marie was shot."

"That can't be true," John said." Eddie told us he was at Mrs. Pickett's house when Marie was shot."

Lycurgis put up his hand. "She may offer contradictions which is not our business. Speak to no one on the subject."

The trial had continued into its fifth day, Saturday. When the bailiff called John Bigger's name, a gangly boy of sixteen loped across the room. On the night Marie was shot, after her trolley ride, John had walked her home to her gate. The spectators in the room huddled into silence, tense with knowing John had been so close to the killing.

Settling into the witness chair, John Bigger nibbled his bottom lip. St. Clair-Abrams had warned him about the trickery of the men of the Bar who would confront him. He might know their names, but he would never be their friend. In the hall, John saw his father's angry face after his own encounter with the gentlemen of the Bar.

In his stiff white collar and Sunday school suit, John Bigger

John Bigger

answered St. Clair-Abrams' questions with precision, his voice unexpectedly firm and clear. "That night, my father arrived home with Marie Louise and told me to walk her home because she was afraid to go alone. He said there was a colored man who had scared her."

"Your father is Lycurgus Bigger, who just testified, correct?" asked St. Clair-Abrams.

"Yes, sir."

"Would you tell us what you observed about Marie on this walk?"

"Nothing. Except she seemed eager to get home. Chirpy. Excited. She said Eddie was coming over."

"Would you say she was looking forward to seeing Eddie Pitzer?" added St. Clair-Abrams.

The boy was clutching each arm of the witness chair.

"Yes, sir. She acted like it."

"What occurred when you arrived at the Gato place?"

"After we got to her house, we stood awhile and talked at the outer gate, the livestock gate that runs by the road. I couldn't go in. I had some lessons to study. I wish now…"

"You wish what?" said St. Clair-Abrams brightly. Bigger shook his head, his lips scrunched. "What happened after that, son?" asked St. Clair-Abrams in avuncular tones.

"When I left her, I walked to 11th Street and turned east toward Main. I walked three or four yards off the old Panama Road when I heard two shots. Then, I heard more shots." There were loud reactions in the room. John quit talking, looking unnerved.

"Go ahead, son," said St. Clair-Abrams.

"I looked back and there were flashes of light, like fireballs, and Marie called out 'Mother' three times. I kept walking towards Main Street."

"Did you see or hear anything else?" asked St. Clair-Abrams.

"I saw Marie Louise falling forward, but that's all I saw." He emphasized the latter.

"How about the house on the corner, the Caballeros,' did you see anything there?"

"I only saw the house."

"Was anyone near the house? I should say, did you see anyone near the house?"

"No, sir. Nobody was there. I would have seen those two colored girls if they came out."

"Objection," said the state attorney. "No foundation. I move to strike."

"Denied," said the judge. "We've all heard the previous testimony of the two colored girls." He motioned St. Clair-Abrams to continue.

Hartridge knew Bigger had not heard the previous testimony, but probably been coached to deny seeing the girls. Hartridge let it pass.

"Did you hear anything coming from the corner house?" asked St. Clair-Abrams. "Maybe a window opening or a shade banging against the window?"

"Yes. I heard a noise at the window."

The two prosecutors exchanged glances again. He admitted to hearing the noise but denied seeing the sisters run out?

"What did you do after you heard the noise?" St. Clair-Abrams continued.

"I reached Mrs. Allen's place near Main and met Charlie Flynn," continued John. "He was running out of his house, chasing after the shots. So, I ran back with him." Bigger stopped talking. He hesitated, then leaned forward. His voice sounded shaky.

"As we ran back, a man turned off the Panama Road onto 11th, coming towards us. He passed us by, then sped around the corner south on Laura. Charlie and I saw him from the other side of 11th. We weren't far away."

"Could you see the man's face?" asked St. Clair-Abrams, watching John closely. Judge Call also inclined his head toward the boy.

"No, sir. I couldn't."

"And why could you not?"

"Because it was too dark, I suppose." John blinked and cleared his throat. "I only saw a large dark man in a long coat. I know Eddie Pitzer, and this man was taller than Eddie."

"I see," said St. Clair-Abrams, pausing. "Why did you mention Edward Pitzer?

"Because he's over there a lot."

"Did you see anyone else that night?"

"After that, Mr. Gato's horse and buggy came trotting down 11th Street from Main. Charlie and I were nearly to Laura so I ran out and grabbed the horse's bridle and stopped the carriage. Mr. Gato scowled at me. I said, 'There's been a shooting at your house. You need to hurry home.' He looked as if he'd been smacked in the face." John wiped his mouth with his hand.

"Then Mr. Gato whipped his horse and took off across the Panama Road into his back yard. He left his carriage there at the side of his house and ran inside."

"What did you and Charlie do?" asked St. Clair-Abrams.

"Charlie and I ran up to the Gatos' yard, and by then the grandmother and the gardener were moving Marie inside. Marie was bent over and hardly walking. Georgia and Mrs. Gato and Elvira and some other people were on the piazza."

"Did you observe anything else?"

"Not really, sir."

"Anything else you want to tell us?"

"No, sir."

"Thank you, John. Your witness." St. Clair-Abrams nodded to Hartridge but it was Duncan Fletcher who rose and approached the witness. A prominent lawyer, ex-mayor of Jacksonville and legislator, now also joining the prosecution team due to his widespread popularity and status.[1, 2] He was added hoping to lend weight to the state's case. Before he spoke, Fletcher studied the papers he held.

Recognizing Fletcher, John braced farther against the back of his chair.

"John, you said your father told you to walk home with Marie Louise. Why do you think he did that?"

"What do you mean?"

"Did your father not care for Marie Louise or was he scared of the dark man, too?"

"Objection," St. Clair-Abrams called out. "He can't testify to what the father thought."

"Sustained," said Judge Call.

"John, did your father ever say he did not like Cubans or that he did not want to walk with Marie Louise because she was Cuban?" Fletcher cocked his head noticeably, waiting for an answer.

"Objection. Leading the witness."

"Sustained."

Fletcher changed the subject.

"Your father and James Pitzer were partners in business for a while, how long had they known each other?"

"I don't know. A long time. Since Ohio and then in Florida. They were friends from church."

"And your youngest brother is named Edward Pitzer Bigger, is that correct?"

"Yes, he is," said John. St. Clair-Abrams stared at his desk, as if he were bored. The gallery behind him buzzed again.

"All right," Fletcher smiled. "Do you think that indicates a very personal relationship between the families, John? A brother named Edward Pitzer Bigger?"

"I guess so. I think so. Our parents are good friends."

The boy took a deep breath and stared at Fletcher, who was looking down at his papers again. Finally, he looked back at the witness. "You testified you were a few steps onto 11th Street when you saw and heard the shots?"

"Yes."

"Would you say that was about fifty yards from the Gato place?"
"I guess so. Yes, sir."
"Were you able to see the shooter?"
"No, sir."
"At what point did you begin to run away from the shooting, John?" Fletcher's voice had turned chilly. "You were afraid someone would shoot at you?"
"No, sir, I didn't run away," John responded firmly. "I didn't run away. I hurried away." He reached out, animated, looking desperate to set things straight.
"You hurried away very fast, John. Then you saw Charlie, younger than you, running towards the shots. Only then did you turn and run after him, back to Mr. Gato's?"
"No, sir. I wasn't running away. Not like you mean it." Fletcher smiled unkindly at the witness.
"You said you were pretty close, still at the corner, when you heard and saw the shots, yet you said you didn't see anyone come out of the corner house? So you were either blind or had run scared down 11th Street, correct?"
The boy did not answer.
Though the room grew hotter and close, nobody stirred, even to pull out a handkerchief or wave a fan.
"John, if you weren't running away, how could you not see Malvina Lockett at the Caballero house window?"
"I don't know."
"You remember hearing the noise at the window, right?"
"Yes, sir."
"Were you on the same side of the street as the Caballero house?"
"Yes, sir."
"Did you hear a blind banging against the window?"
"I don't know what I heard."
"Did you see Malvina opening the blind?"
"No, sir."
"Did you miss the colored girls' running out because you were already further down 11th Street? You didn't see them because you were running away, scared for your life?"
"No, sir. I called out they needed help at Gato's."
"Then why didn't you go over there?"

John stammered. "I don't know. I was a little afraid, maybe."

"So you had no intention of returning to Gato's until you ran into Charlie Flynn a block away, right?"

"Not right then." The boy squirmed in his chair. He stammered, "I mean, yes. I would have gone back."

"So, you saw the shooting from 11th and the Panama Road, and you saw the runner sixty feet from the house, turning at Laura Street, where you had run?" asked Fletcher. "What did Charlie Flynn say about the running man?"

John hesitated.

"Yes?" said Fletcher.

"Charlie said it was probably Eddie. I think he said it because Eddie was around a lot."

"Objection, hearsay," said St. Clair-Abrams, to be heard across the Georgia state line.

"Sustained."

"All right, I am going to change the subject, John," Fletcher said. The boy took a breath, crossed his boots at the ankle.

"Do you remember the evening Mr. Hartridge and I came out to see you?"

"Yes, sir."

"Remember, we asked you to reenact the scene where the running man turned south on Laura Street toward town?"

"Yes, sir."

"Remember, we tested your ability to see and recognize someone you described running past you that night?"

"Yes, sir," said John, looking at his knees.

St. Clair-Abrams objected. "No proper predicate. The circumstances of a different night, the degree of light has changed, the positions of the people have not been described and could not be the same."

"Overruled," said Call, "assuming the circumstances can be described."

"What time was our meeting, Johnny?" asked Fletcher. "When did we come visit you?"

"I believe it was around a month ago."

"Does late April sound right? And on that evening, approximately seven, you took your place near Laura Street, as you did on the night of the shooting?"

"Yes, sir."

Fletcher continued. "And when Mr. Hartridge took turns running around the corner of Laura as you described, you were unable to tell if Mr. Hartridge wore a long or short coat?"

"No, I couldn't tell, but I did say the runner was about the same size as Mr. Hartridge."

"Yes. Quite helpful," Fletcher said. "Moving on. When Mr. Hartridge wore a hat running past you, you couldn't tell if he wore a straw hat or what kind of hat, correct?"

"Yes, that's correct." John's shoulders noticeably wilted.

"Could you say if his coat was open or buttoned?"

"No, I couldn't."

"Could you tell if it was Mr. Hartridge or I running by you?"

"I think I could."

"Well, if you think you could or thought you could, you certainly didn't, did you?"

St. Clair-Abrams, apoplectic, jumped up. "Your Honor, this is an outrage." John stared vacantly to the side. He focused on the brass spittoons. "There is no relevance to these questions and he is hammering the witness," said St. Clair-Abrams. "The state attorney's little games occurred on a different night under different conditions. These charades prove nothing."

"The witness agreed to when and where the meeting took place. The jury will take that into account. I overrule the objection," replied Call.

Fletcher changed the subject again. "How soon did you get back to the Gatos' after the shooting?" he asked.

"Right away."

"Where was Marie Louise?"

"In the house. I was with Charlie Flynn. We didn't go in then."

"Did you ever go into Gato's?"

"We did later on. Marie looked pretty bad. Made me sick to my stomach."

"What did you do after you saw Marie?" asked Fletcher.

"I came out on the porch, then Mrs. Sánchez wanted us to walk her home because she was afraid. Charlie and I saw her to her house but returned to Gato's again."

"And then?"

"We stood on the porch. Dr. Mitchell came in and Mr. Huau. Alphonso Fritot, Mrs. Gato and Elvira Gato were there on the piazza. And some others."

Fletcher stepped back for a moment, then began with a quiet voice. "Why did you make a comparison earlier of the runner's size to Edward Pitzer? You volunteered that without being asked."

"I knew Eddie was going to the Gatos' that night and I thought they might say he shot her. When I heard Charlie say, 'I bet it was Eddie,' I told Charlie the running man was much larger than Edward Pitzer. I said the man wasn't Edward Pitzer."

Fletcher's volume abruptly increased. "Did you tell Mrs. Gato that you walked home with Marie Louise from your house?"

"I already told Georgia inside, then Mrs. Gato asked me afterwards."

"Did you not say to Mrs. Gato and Elvira, in the presence of these people on the piazza, that after leaving Marie, when you were hurrying away, that you saw Edward Pitzer racing by? Did you not tell them, on the piazza, you saw Edward Pitzer running down the Panama Road to 11th Street and turning south on Laura Street?"

"No. I didn't."

St. Clair-Abrams was on his feet but before he could speak, Fletcher continued.

"Well, you're a good boy, Johnny Bigger, obeying your orders, protecting the white boy," drawing his session to a close. "Just remember what you say and do today will follow you the rest of your life."[3]

John Bigger froze as if he'd been slapped in the face.

Part IV – Chapter 20

Mrs. Cornelia Pickett

Edward Pitzer maintained a room, a few blocks west of El Modelo Cigar Manufacturing Company at Mrs. Pickett's boardinghouse, the corner of Bay and Bridge Streets. He did not reside there regularly but the evening of April 20, after the shooting, he had called at the house. The next day, April 21, Marie Louise died.

The coroner's jury, already appointed by A. O. Wright, visited the body that evening and convened the following day to determine the cause of death. Mrs. Pickett, although summoned before them, professed to be ill on the 22nd and did not appear. Her daughter, also named Cornelia, excused from work, attended the April 22 inquest and testified regarding Pitzer's last visit.

Both prosecution and defense were interested in Mrs. Pickett's testimony at the Pitzer trial beginning in late May. Fearing a recurrence of Mrs. Pickett's illness at her scheduled trial date, the opposing attorneys arranged a session on Wednesday, May 5, at the Pickett house to record her statement. They took her affidavit at her dining room table before a stenographer.

As feared, on the fifth day of the trial, Saturday, May 29, when Mrs. Pickett was scheduled to testify, she was again infirm and supposedly unable to attend the proceedings. Although in light of her illness on the day of the inquest in April, her statement was introduced without objection.

There had been reason to believe Mrs. Pickett, a gentlewoman not to be maligned, might not be emotionally capable of a trial appearance. There were signs of her reticence to appear in public the night of the killing, the night Pitzer appeared at her boardinghouse. A young police officer ordered to her house that night reported her resistance.

When he arrived at her house, he blurted out his message to the guests who answered the door. "Someone shot Marie Louise Gato tonight. Edward Pitzer is suspected. He surrendered a few moments ago and claims he was here at the time of the shooting. Chief Keefe wants me to ask a few questions."

The boarders in the parlor fetched the proprietor, and Mrs. Cornelia Pickett soon descended the stairs to her hall. Her long, dark skirt swished on every step. Shoulders back, head high, she opened the door to the young officer, his brass bright in the porch light. She waited for him to speak. The boarders leaned in to listen also.

Under her sharp gaze, wearing a grave but jittery face, the young man repeated, "Edward Pitzer says he was here when Marie Louise Gato was shot tonight. Chief Keefe wants to know if that's true."

Composed, pausing several seconds before she answered, Mrs. Pickett stepped back. "I know nothing of it," she said. Eyes hard, she started to close the door.

"But was he here tonight?" the policeman asked.

She hesitated. "Yes, I believe he was."

"What time was that, madam?"

"I don't know," she said, hurriedly. "Between seven and eight, I suppose. I can't really say."

Her daughter, also named Cornelia, listened to the officer, too. She clerked at Oskey's Curio Shop nearby on Bay Street, where she sold baby alligators and packaged baby gators in Spanish moss for posting. She also sold baby alligator-head purses. "He was here from about seven-fifteen, seven-twenty," she said, as she entered the foyer.

"I'm sure that is correct," said Mrs. Pickett. "And now we must go, I'm afraid." While closing the door, she pushed her daughter toward the parlor, but the policeman stuck out his foot to keep the door open.

"Did you notice anything odd about him at the time?" he asked the daughter.

"Eddie's hair was mussed and he was moist with perspiration," Cornelia added, as she was guided from the room.

"And that is all we know," said Mrs. Pickett abruptly. "I must go. I run a business, sir." The officer withdrew his foot. Mrs. Pickett closed the door and locked it.

"No more," she said to her daughter. "We do not speak to anyone of this, again. It is not good for our reputation. It is not good for our business and Mrs. Pitzer is a lovely woman, active in temperance." Cornelia stared at her mother in silence.

Pitzer never spent the night at the boardinghouse, and he had left the house that evening at approximately seven-thirty. From her second-story window, Mrs. Pickett watched him leave the front yard and head north on Bridge Street. Although she did not say so, she thought at the time he looked very upset and shaken. He later surrendered at the police station, and claimed he had been visiting Miss Cornelia, the daughter, during the Gato attack. That was the last time Mrs. Pickett saw Pitzer, though she heard of him often enough in the ensuing weeks.

Part IV – Chapter 21

Mrs. Cornelia Pickett's Affidavit
Miss Cornelia Pickett

The stenographer read Mrs. Cornelia Pickett's affidavit aloud, which was entered into the record:

"'I reside in the Fitzgerald Block at the corner of Bridge and Bay Streets where I run a boarding house. On the evening of the murder of Marie Louise Gato, Edward Pitzer arrived at my house about fifteen or twenty minutes after seven.'"

"Oh, Mrs. Pickett knows better than that," muttered Pitzer aloud, disgusted at the hours she had declared. He flopped to the side of his chair. The time she stated did not comply with the alibi he gave Lieutenant Gruber the night of the murder.

"Quiet." Judge Call glared at Pitzer.

Straining to see through his wire-rimmed glasses, the stenographer continued to read Mrs. Pickett's words in a voice like a tin horn. His tweed coat hung loose on his skinny frame.

"'Mr. Pitzer rented one of my rooms about a year ago,'" Mrs. Pickett's statement continued, "'although he never spent the night. He said he did not wish to disturb his parents when coming in late, but apparently it was never a problem. When Mr. Pitzer arrived on the night of the murder, I did not notice his appearance or manner. Mr. Prather, another boarder, who actually stays on the premises regularly, arrived about seven-forty. He informed me of the attack at Gato's that evening. Mr. Pitzer had been chatting in his room with Cornelia, my daughter. Mr. Prather spoke to Cornelia and Mr. Pitzer and shook hands with each of them. Twenty minutes later, Mr. Pitzer departed.

"Then seeing my other daughter Florida standing with me in the doorway of her bedroom, Mr. Prather came up the stairs to repeat the news. He said one of Mrs. Gato's daughters had been shot and Pitzer was accused. I didn't speak to Mr. Pitzer that evening but I heard him saying his goodbyes at about eight. I went to the front landing and watched him leave. He wore a dark suit and a derby and he headed north on Bridge Street. I watched him until he was out of sight. I have no idea why I watched him. Curiosity, I guess. Later, a police officer arrived to verify that Mr. Pitzer was at my house the night of the shooting and to establish the time he was there."

* * *

After her mother's statement was read, St. Clair-Abrams called Miss Cornelia Pickett, for the defense. "I recognized Pitzer's voice at the house about seven-twenty that evening," she said. "I went upstairs to greet him two or three minutes later." Her testimony was consistent with her mother's statement.

"Did Mr. Pitzer speak of Marie Louise that evening?" asked St. Clair-Abrams.

"Not much. I asked him if he'd given Marie Louise a little book—a Bible, I think it was—which he had planned to do on Easter. He said, 'Yes,' and he also got her a bookmark with a rose and a little heart and anchor design."

"Did Eddie say he planned to go out to Gato's that evening?"

"No, he said Marie was staying in town at the Huaus'. He had a Columbia Bicycle catalogue in his pocket to show her the next day."

"Thank you, Miss Cornelia," St. Clair-Abrams said. "Your witness, sirs."

Augustus Cockrell Jr., continuing the questioning, remained seated at the State's table. "Miss Pickett, did you notice the defendant's red face and disheveled appearance when he arrived at your house? Your younger sister, Florida, who was also there, was quoted in the newspaper, on this point."

"I guess one could say he appeared a bit ruffled," Cornelia said, "now that you mention it."

"Was he sweating?"

"Yes. April can be a hot month, you know."

"Was his face red?"

"That, I do not remember."

"Thank you, Miss Pickett," said Cockrell. "I have no further questions."

To counter Cornelia's assertions about Pitzer's sweaty condition, St. Clair-Abrams then called James Pitzer, the defendant's father, to explain that his son always sweated profusely and his collar wilted quickly. James also said Edward's face turned red with slight exertion.

Pat Fallon, the jailor and next-to-last direct defense witness, was handed a bundle by Abrams. Opening it, he identified the collar, cuffs and shirt Pitzer wore the night he surrendered. The collar, which the bailiff passed to the jury for examination, appeared only a little soiled and wilted from sweat. Cross-examined by Cockrell, Fallon stoutly maintained they were the identical set which Pitzer had worn April 20 and had never left Cockrell's care and control.

Part IV – Chapter 22

Mrs. Rachel Bixler

"Your Honor, at this time, I have a vitally important surprise witness to call next. She's waiting in the hallway." said St. Clair-Abrams with deep sincerity, rising slowly. "She will testify to events of April 20, the night of the appalling Gato murder. I assure you her testimony will be most relevant to us all."

Hartridge surged to his feet to object.

At this point, the trial had consumed four days, two by the prosecution, two by the defense. Evidence had contradicted evidence as to who had been where on the evening Marie Louise was shot. Witnesses quoted distances, times, order of appearance, many different accounts. The jurors, all gentlemen from the country, listened with extreme patience and apparent indifference.

"This new witness comes forward, unwillingly, but of her own accord, to present her personal recognition of Edward Pitzer on that night," St. Clair-Abrams continued.

Judge Call, eyebrows drawn, glared firmly at St. Clair-Abrams.

Sensing the recently discovered witness planned to create a new timeline, propose an expanded murder scene, Hartridge's voice smoked as he struggled to restrain himself. "Your Honor, I have received no notice of this witness's appearance, although the trial has been in construct for a month. I have no idea of the witness's integrity. I have had no opportunity to prepare a cross-examination, much less to conduct one. I strongly object to this surprise witness as prejudicial to the State's case."

"Nor, sir," St. Clair-Abrams said in quick follow-up, turning slightly to include the state attorney, "have I had adequate time to examine this witness, but her information is invaluable. I am sure you will find an equitable remedy for this young man who has no blemishes on his life and allow us to hear her remarks, which are highly probative."

The people in the gallery glanced at each other, faces open in wonder that St. Clair-Abrams had secluded this woman from their gossip.

The defendant remained quiet, staring straight ahead. He showed no awareness of the new witness.

For protracted seconds, Call sat immobile, looking at the opposing parties. Quietly, the gallery pulled for one or the other side to profit from Call's decision on the surprise witness. The public relied on him for detachment and objectivity, but did not understand a major factor. In the middling town, such people as the primary trial participants, excluding the Pitzers, adhered together, like mud. They worshipped together, knew the same secret club handshakes, gathered for holidays, celebrations, games of whist, hunting and fishing.

Call had been Hartridge's guide and tutor as a young assistant county solicitor. Both families had pioneered Florida. The Honorable Rhydon Call served as pallbearer for St. Clair-Abrams' wife. Many years later, Hartridge would serve as pallbearer for St. Clair-Abrams.

With everyone waiting and staring, Call finally spoke. Looking in St. Clair-Abrams' direction, he said, "This testimony better be all you say it is, sir. I caution you." A dark beat infused his voice. "I hereby adjourn this session of court until three o'clock. The attorneys and this proposed witness will accompany me to chambers where Mr. Hartridge and I will question the new arrival. If this woman's evidence proves to be, as you say it is, an integral part of this trial I'll allow it. We shall see if it is as you say. Let the record reflect this."

St. Clair-Abrams thanked the court, bowing deep from his waist.

After a personal assessment by the court officers, Mrs. Rachel Bixler, the stubby proprietress of the River View Hotel on Riverside Avenue, took the stand for the defense.[1] Wrinkling her broad forehead, she paced headlong across the courtroom before the bailiff finished calling her name.

Flurrying forward, her mauve satin skirt swished as if she were sanding a board. The darker violet lace at her thick neck reached nearly to her ears. Three pink plumes of an unknown, but long-feathered bird waved languidly from her hat as she sailed by the bar, a spectacle in rose hues. The hat all but covered her salt-and-pepper grey hair. On her face, two small lines, timeworn scars, ran from her lip, angled to her cheekbone.

"So what's this?" Hartridge said, mockingly, jerking back when Bixler passed him, pretending to look at her flamboyance with surprise. Judge Call, lifting his bushy eyebrows, shot Hartridge a reprimand. The jurymen, drawn from the hinterlands, watched her flouncing feathers, expensive fashion items, and dreamed of aiming their bores on such a bird or at least grabbing the hat.

"Looks as if she's been shooting in the Everglades," a man in the audience leaned forward to whisper. The ladies lifted their brims and veils to assess Mrs. Bixler's extravagant attire. Except for the unschooled excess, there was little trace of the Ohio farm girl, which many knew her to be.

St. Clair-Abrams stepped forward, smiling, offering to steady her. She placed her chubby hand in his, bunched her skirt to the side, and plopped into the chair. She angled her head, unnaturally.

"I always run things on time at my hotel. I get up at five in the morning to supervise my staff." She pointed to the round gold filigree watch pinned to her bosom.

"I see," said St. Clair-Abrams. "And to what hotel do you refer?"

"I am the proprietress of the River View Hotel, two blocks south of the viaduct on Riverside Avenue. It is the only hotel in town with easy access to the river. Also, the trolley stops in front of it, a major advantage."

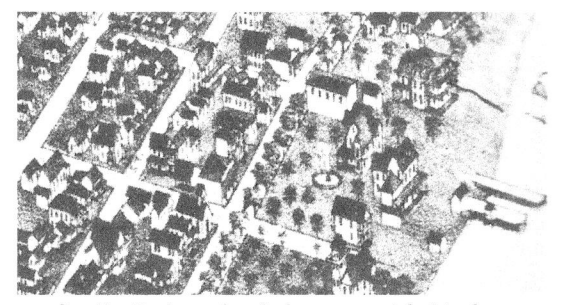

River View Hotel, east of circular fountain, towards St. Johns River.

"Do you recognize the defendant in this courtroom, Mrs. Bixler?"

"Of course, that's him right there." She lifted a hefty arm to point at Pitzer.

"Very good," St. Clair-Abrams said. "Do you ever buy things at the shop of James Pitzer, his father?" James, in the audience, winced at the referral to his mercantile establishment as a shop.

"I do. Quite often."

"And do you remember recently purchasing a cup and saucer there?"

"Of course, I remember the purchase. I bought it on April 20, this year, the same day someone shot Marie Louise Gato. I acquired it for my husband's birthday. It is a large porcelain set, the cup the size of a soup bowl, maybe not quite that big." She made a circle with her hands in front of her face to illustrate the size.

"And why did you buy the gift so early," St. Clair-Abrams asked, "a month and a day before the actual birthday and why have it delivered so soon?"

"I feared someone would buy the thing behind my back or break it. You know how people are."

Hartridge rose. "Objection! What is the relevance of all this? Where is the so-called probative value? She claims to have evidence of Pitzer's activities on the twentieth of April."

St. Clair-Abrams turned, a serene smile across his face. "Surely, we have the right to establish the defendant's whereabouts at the time Miss Gato was murdered?"

"I've heard no word of the defendant, only about this cup and saucer business," said Hartridge, "and I repeat, what is the relevance?"

"If you but sit, you surely will see," replied St. Clair-Abrams. Hartridge looked imploringly at Call.

"Mr. State Attorney, I said I will allow her testimony," Call said quietly and motioned for Hartridge to sit.

Hartridge pushed his lips flat with two fingers, lowering himself to his chair.

"Do you have the cup and saucer in question?" asked the defense attorney.

"I do."

"Did you take possession of it at the time of purchase?"

"Approximately five minutes after the seven o'clock hour, on the evening of April twentieth, Edward Pitzer, the owner's son, brought it out to the hotel." A murmur passed through the watchers. Mention of the coincidental timing caused Hartridge to jerk his hands to the desk as his mouth fell slightly open.

"Are you absolutely sure about the time of this delivery?" asked St. Clair-Abrams.

"Of course, I am. I wear a watch." Mrs. Bixler pointed at it again. "When the chambermaid came out from the kitchen, concerned if I had yet eaten, I looked at my watch and it was the exact time I just said."

Observers more carefully registered the significance of her testimony, which plugged a gaping hole in the defendant's alibi he had assigned to Mrs. Pickett. Their surprised utterances rumbled across the aisles. The people churned. "I told you so," said one. "Not true," shouted another. The temperance girls stood and cheered.

Catalina Huau, stunned at the Bixler testimony, inert and blank, stared at the chunky woman. Hartridge, at his table, quietly parsed Mrs. Bixler's words and planned his cross-examination. Fletcher pushed notes in front of Hartridge offering his own ideas. Call banged his gavel for a full minute to bring the room to order.

"Quiet. Remain in your seats. Bailiff, call the sheriff." The judge directed his courtroom with outstretched arms, the wings of his black robes waving across his desk. Quickly surrounded by uniformed police once again, the spectators settled.

Mrs. Bixler gazed fixedly over the heads of the gallery, ignoring the unruliness. St. Clair-Abrams smoothly resumed his direct questioning, noting nothing unusual. He shook his sleeves free to his wrist and smiled pleasantly at the witness, who met his gaze with indifference.

"How long was Eddie at your place, Mrs. Bixler?"

"A few minutes. I handed the package to one of my servants to take inside. We talked a moment and I walked the boy back out through the side gate where he entered. Eddie Pitzer stood as close to me as Major St. Clair-Abrams stands beside me now," she said, looking at the jury, catching their eye and smiling.

"Hmm," said one.

"Is that so?" said another.

"Not necessary to answer, gentlemen," said Call.

Unbidden, Mrs. Bixler continued, "The cup and saucer will be presented to my husband on his birthday. I wished care to be exercised in delivering them. That's why they were brought to me by Mr. Pitzer's son. I knew he would be accountable." She made the ring of the saucer in front of her pudgy scarred face again.

"Thank you, Mrs. Bixler," said Abrams, and returned to his chair. The gallery still sparked with muted discussion.

The judge nodded for Hartridge to begin cross-examination. "Well, your report was informative," Hartridge said, approaching her. "Thank you for this last-minute news you finally thought worth sharing." He smiled coldly. She did not blink.

"Watch yourself, Mr. Hartridge," said Judge Call, twirling his gavel between thumb and fingers. Hartridge continued toward Mrs. Bixler, smoothing his hair and straightening his jacket.

"When did you first hear of the shooting of Marie Louise Gato?" Hartridge asked her.

"My son came in about eight-thirty in the evening and said that Eddie Pitzer shot Miss Gato." No matter how many times the crowd heard of the murder, it seemed to stun them every time. A general gasp ran up and down the rows.

"Who is your son?" said Hartridge.

"I only have one, Ernest. He sells insurance."[2,3,4] She touched a forefinger to the scars on her lips and looked straight at the attorney.

"Yes, he's been doing so for nearly a year, correct? I've heard the name."

"Yes."

"When Master Ernest told you that the defendant shot Miss Gato, were you upset?"

"Concerned. As anyone would be."

"Did your son seem upset?"

"I think so. He and Eddie were close in age. We attend the same church as the Pitzers."

"The defendant had been at your house an hour before," said the prosecutor. "What did Master Ernest say to that?"

"He's twenty-two years old. Call him mister."

"All right, what did Mr. Ernest say to that?"

"Nothing, I did not tell him," Mrs. Bixler glared and replied.

"For heaven's sake, you didn't tell your own son?" Hartridge sounded genuinely amazed.

"I didn't want the attention. I didn't want to get up before the public, unless necessary to stand by a man. Now, I think it is necessary in this case."

"You equate telling Ernest with getting up before the public?" She stared at him in silence. "When did you finally tell him?"

"Two days ago."

"Strangely late, don't you think?" said Hartridge.

"Objection," called St. Clair-Abrams.

"Question withdrawn."

"Where is your son's office?"

She became less petulant as she spoke about her son. Sitting taller, she said, "His office is on Hogan just around the corner from Mr. Pitzer's store in the second block on West Bay."

Hartridge looked down at notes he was holding. "Ernest will be moving to an office on Bay Street soon, I believe," he said.

"Yes. He's doing well." She smiled that Hartridge knew her son's business.

"He will be working even closer to James Pitzer's store," the attorney mused. "The defendant is twenty. You said Ernest is twenty-two. Are they close friends?"

"They're friends," she said. "They talk during their work breaks. I said they both go to the Congregational Church. Yes, I suppose they're good friends."

"Good to hear it," said Hartridge. He lifted his shoulders and breathed heavily. "Have you observed any special affection your son has for the defendant that might steer you to stand suddenly by this defendant as you are now doing?"

"What do you mean?" She squinted, answering with a surly pitch.

"Never mind," he said. "One hears things is all." She glared at him like an angry street cur, but didn't answer. "What time did you go downtown to James Pitzer's place to purchase the huge cup and saucer?" Snickers came from the audience. She sliced her eyes at the gallery and back at him. She spoke flatly.

"That is my affair and none of your business."

Call interjected at once. "Mrs. Bixler, you are on the witness stand at my discretion and you will answer the question." She glowered at him first and then at the prosecutor.

"When did you leave your house for town, on April 20, Mrs. Bixler?"

"I don't remember. In the afternoon."

"Think of the time, Mrs. Bixler. This is important." Hartridge's tone was sharp.

"I *am* thinking, mister. Do you imagine I want to be here any longer than necessary? I do not recall the time. Between the lunch hour and supper."

"Meaning, of course," Hartridge said, "enough time for you to return and receive your delivery."

She glowered at him again. He began to prod and poke at her itinerary on the afternoon. She thwarted him at every turn with half answers and lack of memory.

"How did you get to town?"

"I walked. I turned east on Bay Street."

"Where did you go on Bay Street?"

"I went first to the Armour Meat Company."

"Did anyone see you there or talk to you?"

"I don't think so. Maybe they did. I don't remember."

"Did you pay a bill?"

"Yes. No. I started to. I changed my mind."

"Where else did you go?"

After many queries, Hartridge, bit by bit, evoked a list of her calls. She walked to Wood's Store, to Pitzer's store, then to Kuhn, a florist, then Furchgott's Department Store, and Cameron's Seed Store. She also entered Armour's Meat.

The defendant sat straight-backed in his chair, nodding his head to affirm Mrs. Bixler's testimony, as if he had accompanied her.

"Does anyone remember seeing you at any of the places?" asked Hartridge finally.

"How should I know?"

"Did anyone see you anywhere else downtown?"

"I also stopped at Mrs. Goodson's dressmaking establishment on Riverside Avenue. Then, I walked to Mrs. Mueller's on Duval Street. I returned to Cameron's Seed Store and caught the trolley home."

"And no one could swear they saw you that day?" Hartridge asked again.

"I said I didn't know," she said. The chased mouse appeared to have beaten the cat, as one of the attorneys later remarked.

George Hosack, the defendant's uncle-in-law, sat with his arms crossed at his waist, staring into his lap. Everyone was certain he had paid for the defendant's defense. Was he pleased with this testimony? Was he as surprised as everyone else when the woman came forth? His wife, Sadie, turned to look at him and placed her hand on his arm.

"Did Mrs. Goodson, or another dressmaker, create that frock you're wearing, Mrs. Bixler?" Hartridge asked with a taut smile. Call raised his gavel but the woman answered before he could rap it.

"She did not."

"Were you dressed in your current attire the afternoon you were paying bills?"

"I was not," she said.

"I would guess not, for if you had been, someone would have remembered you, or at least your lovely feathers." A few more chortles in the room.

"I don't care for your attitude." Her voice rose. "You're a rude man," she almost shouted when she said it.

Call banged his gavel. "Mrs. Bixler, keep to the facts."

St. Clair-Abrams jumped up. "Objection, Your Honor, objection. He's upset her."

"Overruled. I gather she's upset, Abrams," said Call and returned to the witness. "Mrs. Bixler, restrain yourself. If you shout again, you will be escorted out."

Hartridge suddenly turned to the woman and said politely, "And you walked the entire distance alone the day you bought the cup, didn't you? You must have been exhausted. Poor dear. By any chance, do you have a receipt for the day you purchased the cup?" he asked.

As an owl blinks, she squinted her eyes at him and gripped her jaw tightly. "I had no idea my honesty would be questioned," she said, holding the glare.

"I have nothing further, your honor," said St. Clair-Abrams, "but Mrs. Bixler will retrieve her proof of purchase and present it at the next court session."

"Mrs. Bixler, you are excused, subject to recall," said Call. Bailiffs approached to escort her out.

After her testimony on Saturday, the trial adjourned. Hartridge spent Sunday afternoon looking unsuccessfully for someone, anyone, who had seen Mrs. Bixler in the town the afternoon of April 20. He could not find a single soul.

Part IV – Chapter 23

Mrs. Rachel Bixler Recalled

Monday, May 31, 1897

The trial resumed on Monday morning, May 31.

St. Clair-Abrams stood at his table with an enigmatic smile.

"Hello, Gus," he said to the state attorney. Hartridge nodded. The rich color of the younger man's hair shone in the morning light. The difference in their age seemed more striking. "I understand you made a hunting expedition yesterday," said St. Clair-Abrams.

"Do you?" replied Hartridge flatly and turned to speak to Fletcher, seated beside him.

When Judge Call arrived and brought the trial to order, St. Clair-Abrams requested the recall of Mrs. Bixler. Hartridge objected, but Judge Call allowed it. For the second time in two days, crowned by a hat of extravagant plumage, Mrs. Bixler's squat form flurried to the witness chair.

"You testified previously that you bought a cup and saucer from James Pitzer on the afternoon of April 20," St. Clair-Abrams began. "And that his son delivered it to you in Riverside at roughly seven o'clock that evening?"

"Yes, sir." Mrs. Bixler nodded at the jury.

"Is there any written evidence of that purchase?"

"Yes, sir. I have the receipt right here." With a flourish, she produced a folded paper from her purse. "I forgot it Saturday when I testified. I was not expecting to be disbelieved." She shot a foul look at Hartridge. He remained placid.

St. Clair-Abrams took the receipt and showed it to opposing counsel. "So, the receipt shows you bought the cup and saucer on the 20th of April?"

"Yes, but I erred in my testimony Saturday." Hartridge and Fletcher looked up in unison.

"There is no end to her," whispered Fletcher as he stared at the woman.

"I made a mistake," she said. "I wasn't in Armour's Meat at all. I do my business with them by phone and I was confused. I only go there to pay my bill and I had already paid it that month. I'm unclear when exactly, but it wasn't the day I bought the cup and saucer. I checked my accounts Saturday night."

Hartridge sent word to dismiss the Armour's clerk there to deny Mrs. Bixler's presence at Armour's on April 20. As she had corrected her error, he was no longer needed.

"Thank you, Mrs. Bixler," said St. Clair-Abrams.

"You know, those small shops don't give receipts for minor purchases," said Fletcher to Hartridge.

"I know. I know," said Hartridge, shaking his head slowly and rising to address the court.

"I have two questions for the lady, Your Honor," said Hartridge. "He stood, straightening his shoulders. "Mrs. Bixler, when did Mr. Pitzer actually give you the receipt for the cup and saucer?" People shuffled in the uneasy moment.

"I received it on April 20th." She was angry, emphatic. Her face reddened.

"Did anyone else see you receive it besides Mr. Pitzer?"

Her nostrils flared. "I don't know who else was in the store, if that's what you're asking, her words aggressive and bitter. I don't remember," she said.

"Did anyone else see you anywhere downtown that afternoon?" Hartridge continued.

"How would I know?" she snapped.

Sunlight spread through the stained-glass pane and across the scarred floor. Someone opened a window. No breeze blew in or trembled the palms outside.

"So you cannot name one single person who can verify you were downtown on April 20th?"

"I am not in charge of finding witnesses for you," she growled.

"More's the pity," Hartridge said and turned away.

Part IV – Chapter 24

Edward Pitzer

All through the trial, Pitzer twisted in his chair, glowered and grunted at those testifying. He was to be the defense's final witness. St. Clair-Abrams feared he might be churlish while responding, so the attorney opened the examination with a few palliative questions, also drawing attention to Pitzer's own suffering and discomfort. There was great interest in his testimony. Observers in the back climbed on chairs to see the man better.

"How is your food in jail, Mr. Pitzer?"

"It's fine, sir." The defendant smiled sweetly.

"Are you resting well on your cot?"

"And I am resting well. I am glad to be here at last, to answer real questions truthfully. I'll be finally able to straighten things out." Pitzer's words were steady but he made nervous arm movements as he spoke.

"Mr. Edward Pitzer," said St. Clair-Abrams, louder, stepping closer, rising to his full enormity. "In the presence of this court, this jury, this crowd assembled, and the God before whom you expect to be judged, did you shoot Marie Louise Gato?"

In response, Pitzer jumped skyward to his feet and threw up his arms, his voice loud and pleading. "Gentlemen, as God is my witness, I swear I never shot Marie Louise Gato." He leaned his head backward, gulping a noisy sob. "We were engaged to be married, for

His sweet sake, and had been so for a month before she died." His face fell forward into his open hands.

He slid to his chair, then to his knees, hands and head bent, in pious supplication. "I did not shoot or harm her in any way." A moan trailed from him. "I never would. I never would," he keened.

"Objection," Hartridge and Fletcher both yelled and sprang from their seats.

"I move for a mistrial, Your Honor. These histrionics are highly prejudicial to the State's case."

Judge Call roared, "Get up, man. On your feet. Into your chair." St. Clair-Abrams and a deputy ran to Pitzer, each grabbing a shoulder and setting him on his chair.

"The jury will ignore this outburst," Call said to them.

Pitzer's father cried softly. With help, Eddie Pitzer leaned back in his chair resting his head on his hand, gazing at the floor.

"The motion is denied. We will continue, but I warn the jury not to consider the defendant's actions," said Call, fiercely. He turned to the defendant. "Mr. Pitzer, in all my years in a courtroom, I have never witnessed such a ridiculous thing, such outrageous behavior. Strike the thing, every bit," he ordered the stenographer.

"You best control your client, Mr. St. Clair-Abrams." The defense attorney stood and nodded solemnly.

"That was interesting," said one juryman in a rare response to the proceedings. Call glowered at him while straightening items on his bench.

St. Clair-Abrams began again as if nothing odd had occurred. "Mr. Pitzer, you have known Miss Marie Louise Gato for a long time, correct?"

"For years," Pitzer said.

"When was the last time you saw her?" he asked.

"On Monday evening, April 19th, at her front gate," Pitzer said.

"Would you describe your meeting, please?"

"I had my arms around Marie Louise as we stood in front of her yard and we were talking. All of sudden, she drew back and threw a hand over her breast. She was screaming and looking over my shoulder, so I turned to look also. I saw a large dark man with a cigar, standing there on the Panama Road watching us.

"I said to Marie loudly so the man could hear," Pitzer continued, "'A few more lessons and you'll know how to dance the two-step.' I grasped her hands. I meant to walk her to the front door, but she rushed up the path alone. She glanced back a couple of times, smiled quickly at me and went inside."

"Had you seen this man before?" asked St. Clair Abrams.

"No, sir," Pitzer said, "but I can tell you, it made me very nervous, the way he was staring at us." Pitzer's eyes widened.

"What happened next?"

"I looked back again and he was gone."

"Can you describe the man?"

"He was tall. He was dark. I've never seen the man since and I never had the chance to discuss it with Marie Louise. She was shot the next day. The man could have been a spy. Cuban and Spanish spies, both sneak all over town. At first, I didn't think she was in any real danger. She wasn't part of the revolution, but obviously he was a danger to her for some reason. Someone should be looking for him."

"They are, Mr. Pitzer," said St. Clair-Abrams. "I assure you. We all are."

"Objection," said Hartridge. "Counsel is testifying about his own assumptions. The State is simply trying the defendant for the Marie Gato murder."

"Sustained," said Call.

Pitzer stuck a finger in his collar and pulled it from his neck. The afternoon sun, slanting through the windows, broiled the courtroom.

"Watch to see if he sweats," said Fletcher, with a smirk.

"Eddie, I want to clarify where you were the day of the murder," St. Clair-Abrams continued. "Tell us your whereabouts the afternoon and evening of April 20th this year."

"After work, I go to Springfield almost every afternoon for exercise and did so the day of the murder."

"At what precise time did you leave your father's store the evening Miss Gato was murdered?"

"Between four and five," Pitzer replied.

"Tell us your precise movements during this time, please, sir."

"I took the trolley north and got off at Beaver Street. From there, I walked for exercise north on the shell road, Main Street, to the West 8th Street trolley barn, the end of the Main Street line. I was only there a minute. I figured that was enough exercise for that day and I had other things to do.

"So, I hopped back on the southbound trolley, rode to West 2nd Street and decided to get off again. I like to look at the impressive houses on that road. I had planned to walk to the bicycle store on Adams to examine a Yellow Fellow bicycle, a Stearns wheel. Marie Louise liked that model and I intended to buy it for her. I walked over to Laura. Then, down to 5th Street and headed south from there to Springfield Park. It seems I got carried away with my stroll and forgot where I was headed."

"You are quite the wanderer," said St. Clair-Abrams.

"Yes, I like to exercise," Pitzer returned.

"What was your next engagement?"

"I stood in the park and watched two men at work. Let me think, I believe I had my hands on my hips." Pitzer smiled but St. Clair-Abrams did not. "Oh, yes, they were digging, and, no, sir, I was not close enough for them to see me or identify me."

"Did you see anyone else while walking that afternoon?" St. Clair-Abrams asked.

"Walking on West 2nd Street, I saw the big judge, Judge Dzialynski, rocking on his piazza, smoking a cigar. I tipped my hat to the judge who nodded in return. He's always nice to me. He likes me."

"Did you see anyone else?"

"Yes, there were others, but I didn't know them and they didn't know me." Pitzer sat with intertwined fingers in his lap, his leg jiggling. "In case you were going to ask."

"After you passed the judge," asked St. Clair-Abrams, "did you venture north of 2nd Street toward the Gato place?"

"I did not, Mr. St. Clair-Abrams." He rubbed his open hand across his face. "I headed to the bicycle store, remember? On the way, though, I recalled my father told me to deliver a cup and saucer to Mrs. Bixler in Riverside. So, I walked to the store, collected the cup and saucer, and caught the Hogan Street car to Bridge Street and the River View Hotel. The trolley stops right in front of the hotel. Mrs. Bixler owns it and the trolley stop is part of what she advertises. She also advertises hers as the only hotel with a dock on the river." He paused.

"Yes, please go on," said St. Clair-Abrams.

"When I stepped off the trolley, I saw Mrs. Bixler outside, so I went through the side gate to the backyard. We talked a bit. Her niece was there, too. Then the maid came out to tell Mrs. B. her supper was ready. I left the package with the maid."

"What time was this?" asked St. Clair-Abrams.

"Around seven."

"What did you do after delivering the cup and saucer?"

"I hadn't eaten either and I was hungry, so I started to Pigniolo's. I dine there often. When I left the River View," Pitzer continued, "I walked up Bridge Street, then over to Conover's Drug Store for some Coca-Cola. I finished the drink, caught the trolley and headed south again on Julia toward Pigniolo's."

"Did you eat supper?"

"No. Suddenly, I remembered I owed Mrs. Pickett five dollars for the room I rent at her place. I got off the trolley and turned back to Bridge Street and Bay. Her house is in the Ferguson Block. I met Mrs. Pickett at the top of her stairs. She called her daughter, Cornelia. We talked a minute or two. Then, I went to my room. I forgot to pay Mrs. Pickett, though."

"How long have you rented this room, Mr. Pitzer?" asked St. Clair-Abrams.

"Eight or nine months." One of Pitzer's legs started to bounce again.

"So, it is not a room you engaged recently or in connection with any recent events?"

"No, of course not," Pitzer scoffed.

"Did you change clothes there the evening of April 20th?" continued St. Clair-Abrams. He stood soberly beside his client.

"No, I did not," Pitzer responded. "I had no reason to do so."

"Why do you maintain the room?" asked St. Clair-Abrams, his expression very somber. "Did anyone else ever use it with or without you?" The audience rustled. They thought the probe suggestive.

"No, none of that," Pitzer said emphatically.

"All right, then," said St. Clair-Abrams, stepping back. "Paying for an unoccupied room may seem problematic to some is why I ask."

"I took the room when my family moved to town so as not to disturb my parents if I came in late." The Pitzers had recently moved ten blocks south across Hogans Creek, a more populated area.

"Have you ever spent the night at Mrs. Pickett's?"

"No, sir, I have not." Pitzer dipped his head rhythmically. He seemed to be growing more nervous. A few in the front row unintentionally nodded their heads, aping his movements.

Willie Gato leaned to his Aunt Catalina Huau, hiding his grin with a hand to his face, whispering, "I bet he's spent the night there. I don't care what he says. Have you seen the lovely Cornelia Pickett?"

"*Silencio*," Catalina whispered, eyes blazing. Elsewhere, she would have slapped his face for his crudity. Her own unmarried daughters were chaperoned everywhere they went, or so she believed. She was almost certain her eldest, the strong-willed Katie, had abided by her mother's rules.

A forlorn look suddenly shaded Pitzer's eyes. They sagged at the corners. "After I left Mrs. Pickett's, I first heard of the shooting from Clark, the barber's son, next door to our store. He said everyone thought I did it. I went straight to the police station and turned myself in. I met Officer Gruber, a fine man. He would have caught who did this, if he hadn't been killed." Pitzer leaned back in his chair. Dead air filled the room.

"All right," said St. Clair-Abrams. "How long had you known Miss Gato?"

"We were acquainted for six years. We went together for three years." A loud guffaw rose from the crowd.

Call pummeled his gavel and Pitzer, his face reddening, looked fiercely into the gallery. He examined a group of the temperance girls sitting close, their countenances taut. They smiled when they saw him look at them. He should never have doubted that group.

"Were your relations with Marie Louise friendly before the shooting?" asked St. Clair-Abrams.

"Relations between us were always friendly," Pitzer smiled.

Another snort came from the audience. Pitzer twisted toward the Gato family but they, too, appeared serious, attentive.

"Quiet," said Call. "No more noise." He scanned the courtroom. The gallery sat quietly, their expressions bland.

"Mr. Pitzer, I am now going to ask you a very personal question," said St. Clair-Abrams. He paused. "Did you love Marie Louise Gato?"

Hartridge looked at his desk, running his fingers through his chestnut hair, laughing to himself with a straight face.

Pitzer sat up, astonished. "Of course, I do," he said with great feeling.

St. Clair-Abrams offered him a small stack of pictures. "Do you recognize these?"

Pitzer glanced at them and quickly returned them. "They're all of Marie," he said through flat tight lips. His eyebrows drew together. "She gave me two. I took two from tables in the house."

"And these?" questioned St. Clair-Abrams, displaying a silver-mounted *Pocket Book of Common Prayer* and a bi-fold leather wallet.

"They were gifts from her to me," Pitzer said, looking up.

"Do you recognize this Christmas card that reads, 'With love and best wishes for a Happy Christmas to Eddie from Marie'? Naturally, I suppose you saw the salutations inscribed on it," St. Clair-Abrams said. "This tender Valentine card, I also suppose you recognize." Pitzer glared at him. "Do you recognize this silver matchbox? Also, a gift from Marie."

"I smoke cigarettes," said Pitzer. "And yes, we exchanged gifts and cards."

"What about this lovely handkerchief?" St. Clair-Abrams held a dainty cloth in the air by its corners.

"I took it. It was hers. She left it on a chair in her parlor, so I took it. It was a comfort to me." The muscles of Pitzer's jaw tightened. His eyes teared.

"May the defendant have a glass of water?" St. Clair-Abrams asked Call.

"Of course," said Call. "Would he like anything else?" He sounded peevish, then motioned to a bailiff, who left, returning with water.

"I'd like one of those," said the same juryman who had spoken aloud before.

Call ignored him. "Resume, Abrams," he said.

"Mr. Pitzer, I am going to ask you a series of questions to clear up some pending matters," said St. Clair-Abrams, stepping back, clearing his throat. Pitzer stretched his neck, chin upward, and waited. "Let's turn our attention to the night of the murder," said St. Clair-Abrams. "Had you planned to visit the Gato place that night, April 20th?"

"No, definitely not, sir. Marie Louise told me she planned to stay in town at the Huaus'. We planned to go to the Columbia bicycle store the following morning. So an agreement floated, of sorts, to see each other. But not that night, not the night of the shooting."

Part IV – Chapter 25

Pitzer Cross-Examination

Hartridge rose to cross-examine the defendant. "Mr. Pitzer, I am going to ask you questions regarding your specific whereabouts on the afternoon before the killing," he said.

"Yes, sir, Lieutenant," Pitzer responded.

Hartridge, an officer of the Jacksonville Light Infantry, a unit Pitzer had recently joined, pinned the defendant with an unfriendly stare. The attorney's eyes narrowed.

"Very well," said Hartridge, momentarily looking out the window and then, back at Pitzer. "Mr. Pitzer, did you say, on a recent occasion, that you were jealous of the Cubans?"

"I did say that, Mr. Hartridge," Pitzer sat erect, "but someone twisted what I said. And I can bet who it was." St. Clair-Abrams also sat erect. "I said to Marie's cousin, Flora, I was jealous of the Cubans. I know she told you what I said, but she didn't understand how I meant it."

"How did you mean it?"

"I meant to say I very much supported the Cuban Revolution and I wished to travel with the men to aid the insurgents and to fight beside them as a brother. I was jealous of the fighters."

"Then why do you not volunteer with the Cubans?" asked Hartridge.

"My primary responsibility lies with my parents. They are here in Jacksonville. I assist my father with his store and I am a comfort to my mother. I am their only child and their only nearby relation."

"Did you know that Marie was dating a Cuban army officer, Eddie?" Hartridge continued.

"What? No, I don't know that. I don't think so."

"Do you know a Cuban officer named Domingo Herrera?"

"No. Maybe. I might have heard the name."

"Were you ever informed that Marie was engaged to him?"

"Definitely not."

"Marie Louise was engaged to Domingo Herrera. Did you, by any chance, see the article in the paper from the *Detroit Free Press*? It mentioned José Carbonne also supposedly, Marie's fiancé. He plans to come to Jacksonville to find her killer."

"I didn't see it," Pitzer mumbled.

"Could these be reasons you are jealous of Cubans, Edward?"

"I didn't mean it that way. I told you." He flattened his mouth and his shrimpish coloring deepened.

"Do you know of any other men Marie was dating?" said Hartridge. Pitzer started but did not answer. He breathed deeply.

"Don't know the answer or don't want to talk about it? Okay, we'll change the subject to something familiar. You often visited Miss Gato in Springfield on your exercise jaunts and later in the evenings, right?" asked Hartridge.

"Yes."

"But Marie Louise often turned you away or refused to see you, true?"

"No. Not often. But she was sometimes busy." Pitzer clipped his answer, his expression sour.

Hartridge raised his voice. "Is it not true that on the evening of her murder, when she got off the trolley, you were waiting for her in Springfield with a gun?"

Hartridge's audible force for this question shook Pitzer free from his sullenness. "No, it is not true," he responded calmly.

"And except for all this running around you concocted at the last minute, after running past Mrs. Pickett's boarding house, the alibi you originally told Lieutenant Gruber when you surrendered. Next you said you stopped at Conover's Drug Store, where you sat and drank Coca-Cola, even though you were hungry and heading to Pigniolo's for supper. Then, you wandered to Mrs. Bixler's to make a delivery still having time to shoot Miss Gato. I am confused, Mister."

"No, I didn't run around. I was attending to errands, and I didn't shoot Marie Louise. I loved Marie."

"What do you mean, not true? Mrs. Pickett's is exactly where you told Officer Gruber you were."

"Not true. He must have misunderstood."

"Then, when you realized Mrs. Pickett did not support your alibi, you suddenly produced Mrs. Bixler, who places you at her hotel at the precise time of the murder. But you never mentioned Mrs. Bixler to Lieutenant Gruber the evening you shot Miss Gato, did you?"

"I told Lieutenant Gruber the best I could remember. I was upset about Marie."

Hartridge paused. "Yes, I imagine you were very upset. He turned to Call. "Your Honor," he said, "my co-counsel, Mr. Duncan Fletcher, has some questions of Mr. Pitzer."

Fletcher, the round-faced Jacksonville politician, with slicked-back greying hair, stood again to approach the witness stand. His wide handlebar mustache, also greying, concealed his expression, but not his eyes. They were alight.

"Now, about this engagement to marry Miss Gato," Fletcher said to the defendant, "Did you ask Miss Gato's father if you could marry Marie Louise? Was it all very formal? The mother and sisters hiding in the hall to listen while you requested Marie Louise's hand in marriage?" Fletcher looked down to straighten his diamond tie pin. It had slipped a bit on his crimson silk tie.

The defendant's eyes flashed. He recognized the irony. "I did not ask such a thing or in such a manner. I knew Mr. Gato would say no to our marriage. He and I have never been friends."

"Then you expected to carry off the marriage without his ever knowing?" Fletcher delivered.

"She was not forbade to marry me," Pitzer snapped.

"Well, there's a compliment for you," said Fletcher, glancing wide-eyed at the jury, tugging at his mustache. Two of them grinned a little. "Mr. Pitzer, you testified, after turning yourself in the night of the murder, you went to the Gato place in the company of two policemen?"

"Yes."

"On the ride to the Gatos' with the two officers," said Fletcher, "did you not remark you were afraid and wished to turn back to the station house?"

"No, I did not say that. I said I hoped there would be plenty of officers to keep the Cubans under control. I knew their disposition."

"That's not what I heard," Fletcher said.

Booing rose from the audience. "Come to order," Call said, looking towards the temperance girls and banging his gavel.

"Did you really think the Cubans would have killed you in front of two police officers?" Fletcher asked, goading.

"No," Pitzer retorted, "but I didn't want to take any chances."

All right, let's talk about the incident where you showed up at the Gatos' with a butcher knife and a pistol. Do you remember that?"

St. Clair-Abrams ascended, his face on fire. "Objection," he said. "There is not one whit of evidence the decedent had knife wounds, and counsel knows it. He's trying to confuse the jury."

"Overruled, Abrams," said Call. Call and Fletcher both stared at St. Clair-Abrams, while the witness continued.

"I would have never hurt Marie in any way," Pitzer replied.

"You didn't answer the question," said Fletcher. "Isn't it true that you appeared at Miss Gato's house once in possession of a butcher knife and a pistol?"

"An incident occurred when I possessed a butcher knife while visiting Miss Gato."

"A gun, too?"

"Yes."

"Tell us more about that, Edward."

Pitzer folded his restless arms. There was dead silence in the gallery.

"One day I had been showing the knife to a customer at the store but the customer didn't buy it. By mistake, I stuck it in my coat pocket and forgot it was there. Afterwards, I jumped on my wheel to ride to Gato's and brushed my hand against it. I cut my wrist on the point of the knife."

"Very foolish, sir."

"Yes, it was."

"Do you own a .38 Smith & Wesson pistol?" Fletcher said.

"Yes, sir."

"Do you often carry it with you?"

"For my own protection, yes, sometimes I do."

Fletcher stepped closer to the witness.

"And you had it with you at the Gatos the night you had the butcher knife?"

"Yes."

"And you displayed the knife and gun to her that night?"

"Yes."

"Did Miss Gato think it strange you came to visit her with a butcher knife and a gun?" The ends of Fletcher's mustache stiffly framed his cheeks. His demeanor had grown grimmer. "Or did you often carry lethal weapons to her place?"

"Of course, she thought it strange, but I explained the knife business to her, and I also showed her my pistol. She was only afraid for my safety." He hesitated. "She worried I might fall off my bike pedaling home and cut myself again."

"What did she do when you showed her your weapons?"

"She called me a coward."

"Then what happened?"

"She ran upstairs to her father. Maybe she was scared."

"What happened to scare her?"

"I'm not sure. Calling me a coward made me a little mad, I'm afraid, and I slammed the knife blade into a stair step. I tried to get the knife out but the tip broke off."

"When Marie Louise ran upstairs to her father, what happened next?"

"Mr. Gato came downstairs."

"Did he send you away?"

"Yes, of course. I don't blame him. I had unintentionally scared his daughter."

"Were there other nights you were sent away by Marie Louise or her father?"

"At times when Marie was busy or indisposed, her father asked me to leave."

"Did that make you mad?"

"No."

"Did you throw things, like candy, in their fountain when you were asked to leave?"

"No."

"Did you hide in the yard and spy on the family instead of leaving the premises when they had asked you to do?"

"That's ridiculous. No, I didn't."

"Where are your knife and pistol now?"

"I sailed them off the Gato porch the same night I took them out there. I left them in the yard. I don't know where they are now. I already told the police this. I didn't want Marie Louise to think I was afraid to come see her without an arsenal in my pocket."

"Are you aware," Fletcher asked, "that Mr. Gato found the broken knife in his yard the next day but not the gun?"

"No, not really."

"Where is your gun at this moment?" Fletcher said.

"I don't know," Pitzer said. "The police went through all my things and didn't find it. Maybe someone found it and took it to Mrs. Pickett's. Maybe it got lost there. I have no idea."

"You didn't go back to the Gatos' and try to retrieve the gun or even look for it?" Fletcher asked.

"I did not. Somebody must have stolen it at the boardinghouse. We had no locks on our rooms."

Fletcher paused. "That doesn't make a lot of sense, does it? Someone gathering the gun from the yard the very night you toss it into the yard. It disappears to the boardinghouse, then disappears again?"

Pitzer shrugged and Fletcher plowed forward, more intense, leaning forward. "On the night of the shooting, Mr. Pitzer, obviously, there was a pistol involved."

Pitzer looked disgusted. "I don't know," he whined. "I'm not aware of any of this. I simply know I'm not a coward."

Fletcher raised his voice more. "Are you aware that a .38 Smith & Wesson is the model gun that killed Marie Louise Gato?"

"I don't know what killed her."

"And you owned such a gun and now, it is strangely missing?"

"Objection," said St. Clair-Abrams loudly. "The prosecutor is asking insinuating baseless questions. Prejudicial."

"Overruled," said the judge.

"Answer the question, Eddie." Fletcher put a spin on the defendant's name as he said it.

"I don't know about the gun," Pitzer clamored. "I don't know anything about a gun, any gun."

"Especially your own gun, isn't that right?" said the attorney. Pitzer shoulders slumped forward but he looked up into Fletcher's face, wide-eyed, breathing deeply. Fletcher stood, staring back, allowing the onlookers to absorb the exchange between them.

After the short silence, Fletcher said, "You don't like Mr. Gato much, do you?"

"As I said, he and I have never been friends." Pitzer spoke quietly again.

"Is it because he didn't like you in his yard at night?"

"I'm not in his yard at night except to pass through it." He spoke with restraint.

"You usually eat supper at home with your parents, do you not?"

"I hardly ever eat supper at home. Maybe twice a week, but I always spend the night there," he said, still subdued.

"So when you were chased out of Gato's yard for spying through the windows, or when Marie Louise refused to see you, it was a quick trip home to your parents?"

"I've never been run out of the Gatos' yard," he said. "Marie Louise refused to see me for a short time before the shooting, a few months before." He hesitated. "There may have been a few other times. I can't remember when. But we made up."

"You testified you and Marie Louise gave each other gifts. On one of your numerous visits to her home, did you have a conversation with Marie Louise about some piano music you wished to give her?"

"No." He shifted in his chair.

"Are you saying you and Marie Louise never discussed your giving her piano music?

"No, we did not," Pitzer snapped, "because she refused to accept it."

"Did you not threaten to kill her if she refused the sheet music?"

"I won't even respond to that," Pitzer growled. "I did not!"

"I have nothing further, Your Honor," Fletcher then announced, and St. Clair-Abrams rested the defense case.

Part IV – Chapter 26

Mrs. Enriqueta Gato

Following the defense testimony, the state attorney rose to announce his intention to call a rebuttal witness.

"Your Honor, understandably, Mrs. Enriqueta Gato, Marie Louise Gato's mother, has been absent from the courtroom during these proceedings. In her despair over the heinous murder of her daughter, she was unable also to bear the contentions and assertions alleged this week. She is able to join us for a brief time today and I call her now for rebuttal to the testimony of the defendant."

"Objection." St. Clair-Abrams was on his feet. "I had no prior notice of this witness, nor opportunity to examine her."

"And you should not expect such opportunity, Mr. St. Clair-Abrams," responded the judge. "Considering the leeway you have been granted for the appearance of your surprise witness only two days ago."

When Enriqueta emerged from the witness room, an excited intake of breath fluttered through the audience. Enriqueta was rarely seen in public. She advanced slowly. Her rosey copper skin shone beside her silk black hair which swirled behind her head. Erect, bosom high, she presented as a fine lady; to some, as an exotic.

That day she strode to the witness stand, dark circular shadows smoldered beneath her eyes. She turned to Hartridge who guided her to her chair.

"You have been sick through most of this trial, correct?" he said.

"I have been sick," she answered evenly, looking straight at Hartridge. Having lived abroad in her youth as had her brother José, her voice reflected only a light Cuban accent.

"Mrs. Gato, you've known the defendant for several years, correct?"

"Yes, for many years."

"Did he ever make threatening remarks about Marie Louise to you?" The room grew soundless.

"He told me once if she didn't love him, he would kill her. He said that some time back. I can't be positive when." Her voice was low. There was general stirring through the room, the sound of shuffling shoes and chairs. The jury and defense lawyers twitched when they heard her words.

"Do you remember the circumstances in which the defendant said this to you, Mrs. Gato?"

"It was not part of a conversation. He made the remark as we passed in the house. He was very angry." She covered her cheeks with her tan shapely fingers.

"Mrs. Gato, did you hear other threatening remarks the defendant said regarding Marie Louise?" asked Hartridge.

Pitzer froze. He lay his head on his arms, resting on his table. The room remained quiet, stuffy heat forgotten, paper fans at rest. Even St. Clair-Abrams remained silent.

"Edward brought Marie many presents and sometimes she refused them. He would be angry and throw them in all directions. He threw candy in our fountain more than one time.

"One afternoon I was on the piazza and I could hear him and Marie Louise talking inside through the window. He had brought her some music for the piano. She didn't want it and told him so. He said to her 'You will take it or take a bullet.'

"As I got up to enter the house, he slammed out the front door. I intended to ask Marie Louise if she were all right but she had already run upstairs. A half-hour or so after Edward left, I went back to the piazza. I heard some noise and looked over the railing. There he was, crouched in the bushes."

"What did you do when you saw him?"

"I told him to go home," she said softly.

"Does he often crouch in your bushes?"

"On many occasions. We can see him looking through the windows. The children laugh."

Pitzer blew a ruffled sound through his lips.

"Mrs. Gato," continued Hartridge, "do you know John Bigger, who walked Marie Louise home from the trolley the night she was shot?"

"Yes, of course."

"Did John Bigger speak to you the night of the murder?" asked Hartridge.

"Yes, he did. He came to me first while I was standing on the piazza. My daughter Elvira was with me when the boy walked up. The doctor was attending Marie."

"What did John Bigger say to you on the porch?"

Mrs. Gato put a lace handkerchief to her face. Her voice wobbled. "John told me he had seen Eddie Pitzer race by him on 11th Street right after the shooting. He said Eddie was running extremely fast and he turned onto Laura Street towards town." Mrs. Gato's words caught in her throat and her answer came in foggy gulps. Her head bent forward to her chest. Hartridge looked at Call and stepped back from the witness.

"Objection," said Abrams. "I move for a new trial." His words were lost in a roomful of quiet concentration.

"And this statement was made by John Bigger on your piazza following the shooting?" Hartridge continued, glancing at the deathly still jury.

"Yes," she said quietly to the prosecutor's last question.

"No," said Pitzer quietly, sitting up, lifting his head from the table.

"Objection overruled." said Call.

Part IV – Chapter 27

Fletcher's Closing Argument

June 1, Seventh Day of the Trial

    The previous day's proceedings had not closed until 7 p.m. The next morning, countless hopeful spectators rushed through the streets for seats at the closing arguments of the trial. Some people arrived hours before schedule. Late arrivals continued to pound the locked doors as the trial progressed. Colored men and women and white men sat on one side of the courtroom, and white ladies sat on the other.

    By an act of God, apparently, the attorneys had agreed upon a rotation for the closing arguments. Lined before the trial bench with grave faces and lavish mustache tips diving toward their collars, the judge entered, happy to be approaching the trials's conclusion. The jurymen emerged alert, looking ready for the drama they expected from closing arguments.

    Duncan Fletcher, facing the jury, opened for the prosecution at a little past nine-thirty in the morning. The pounding on the door by the latecomers persisted throughout most of Fletcher's remarks.

    "This case is unparalleled in the history of Duval County," he said, "and when a beautiful young girl, without a single enemy, is shot down like a dog from point-blank distance, the crime deserves the greatest punishment. The criminal should hang."

The audience sobered. Pitzer's Aunt Sarah Hosack covered her mouth with her hands. Her husband remained still, nothing in his expression flinched. Pitzer's eyebrows furrowed and his father leaned towards his son with an open arm.

Fletcher continued. "In her front yard, after the terrible shooting, Marie Louise told her grandmother, Mrs. Eliza Huau, who ran from the house first that Pitzer had shot her…."

St. Clair-Abrams interrupted at full volume. "Objection. As Marie Louise's dying declaration was declared inadmissible," he barked, "references to her naming Edward Pitzer as her attacker should now be stricken also."

Fletcher propelled to face the bench. "Your Honor, these remarks were the subject of no little comment and debate during Mrs. Huau's testimony. At the time, you ruled the remark an admissible hearsay exception, a natural and spontaneous utterance."

Judge Call nodded in agreement.

"Mr. Pitzer had a different story, of course. He first said he went to Springfield that night to exercise," Fletcher said, "but exercise could not have been his major objective because he took the trolley. To ride home, we know he walked to the 8th Street terminal, again avoiding exercise. He said he departed the trolley at West 2nd Street to examine a bicycle to purchase for Miss Gato. But he didn't do that. Why not?" Fletcher flat-handed his forehead as if an idea had struck him. "Pitzer remembered something else.

"Mr. Pitzer remembered he had to deliver a cup and saucer to Mrs. Bixler that night. The defendant decided to deliver the cup and saucer rather than keep his bicycle appointment. So why did he get off the trolley at 2nd, his father's store being on Bay Street?

"I'll tell you why the defendant got off at 2nd Street," he said. "He got off to run north to Marie Louise's home before she got there. She had told Mr. Pitzer she would be spending the night at the Huaus'. The sight of her on the trolley going home infuriated him. She had lied. She didn't want to see him.

"Pitzer jumped off his car at 2nd Street at approximately six-thirty. It took him about twelve minutes to run to hide in her rose bush." Fletcher raised his voice and jabbed his finger in Pitzer's direction. "Edward Pitzer ambushed and murdered Marie Louise Gato."

Even the young women, Pitzer's admirers, sat quietly with their hands folded in their laps. Fletcher stepped back from the jury and smoothed his coat. He brushed the end of his mustache, then turned back to the panel.

"Edward Pitzer claims that on one of his frequent incursions to the Gato home, he and Marie were surprised by a tall dark man standing near them on the Panama Road. The defense wants you to believe this is the same dark man, who supposedly frightened Marie Louise on the night of the murder. This, according to Lycurgus Bigger, close friend of the defendant's family, who had a son named Edward Pitzer Bigger.

"If all Pitzer says is true about the dark man and Pitzer's ridiculous pretend dance at the Gato front gate, why wouldn't he simply ask the dark man who he was? Why wouldn't he ask Miss Gato if she knew the man? Perhaps the man worked as a messenger for Domingo Herrera? What a flimsy effort on the part of the defense to concoct this story! It's a lack of defense. No defense at all and it is plain silly."

The sun now beamed in the room through the arched window. Fletcher blotted his sweaty forehead with his handkerchief. He took a deep breath and smiled towards the jury, and two nodded back. Fletcher cleared his throat to continue.

"On the Gatos' piazza the night of the murder, Johnny Bigger admitted he saw Edward Pitzer running on 11th Street away from the Gato front gate. He said so to two people. Soon after, he changed his story. He also decided the man running away was not Pitzer, but a tall dark man he didn't know. Presumably, the same dark man, a handy creation for mystification, who watched Pitzer's absurd dance routine teaching Marie the two-step.

"However, the night Mr. Hartridge and I tested John Bigger's ability to distinguish someone in similar circumstances; John could not discern a thing. He couldn't tell if Mr. Hartridge wore a long or short coat. He couldn't tell if he wore a straw hat or another kind. He did say the dark man was about the same size as Mr. Hartridge, but he couldn't distinguish if it were Hartridge or me running. His testimony was unconvincing, at best."

"Remember, Pitzer initially told Lieutenant Gruber at the station, when he surrendered, that he arrived at Mrs. Pickett's to visit Miss Cornelia at close to seven. Now, he says he was at Mrs. Bixler's making a delivery at that time. When Mrs Pickett did not support his timing of the evening's events, the defendant modified his alibi from visiting with the Picketts to visiting at the River View Hotel with Mrs. Bixler. He had already passed Pickett's boardinghouse twice without stopping," said Fletcher.

Edward Pitzer, the accused, has gotten himself into too many places, too close together. Too many alibis."

Part IV – Chapter 28

St. Clair-Abrams' Closing Argument

When the court officers returned to court on Wednesday, June 2, they found St. Clair-Abrams motionless, sitting quietly, staring at the judge. The repopulation of the room was a noisy affair but St. Clair-Abrams did not notice. Call paid little attention to him but Hartridge and Fletcher shot each other curious glances.

After all settled, Call summoned St. Clair-Abrams to begin. The subdued man pushed himself up with one hand from his table, the other on his walking stick, squared his shoulders and proceeded slowly across the room. He approached the jury, staring upward as if spellbound with something above their heads. His opening gambit in low tones introduced a new quiet St. Clair-Abrams into the proceeding. Hartridge grew more concerned watching the old bird, knowing St. Clair-Abrams' propensity for any histrionic moment.

"It is Edward Pitzer who speaks to you now," St. Clair-Abrams began in a low-pitched delivery. "It is his voice who speaks through mine and it is the last opportunity he has to speak, so I beg you to listen attentively to the young man." It was an eerie beginning.

"This is not flattery," St. Clair-Abrams continued, "but State Attorney Augustus Hartridge is known for his zeal to prosecute. However, in this case, I believe you can see, as I do, that he has stepped beyond decorum.

"When we see men with such legal standing as Colonel Cockrell and the Honorable Duncan Fletcher employed to aid the prosecution, one must realize the personal desire to avenge and to hound our boy defendant, Eddie Pitzer, and to see him dangling from the gallows." Gasps and groans loosed from the audience at another "hanging" remark. Catalina Huau stared at Abram's head, imagining machetes being thrown at his cranium.

"The family, of course, feels the same," he continued. "There is no impropriety in that; it is to be expected, but it is nonetheless extreme bias. So keep in mind, that the total prosecution testimony, comprised of Gato family and neighbors, raged with extreme favoritism. Whereas, we, the defense, gave an objective narrative, presenting testimony of nineteen witnesses, seventeen unrelated to the Gato family.

St. Clair-Abrams suddenly raised his voice to great force. "Having said that, words cannot express the horror of how I view this crime. He who committed this deed, may he never enjoy a woman's love, a woman's confidence, press a baby's cheek to his. Such men should be cursed by God. Hell should refuse to receive him. If that boy did it, may he be cursed in heaven and hell.

"But of this horrible crime, this is what you should remember. Marie Louise could not have seen the culprit's face. Proof demonstrated the perpetrator was on his knees as she attempted to run away. Never did she turn toward the shooter. In fact, while she tried to flee, the killer's last three shots were fired into her back as he held her skirt. This observation does not require the keen insight of the gentlemen employed to prosecute this case. Even a country lawyer, such as I, knows Marie Louise did not see her assailant.

"Moreover, she had already been dosed with morphine when she later identified the defendant as the man who shot her. But what did the drug slow? Her heart and her brain, both, were reeling from the drug. Marie Louise's words about her killer that evening were not sustained in a court of law as she had been given morphine. A young woman, susceptible by nature, as all young women are, was rendered more susceptible by the injection of this powerful drug, which was why she did not mention the tall dark man she and Edward encountered on the Panama Road. Nor did she remember her fear of the mysterious stranger on the streetcar. Nor, the man of the same description, John Bigger saw running away from the scene of the shooting.

"Instead, Marie Louise heard her sister, Georgia Gato, shout that Edward Pitzer was at the gate. Georgia, on the piazza at a distance of sixty feet, said she recognized him, but Georgia couldn't tell who fled the gate." St. Clair-Abrams exaggerated actual distance to the gate from the piazza and the state of Marie's mind. He proposed that the lights were too dim for Georgia to make an identification. Even the drooping branches of the banana tree blocked its glow. The hall light alone shone toward the gate.

"Georgia hated Edward Pitzer," said St. Clair-Abrams. "A snap of her eye indicated her hatred. So, she tagged Edward Pitzer in loud terms by the cut of his suit. The name was suggested by many to Miss Gato's drug altered mind that night. The family did not like him and this was a chance to say so.

"As to Marie Louise's dying declaration, the court deemed it unworthy and Marie Louise mentally incapable of making it. Its introduction as evidence was denied. Instead, the state lawyers, as learned and astute as they are, created an alternative to the dying declaration. And even I, as a backcountry, piney-woods lawyer, can recognize the ruse that it is.

"The testimony of Mrs. Eliza Huau, Marie's grandmother, was created in case the dying declaration proved inadmissible. When Mrs. Huau rushed from the house to help Marie Louise, the girl supposedly said, 'It was Eddie Pitzer who did it.' The good lady lied for that statement to be admitted as *res gestae*, a spontaneous utterance connected to an event. It was nothing more or less than substitution for the dying declaration."

At St. Clair-Abrams' wholesale condemnation of Mrs. Eliza Huau, the erstwhile fairy godmother, some listeners frowned, registering displeasure at his spirited remarks about her.

St. Clair-Abrams then addressed each prosecution witness to refute the individual testimony. "Fritz Aberdeen is a servant and when the Gato family takes snuff, Aberdeen sneezes. When they say that the moon is made of green cheese, he is ready to swear to that also. He cannot be believed.

"Those colored girls, walking home from a day of cleaning, could not see well enough in the dark to identify anyone. Much less, they couldn't see far enough to see someone rolling up his pants leg a block away, as they testified. They do not speak the truth. They lie.

"Lula Lee beguiled State Attorney Hartridge with what appeared to be charming infantile innocence. In fact, Lulu had been religiously taught and drilled in her testimony. When the blinds rattled at Caballero's, Lulu's sister, Malvina, was peeking out to see the commotion. John Bigger has testified he heard the blinds rattle, but saw no one run to Gato's old gate as Lulu said she and her sister had done. That would be because she didn't do it. Neither did Malvina. Those girls did not run out of the house and into Eddie Pitzer."

Many in the audience nodded their heads in agreement as St. Clair-Abrams attempted to discredit the small colored girl. "Not only was she too little to matter, but more importantly, she was blacker than black."

"No more of that, St.Clair-Abrams," scolded the judge. St. Clair-Abrams gave a quick nod in response.

"Mrs. Bixler, poor Mrs. Bixler, totally unimpeachable," said St. Clair-Abrams. "The state attorney reminded me of a tomcat tossing a half-dead mouse. He slapped her this way, then the other, but she whipped him nonetheless. Mr. Hartridge as much as charged the lady with perjury, saying she purposefully created a missing link for Eddie's alibi. He implied she lied and that her timely receipt for the purchase of the cup and saucer was backdated. How dare he impugn this upright citizen?"

James Pitzer looked up at the judge and quickly away. Sarah Hosack covered his hand with hers. She smiled at him reassuringly.

"We must remember, gentlemen," St. Clair-Abrams continued, "Edward Pitzer had no motive to kill. Even if he did so, using the State's timeline, for him to run over two and a half miles in less than fifteen minutes or twelve minutes or whatever they say it is, would be a physically impossible feat for this boy. Edward Pitzer is not an athlete; he couldn't do it."

Although Pitzer glared at St. Clair-Abrams for saying he couldn't do the time, the attorney shook his head kindly to console the defendant.

Then, St. Clair-Abrams changed his style. No longer intense, he said to the jury softly, "Eddie Pitzer is an only child. The boy cannot be taken from his parents. So, I beg you twelve American jurors to protect this good American boy."

Then in closing, looking upward, St.Clair-Abrams began to pray invoking God to provide guidance to the jury. Hartridge also looked heavenward with an exasperated expression.

"I pray He will direct you in the deliverance of your verdict," continued St. Clair-Abrams. "I pray for the speedy delivery of this son to his mother." The invocation met a silent courtroom. The audience, nervously tense, some faces lifted in surprise, other heads bent in prayer. Judge Call, his mouth cracked ajar, gaped.

When done praying, Alexander St. Clair-Abrams staggered towards the judicial bench. His impassioned delivery had lasted six hours. Bracing with one hand on the bench, swaying against it, he began to tilt and then to fall. A deputy sheriff and one of St. Clair-Abrams' young assistants caught the older man beneath his shoulders. They assisted him to the judge's chambers, where the outsized attorney fell onto the cot. The man's son later said his father had collapsed from hunger and exhaustion, but some considered his near tumble, a mere performance.

After St. Clair-Abrams retired. Call addressed the state attorney. "I assume you would like to proceed with a rebuttal, Mr. Hartridge." Hartridge strode to stand before the jury.

As Hartridge spoke, although unseen from the courtroom, St. Clair-Abrams lay in chambers with the door open to the gallery, moaning and crying out so all could hear, "Don't let them hang that good American boy." He repeated it over and over at such volume that Hartridge had difficulty being heard. The people were also treated to Mrs. St. Clair-Abrams murmuring over her fallen husband as she disregarded his unflagging mouth. After a quarter of an hour, Judge Call inquired of the defence attorney's health and adjourned the session until the morning.

Part IV – Chapter 29

Hartridge's Closing Rebuttal

The next morning, Thursday, June 3, St. Clair-Abrams entered court, looking delicate. He flopped into his chair and Hartridge began again. "I know we all wish Mr. St. Clair-Abrams a fast return to vibrant health, but we must proceed with our work here and so I must continue."

Watching the seasoned athlete with a crisp-cut jaw, the jury and his other listeners expected Hartridge's closing to be the equivalent of a one-two punch. It was not. It might have been without the active vocal presence in the courtroom the day before, which Call did not attempt to quiet.

"It seems," said Hartridge, at last beginning in earnest, looking at each of the jurymen in turn, "the defense is presenting a theory that every state witness came to this trial determined to convict the defendant. The defense seeks to undermine the State's witnesses as all family members, neighbors, or employees. So, I ask you, who else could the witnesses be? Should the State have brought forth people who reside on Bay Street or Adams, who only later heard of the murder, and who were also free of conspiracy charges and mistrust. They could stand before this court and testify to their knowledge of nothing. I say instead, there is a conspiracy on the other side.

"Let me correct any conspiracy theory expressed by any prosecution witness," he said. "Dr. Neal Mitchell, the State's first witness, a legendary pillar of this community, has guarded our collective health, delivered our babies, and set our broken bones. He saved many of us from the streets during the tropical fevers.

"Mr. José Alejandro Huau, also a witness for the prosecution, is a preeminent Florida businessman, a civic leader, strong in family and church. Huau is a booster of our city and nation and a freedom fighter for Cuba, the home of his birth, where he was jailed as he fought against Spain. Even to avenge his niece, the victim, would he lie to convict a man without cause? No, he would not. Surely he has seen enough innocent bloodshed for a lifetime.

"Mr. Fritz Aberdeen," Hartridge continued, "the gardener at the Gato place, had no time to compose a fiction for the benefit of his employer. Fritz Aberdeen pointed the very instant he was asked to the exact spot where he and the dying girl stood.

"Then, as to defense witnesses, John Bigger, a sixteen-year-old, gave a conspired testimony, saying first that he had seen Edward Pitzer running from the Gato place, then changed his story that night. Why would he do that unless someone told him to do so? When tested, he could not identify anyone running out there at night.

"And what of the peculiar Mrs. Bixler, who shows up at the last minute, who does not tell her son an accused killer, being hunted, supposedly visited her home the exact time of the murder? Why did Mrs. Bixler reserve her cup-and-saucer story until the end of the trial? A cup and saucer delivered by the defendant himself at the very moment of the shooting. That would seem to be an important point to mention to one's son.

"But after my unsuccessful search the next day to verify her story, she returns augmented with a crisp handwritten receipt for the cup and saucer purchased from James Pitzer, the defendant's father, written God knows when. She also modifies her shopping day sequence to cover her lie. By the way, Mr. Pitzer did not hear of his son's delivery to Mrs. Bixler, the son's latest alibi, until several days later.

"The defense will tell you that Marie's own words naming her wicked attacker, Edward Pitzer, were uttered under the influence of morphine and must be disregarded. They will say this even as it has been sworn by our respected medical men that the amount of morphia she received was to help her relax and would not have affected her mind. Remember Marie Louise identified her killer in the yard to her grandmother and the gardener before she received any medication.

"And as for the notion the victim did not see her murderer's face, where might she be looking when he first shot at her head with bad aim, blowing off her hat instead? Is the defense implying she entered her gate staring down at her shoes? And was she not looking straight at him when his next bullet ran through her arm up her left thumb, blowing it off?

"What kind of man brings a gift to his love, in this case, sheets of music, and when she refuses his gifts and overtures, threatens to kill her? 'Take the music or take a shot,' he says. He says it and her mother hears it, unbeknownst to him. He is also cocky enough to tell Marie Louise, on another occasion, he will kill her if she does not love him. Such a man is demented and not to be believed.

"What kind of man steals a letter to the girl written by another of her suitors, nay, fiancé, and opens it? The defendant snatched this note from a child on an open trolley, then blamed the child for the disturbance it caused. He is demented.

"What kind of man is so anxious to show his fearlessness, his toughness, that he agrees to a duel and heads into the night to shoot, knowing nothing more? He is not naturally aggressive but he is a bully and a coward, who hides behind a tree to ambush his love. He is demented and cannot be believed," said Hartridge.

"There are too many coincidences with the Biggers in this trial, the long time friends of the Pitzers. John Bigger has a brother named for the defendant, Edward Pitzer Bigger. There is no testimony as to the dark man at the Gato place except from the defendant Pitzer and his good friends, the Biggers. The mysterious dark man will not come forward to explain his presence because there is no such man. Revelations of the dark man came to light only as the defendant shaped his alibis.

"The defendant's convenient incidents, which emerged as the trial progresses, are too coincidental and too convenient and too much for us to consider. The dark man, as well as the battered little mouse, as the defense attorney calls Rachel Bixler, whose memory of rambles about town come and go from moment to moment, are fruit from a creeping vine of sham and deceit.

"There's another element at play in this tragedy. The defense will try, and already has, to damn certain testimony because the witnesses are colored. They want you to feel enmity towards them. But the State would remind you these Negroes were the closest eyewitnesses to the defendant that night.

"When Drucilla and her sister Serena overtook Pitzer on North Hogan Street on April 20, Serena recognized him at once.

"Lulu Lee, the little girl from across the street, brushed by the defendant in search of her good dog, thinking it had been shot. She knew the defendant very well. The defendant also bumped into Lulu's older sister, Malvina, as he raced between the Gato fences.

"These coloreds can see and hear as well as anyone. The State is asking that you listen fairly to the things these Negroes have told us. They testified to incidences from closer range than any other witness before you.

"Is a white man who leaps into the air and proclaims, 'I didn't kill my sweetheart,' any nearer to God than Lula Lee, an innocent Negro child, who swears to the judge she will only tell the truth for fear of going to the bad place? Is she not to be believed when she testifies a man she knows well knocked her aside at the scene of the killing?

"Gentlemen, I fear, black is not the only color-bias lurking in this room. Look around you. These Cubans are kind, Christian, family-oriented people, and as prosperous as anyone here. We are schooled with them. We shop together. We worship together. Many of us have traveled or lived on the island of Cuba. We support their causes and we certainly smoke their cigars. It matters not whether Marie Louise Gato was white or tan in color. She was an American, born on American soil, entitled to the benefits of our grand American justice system which protects us all. This defendant, Edward Pitzer, is guilty. That is the only verdict supported by the facts of this trial."

In total, Hartridge spoke for more than three and a half hours. His address was "devoid of oratorical display," according to the newspapers, but closely attended by both the jury and the gallery.[1] As for Pitzer, he glared at Hartridge during the entire homily, shifting uncomfortably in his wooden chair. The influence of St. Clair-Abrams' disruptive performance on Hartridge's rebuttal could only be imagined.

Part IV – Chapter 30

JUDGE CALL'S JURY INSTRUCTIONS

The courtroom observers although mesmerized for two days by the cast of prominent attorneys launching their last sorties, found pleasure in Hartridge's conclusion. Heads tilted together in fraternal nodding and talking, onlookers congratulated themselves on securing seats for the occasion and for lasting into the ninth day of the trial.

Pitzer's hands, now folded, slipped between his knees. Settled at the defendant's table, he stared forward, thoughts obscured. At times, a sad cloud swept his face and he grabbed the arm of his chair so tightly, the veins in his hands expanded.

Marie Louise was dead six weeks, truly gone. Pitzer winced. Her thoughts, her words, her behavior had once consumed him: Would she smile at him that day? Would she invite him inside that afternoon? Or abandon him in the parlor that night? He held his stomach and tipped forward. What would he think about now: A big man in a black hood? A nun who prayed with the condemned? His neck cracking? His free-fall swing?

Judge Call, having listened to the closing arguments with dispassionate expression, now approached his own task: instructions to the jury. He smoothed his plump mustache, which beyond the courtroom often framed a good cigar, then rubbed his hands together as if to wash them. Some saw this as a cleansing assurance the nine-day ordeal was ending.

But there had been something else about the trial. An intuitive person, a razor-sharp someone, might have noticed it, might have detected an emanation, transparent, floating in the fabric of the trial. So private, so veiled, so blatantly not a friend of Marie Louise. A hint of it may have shrouded Rhydon Call.

Then, Call looked up and saw Katie Huau Lorraine, now married, seated in his courtroom.[1] His gaze rested on her, Marie's first cousin, Catalina and José's daughter. He looked away quickly when he saw her.

He began to read his handwritten charges to the jury. The manuscript lay on the desk before him, but Katie Huau was present. Who didn't remember Katie? With her long, snapping fingers, razor-sharp witticisms, multiple escorts, carriage races. And then the infamous carriage ride with her brother: the baseless implication of her responsibility in her brother, Henry's, death. Her younger sister, Flora Huau, who lived in Cuba, and deceased cousin, Marie Louise, were the only ones who might know the details about the carriage accident. They would not be talking.

* * *

On a temperate day in February 1894, Katie, twenty-four, insisted her twenty-two-year-old brother, Henry, escort her on a carriage ride. A musician and composer, working at the piano, he refused to go. Katie, after pleading with him, always determined, closed the fall of the grand piano over his hands.

Marie Louise Gato heard Katie harassing Henry in the next room. She walked into the room where they were, saying to Katie, who was standing beside the piano, "Leave him alone, Katie. He doesn't want to go with you."

Katie turned abruptly toward Marie Louise. "How could you possibly know what he wants?" Katie said, smiling, beginning to speak in the sweetest tones.

"I heard him say it," said Marie. Henry, knowing Katie, looked between their faces. No one ever challenged Katie.

"You know that's very peculiar, Marie," said Katie, still speaking sweetly, "taking such a heartfelt interest in your first cousin. I wouldn't mention how you feel about him to anyone. Such interfamily matters are against the law and mostly considered scandalous."

"Katie, for heaven's sake, be quiet and we'll go." Henry stood and reached for his coat and hat. "Pay no attention, Marie," he said. "She's not as bad as she sounds."

"She really isn't," added Flora. "But she may take some time to forgive you," she joked.

Marie Louise laughed out loud. "Forgive me?" she said with a crimped snort.

Katie turned away from Marie. "Let's go, Henry. Goodbye, Marie. Flora." She circled her hand above her head with a brief wave as she left the room.

When Henry and Katie collected the horse and carriage from the stable, Katie decided to take a route through town. More people could admire her in the city.

The newspaper reported the next day that the wheel of the carriage knocked an impediment when Henry guided the horse around a corner at the St. James Hotel. The word on the street was a colored woman had popped up a red umbrella near the horse's head and scared it. When the horse reared in harness, the top-heavy vehicle tipped to the hard pavement, slinging Henry against a light pole and breaking his neck.[2] He died at the spot where he landed. Katie, bruised but uninjured, was inconsolable at first but never again spoke a word about the accident.

Alphonso grieved for Henry at the Old City Cemetery as he had his cousin, Louie, years before. This time a pallbearer, he helped carry the casket.

"Murder in the first degree," read Call's charge, "is defined as a premeditated and unlawful killing. Premeditation is a question of fact for the jury. And remember," he said, "the accused is always presumed to be innocent.

"Gentlemen of the jury," he carried on, "the benchmark of guilt is the exclusion of all reasonable doubt. If you have reasonable doubt, you must give the benefit of such doubt to the defendant. You cannot determine a guilty verdict by a mere preponderance of evidence or probability of guilt."

Katie Huau Lorraine's presence continued to float on the skirts of Call's thoughts. He struggled to project a reasonable voice. He spoke louder than he meant to do, at a volume he had seldom used throughout the trial. "As you know," he pressed forward, "this defendant is charged with first-degree murder.

Was the act planned beforehand? You must decide beyond a reasonable doubt."

Head down, he read without pause. Hand-held fans in the gallery paddled against the heat and the tension.

"Take into consideration also," he said, "the interest a witness might have in the case. If you believe the testimony of the Gato family is tainted because they are too interested in the case, then you may disbelieve their evidence. Assess the witness' bearing while he's testifying. Consider other material facts." St. Clair-Abrams beamed.

Willie Gato's mouth flew open at Call's remarks as he whirled to look at his aunt. One juryman pulled at his earlobe. Another's eyes darted between opposing attorneys.

Members of the audience glanced furtively at one another. Some stared at Call. One played with his unlit cigar, spinning it through his fingers. Hartridge turned to Fletcher. Their fixed gazes linked. Was Call committing reversible error? Were his instructions prejudicial?

The old palm tree curved across the leaded window. The slender trunk swayed in the wind, preceding dark grey clouds. Call forged ahead with his instructions. During the trial, the jury sometimes dismissed from the room, the judge had heard arguments for admitting the dead girl's dying declaration. He had excluded it then, but in his jury instructions, he raised it again.

"As you have heard the dying declaration of Miss Gato, I know it is difficult to strike it from your minds." His voice grew more expansive. "Nonetheless, the court charges you, if you consider this dying declaration, you violate your oaths as jurors."

Judge Wright, Justice of the Peace, who rendered Marie Louise's dying declaration according to her dictates, sat several rows behind the bar. Head bowed, he watched his crossed fingers and circling thumbs that lay in his lap. Catalina braced herself, a hunting cat with pulsing paws. Her eyes grew rounder and blacker. Still, Call forged ahead.

"Mind you also, jurymen, if you consider any utterance of the deceased, repeated by the family or anyone else, you are also false to your solemn duty. You will be wrong to think of it. All such words are dying declarations and all are inadmissible, and not to be deliberated.

"Consider, especially, spontaneous statements expressed as part of an occurrence accepted into evidence. The spontaneous statement to consider here, repeated by the deceased's step-grandmother and now in evidence, is as subject to impeachment and rebuttal as any other evidence. Are the deceased's statements believable beyond a reasonable doubt? If you believe the deceased correctly named the person who shot her, were her words really hers? Or were they impressed upon her by those surrounding her?

"If you have any reasonable doubt in your minds as to whether the accused was at the scene of the shooting or rather on Bay Street, in the vicinity of Broad Street, at the time of the shooting, it is your duty to give the accused the benefit of the doubt and acquit him."

Catalina yearned to propel herself forward, to remind Call of the tortuous session her husband, José Huau, and nephew, Alphonso Fritot, had endured when he tricked them with a single syllable. She jumped. A sudden voice she knew too well boomed at her side. Enormous ribbons and tatted lace, flowers and feathers framed Katie Huau Lorraine's flashing eyes.

"Balderdash!" shouted Katie. Standing at her seat, demonstrating to Rhydon Call how fortunate he was that she now lived in Orlando. "Have you lost your decency, sir?" she said. "How do you say these things? Have you no regard for my family, my poor little cousin? How dare you, sir? How dare you?"

Her outburst fired the room with gasps and flutters. Catalina peeked below her heavy dark eyebrows, suddenly becoming a wary mouse. Call's stare at Katie was fierce. He banged his gavel. The corners of her mouth turned downward. Her beautiful face returned pure revulsion to him. Surely, she remembered him. He certainly hadn't forgotten her. Once again he slammed his gavel, staring at her.

She had captured the pulse of the audience. They whispered through a blanket of worry. They knew the extremes of what Katie Huau could say or do. What would happen now?

Call banged his gavel again with less force. Breathing deeply, he appeared to calm himself. "Quiet, Katie. Mrs. Lorraine, please."

She continued to glower at him with undiluted rage. Seconds passed. His face burned red, as it had with her often in the past. He prayed she would be quiet. He signaled the sheriff's deputies. They shifted towards her, lodged her in her place. One man reached for her arm. She snapped it away from him, imparting her ferocious look. She whipped her shoulders, swung her skirts across her knees and sat, still glaring at Call.

Not recognizing the encounter for other than an odd interruption, Cockrell, the assistant state attorney, whispered out loud. "The judge is making drama of mere hearsay, which is not admissible as such, by all lights."

Shakier than ever, Call resumed his instructions. "The alibi defense is recognized in law and need not be proved by the defense beyond a reasonable doubt. However, the jury must determine the truth of the alibi beyond question. If you believe the defendant went to the River View Hotel, as has been testified, you must acquit him. If you believe testimony against the defendant is mistaken, and you have reasonable doubt he was at the murder scene, you must acquit him."

"Good grief," one observer expressed. "You don't believe that Bixler woman." An exclamation shot from the back of the room. Another man, in a three-piece suit, scrambled from his chair. Gripping his hat, he banged out the door.

Katie, looking wide-eyed at the ceiling, slowly shook her head. Judge Dzialynski, who last saw Pitzer run by his porch, had attended the trial to see how the boy would fare. In the second row behind the bar, he sat with his mouth drawn, perplexed. Call's jury instructions seemed to him out of the ordinary.

Call motioned to the bailiff for water. At the end of the long hall, the bailiff found the ice box empty. He returned with tepid water. He eyed Call solemnly over the glass he passed him as if to convey a cautionary message. Call ignored his look.

The newspapers reported Judge Call's jury charges as long and exhaustive.[3] St. Clair-Abrams opined they were the ablest delivered for many years. When asked, Hartridge and the other prosecutors refrained from endorsement.

Catalina's tiny form slipped out of her aisle barely touching anyone she passed. Marching from the room, though, her footfalls reverberated. Willie Gato rose to follow her but she waved him back to his seat. The people stared as Katie Huau Lorraine stood slowly, head high, and exited behind her mother. The people turned to watch them retire from the courtroom.

The case shifted to the hands of the jury an hour past noon. Pitzer's father, fearful of what jury deliberations might presage, fidgeted and twisted in his chair, while Pitzer was walked to a holding cell.

The lawyers gathered in the judge's office to wait for the verdict. Call pulled out a bottle of whiskey. People assumed the attorneys were discussing the case. Instead Call, an avid fisherman, began to describe his recent angling adventure from Fernandina, Amelia Island. He caught a kingfish weighing almost thirty-five pounds. He passed around a photograph showing a number of men and many large fish, each roughly four feet long, strung for display. Call stood in the middle, wearing his hat and a vest.

Killing time, the judge described the sunny afternoon, the color of the sea, how the boat took the waves. When he began to chronicle who caught what, St. Clair-Abrams stood to begin his goodbyes and to leave. Call was not done talking. With a curt hand signal, he gestured St. Clair-Abrams to sit. Feet scraped the floor and knees jiggled, as the other attorneys half-listened to Call. He talked breezily, not needing their attention, but not releasing them to the courtroom.

Judge Call (Courtesy of Amelia Island Museum of History)

The day of his fishing trip, Call had seen Katie Huau for the first time in years. She boarded a boat in Fernandina with her cousin Alphonso. More beautiful than Call remembered, Katie had married a man, also a judge and heir to great wealth, and lived elsewhere. When she returned to Jacksonville to visit, she did not visit Call.

His face had flushed when he saw her that day at the dock. She nodded her broad hat his way and smiled when she saw him, fat and tousled, standing on the dock with his tackle, staring at her. Had she even known him? Was she still a tease? Weren't all Cuban women? She was still beautiful but his appearance had changed.

Outside the judge's quarters, loyal trial watchers, family members and loiterers from the street rested in the half-full room. Only the naive expected the jury to return in minutes, and many people had left. Hours passed without word. Some reasoned the chance of acquittal lessened as time wore away. Pocket watches snapped open and closed. Hands on the large round wall clock crawled. The brass spittoons floated with froth, more heavily utilized than during the trial.

Justice of the Peace Wright sat quietly alone and waited. As he remained for the Pitzer verdict to be announced, he mused again on the death of Lieutenant Gruber. Wright felt certain Gruber's abrupt removal by brutal bloodshed could affect the resolution of the Gato murder. The police might continue to search for Gruber's murderer but the Gato death would be forgotten. Wright believed the right man had been arrested. He knew Marie Louise had known her killer and had been clear about that in her dying declaration.

Wright had attended both funerals. For Gruber's wake, two coppers had draped the police headquarters in black and white swags to mourn their colleague. When pallbearers lifted Gruber's rosewood and silver coffin, for burial at the Old City Cemetery, Kate Gruber, the lieutenant's wife, dressed in heavy mourning, leaned on Gruber's friend, Joseph Marzyck, and spoke through tears. "Come back to your Kate! Oh, come back, my husband, so faithful, faithful unto death!"[4]

Kate Gruber later married William Marzyck, a great surprise to all.[5] And Lieutenant Gruber's casket was interred roughly five feet from the spot Marie Louise Gato lay, an even bigger coincidence.

* * *

When dim lights lit the shadows of the darkening courthouse building, Judge Call rose and led the lawyers from his chambers. On the bench, he directed inquiries be made to the jury. Would they return a decision within a short time? The answer arrived they would not. Accordingly, Call adjourned court at six-thirty that evening to be reconvened at nine-thirty the next morning.

Fearing the following day, the parties retreated into another night of haze. Gripping Pitzer's upper arm, an officer led him out the back door and walked him to the jail. After the blistering hot day, the night grew dark and the rains began. Huge heavy drops slammed the wooden roofs and sidewalks along the city byways, splattering against the brick streets and muddying those of sand. Heavy beads of water resonated, hitting the bottom of rain barrels and startling horses bedded for the night, pawing and snorting in the stables.

Occasional rickety carriage wheels turned and clacked over the uneven pavement outside the barred prison window. Racing through sheets of sheering water, Pitzer ran with his jailer to his cell. At first, he found it oddly comforting, dry and warm. Flashes of lightning illumined Pitzer's stark cage. He was the center of a great storm.

Part IV – Chapter 31

THE LAST NIGHT

The jury had not yet rendered a verdict. Pitzer was wet from running in the rain to the jail. Inside, the officer handed him a towel, then took it away before he left.

Pitzer stood beside his cot, a hand on the brick wall of his cell, the other pressed to his chest. He felt the quick stirrings of his heart. Unrelenting rain fell through the glow of the streetlight. The storm's damp invaded the cell and the temperature dropped. He lay back down and closed his eyes again. The pillow was thin; the mattress flimsy and knotted. He pressed his hands to his head. He doubted sleep would come that night, the night he wanted it most. The trial was ending. Terror filled him.

He remembered leaving the store early that afternoon, heading to Marie's. She said she would be gone that night but he had decided to journey out to see Willie, her brother. He liked being at her home. He hurried past Huau's tobacco shop. He swung by Huau's house on Main Street, where the Fritots lived next door. Mr. Huau, with his smiling face, had been nice to him in the past, but he grimaced thinking of Alphonso Fritot and Henry Huau, tall and handsome, Cuban dandies. He hated those boys, their courtly faces and fancy parties.

Then he turned northeast toward the Panama Road and the Gatos. When he arrived at the Gato house, smells of fragrant *sofrito*, onions and garlic, floated through the open windows. He imagined supper bubbling on the stove. Now, lying on his lumpy bed, he gazed at Marie on her porch trimming flowers. She turned towards him in her breezy remoteness, elusively sunny. She had stayed home after all. He sighed with relief, almost joy, and stretched his legs to the end of his cot.

But when he looked again, the piazza was empty. No one was there. He realized she had gone to the Huaus' to spend the night, just the girls, just as she'd told him. He felt calm. Yet, he had just seen her on the train, when he was stopped at the switch. She was heading towards home. He was confused. Where was she?

The next second, he saw her vision back on the porch. She looked contented and happy. He gazed into her deep black eyes. She was oblivious to him. "Don't come by. I won't be home," she'd said. But she lied. She was home or she would be. She was riding home on the trolley, avoiding him, fending him off.

A peculiar feeling had immersed Pitzer on the trolley the day she died. The memory was returning. In the bright afternoon sun, he felt drenched in a thick fog, seized in its mist. He could see a single cloudy light roaring at him in the distance, a train headlight, rushing up from the dark. The image was brief but vibrated through his skin, his heart, the blood in his veins. The trolley cars scraped from opposite tracks so close, rusty scratches scarred metal. It smelled like the friction or rubbing two stones for a fire. Something provoked an unfathomable menace in the fatal switch. The moment had struck. At last he knew. She didn't love him. Finally, he knew.

On his cot, his hands were cold and trembled. Shoving them under his arms, he listened to the pounding rain and the branches blowing gusts of wind. The cell windows rattled. Pulling the light blanket around his neck, he remembered the coolness of the gun in his pocket. He had scuttled past the front of her house and knelt in bushes beside the gate.

All he felt was solid resolve, without thought or emotion. No racing heart, no churning stomach. He had hidden in the Gato bushes before. Shuddering with embarrassment, he remembered Marie's mother and father chasing him away. The laughter inside the house. Laughter at him.

The shrubbery scratched his face and he rubbed his cheek. He waited so long for Marie, his knees ached. He heard two voices on the Panama Road. Marie Louise and Johnny Bigger. He knew the Biggers from the church and from years ago in Pittsburgh. When Johnny left, Marie floated towards Pitzer. He watched her gaze airily from side to side. She swung the gate open with a grating screech, wood on wood. Light from the piazza exposed him. She met his eyes and gasped, uttered a startled scream. He was aiming a gun at her head.

"What are you doing? Eddie, that's not funny. Put it down," she yelled. She threw her arm across her face. He fired. He missed. He blew off her hat. He shot her elbow. She turned to run. Kneeling forward, he grabbed her skirt, pulling it downward and shooting up into her back. Five shots exploded. They rang in his ears. Five. The gun was warm. He smelled the smoke. What had he done?

He grappled with the new latch, kicked the gate open and ran. He stumbled over two little niggers, outside the gate, one hollering about a dog. He ran and ran, a wild hare careening towards town. Past Johnny Bigger and a smaller boy. In the darkening twilight, he heard neighbors' sharp cries as he passed. His heels banged the wooden bridge crossing Hogans Creek to the city. Moonlight drifted on the thick black swamp.

A small glow flickered at the coal gasification plant. The sawmills lay quiet. Floating logs drifted. Foul odors of the fertilizer plant mixed with the reek of Hogans Marsh, runoff, creosote, oil spills, the filthy black pitch of the swamp. He took the gun from his pocket. He tossed it high, over and up. He heard it break the water's surface, a loud plop. The water splashed, then gulped and swallowed.

Pitzer always confided in Marie Louise. He would remember all that night's details, all the strange things that had happened to him. He would tell her tomorrow. She would think he was brave. She would apologize and tell him she loved him. Everything would be as before.

He tossed his head on the pillow and thrashed against his cot. He smelled his attorney's cologne. St. Clair-Abrams, the stodgy fat bully, always wore the same sickening sweet scent. Then, Pitzer imagined the judge turning towards him, a questioning look, a verdict in hand. Saying what? Pitzer snapped upright. His chest clenched. Morning would come. He lay back on his cot and sobbed.

Thunder rolled in the distance and streaks of lightning lit the dark cell before tearing off into the night. A familiar shadow wavered in the window. She smiled. He reached toward it, then, it, too, expired. Outside on the street, the night continued to rain and rain and rain and rain.

Part IV – Chapter 32

Verdict

"Has the jury reached a decision?" Judge Call asked Deputy Sheriff Vinzant at nine-thirty on Friday morning, June 4, the 10th day of the trial.

"No, sir, they have not," said Vinzant. "I fear a mistrial. They are now at seven to acquit and five for guilty."

Call returned to his quarters and waited alone. The defense attorney, dawdling at his table, when asked by a reporter, said, "Be sure, I do not remotely consider my client guilty." Edward Pitzer and his father sat together in a holding cell, enduring the delay.

At eleven the signal came; a decision had been reached. "They knocked, sir," Vinzant informed the judge. "The foreman sent for stationery."

The lawyers took their places in the courtroom. Pitzer was led to his seat. He showed no emotion as he returned. St. Clair-Abrams covered his mouth with his fist and drew a deep cough that ruffled his mustache. Hartridge and Fletcher sat upright.

"Any demonstrations, for approval or disapproval of the verdict, will be severely punished," Judge Call said. He looked towards the rowdy young women. He signaled Vinzant, who nodded to the deputies surrounding the courtroom. They stood upright, feet apart, their billy clubs behind them.

The spectators hushed, but every scratch, breath of air, brush of clothing was audible. Some bowed their heads.

"Escort the jury into the courtroom," said Call, and the twelve jurors lumbered in, single file, thudding into their seats. A few stared at the floor. Balled fists rammed into their pockets. Pitzer's father trembled. Catalina, who had returned, covered her mouth, her large eyes focused on the twelve men. The lawyers and Pitzer stood.

"Gentlemen, have you reached a verdict?" asked Call.

The foreman stood and answered, "We have, sir." He handed the written decision to the court clerk, who handed it to the judge. Call studied it several seconds, brushing down the sides of his mustache. Handing the paper back to the clerk, his face remained blank as the clerk read it aloud. "We, the jury, find the defendant not guilty."

Call spoke immediately. "Hearken to your verdict, as it will be recorded by the court." More softly, he turned and spoke to the jury. "Thank you for your hard and diligent service," he said. "You are dismissed." To the defense table, Pitzer and St. Clair-Abrams, Call said, "The defendant is discharged."

Pitzer, stunned for a second, sprang to his feet the next. St. Clair-Abrams slammed his big paw on the table and then on Pitzer's back. "Well, boy, well, well, well. We have done it. We have done it, indeed," his round face, a smiling moon. Pitzer turned to the throng gathering behind the bar and began to pump the outthrust hands.

Some expressed joy with smiles and hugs. Others filed out the doors, quiet and morose. There were some groans of disgust. The police still stood at attention. Pitzer's father remained seated, head bowed, tears trailing down his cheeks.

In the bustle of excitement, one young woman rose from the audience, wildly clapping. She fell in a faint. Two deputies carried her to the cot in the judge's room. When she revived, she wandered off in the excited crowd, never receiving the punishment Call had promised disrupters.

"Get out of here, young man, and don't delay." Call spoke over the din to Pitzer, then left the room.

Pitzer remained, vibrantly shaking hands with relatives and jurors, thanking them and wishing them well. He returned to the bar, greeting anyone who extended a palm. Vinzant at last took him by the shoulders, turned him from the crowd and escorted him out the rear door of the courtroom. "You can hold your reception outside," he said.

Pitzer climbed in the carriage ordered for him by the clerk of court and returned home to his mother. Hundreds came to congratulate the family, filling the small yard and blocking access to the modest rented house. Crowds also waited at the Pitzer home goods store. When the Pitzers did not arrive, they contented themselves peering through windows to spot a likeness of Mrs. Bixler's famous large cup, the cup that had saved the accused's life. Never had the little row store appeared so stately beside its great neighbor, Gato's three-story, block-sized El Modelo Cigar Manufacturing Company. Both businesses were locked down.

It was said that on its first ballot, the previous day, the jury stood at seven for acquittal and five for conviction. The vote continued unchanged through the morning. Yet, after twenty-two hours sequestered, the five holdout jurymen sprang to the majority. The acquittal became unanimous. What had most influenced the men? What had changed five jurors' minds? Marie's inadmissible dying declarations, nevertheless communicated? St. Clair-Abrams' histrionics? Prejudice against Cubans or Negroes? Conflicting evidence left nothing to fathom from the verdict. Perhaps, a cigar to smoke, or a bathroom call, had hurried along the decision.

On June 7, three days after the verdict, Pitzer boarded a train to Pittsburgh from Jacksonville.[1] Chief Keefe sent three officers to escort him safely to the station. They rode with him in a carriage to the Union Terminal on West Bay Street, past Huau's store, *La Favorita*, with the two small brass cannons on the sidewalk, flying the Cuban Revolutionary flag.[2] Pitzer glanced at his father's store and El Modelo, both closed. Some of his friends ran beside waving their hats in the air.

On the train, he rolled past the courthouse, the jail, and Old City Cemetery where Marie Louise was buried. Trolleys ran and wagons clanked, and a crowd stood immobile, staring at his departing train. He rode north, alone in a car, on the outskirts of the Gato place, across the 12th Street track where he and Marie Louise had walked. Leaving Florida's sandy soil behind him, the train motored across Georgia's red clay and through virginal pine forests. Pitzer, rocked by the train, bent forward touching his knees and holding his face in his hands. His day in the limelight had come and gone. As had the love of his life. Perhaps she was gone forever. Perhaps he was responsible.

Epilogue

Marie Louise Gato, the alluring daughter of Gabriel H. Gato, had been buried in the city's congenial Victorian graveyard, Old City Cemetery, for a year and three months. Aged palms and palmetto fronds mixed in the surrounding Southern pine forest. Muscled oaks brought to mind age-old connections to buried loved ones.

It is said that hometown boys, after the Pitzers moved to Pennsylvania, seethed about Marie's tombstone. They had convinced themselves Edward Pitzer's name had been plainly inscribed on it and they waited impatiently for Gabriel H. Gato, her father, to die.[1] At 52 he died, a year after Marie Louise, and freed the boys to do their ghoulish work.

According to a forgotten neighbor, Marie Louise's tombstone in the little cemetery, probably a slab of concrete the length of her grave, may have read rather like this 19th century verse:

> *Cut down in blooming youth by a blackguard with a gun.*
> *God in Heaven knows the truth and His justice will be done.*
> *An angel she was on earth and angel she is above.*
> *Mere words cannot describe her worth and we've only tears to prove our love.*[2]

Gabriel's grave, a rectangle of fresh stripped earth, recently tilled and shaped, lay even blacker in the shadows of the graveyard where the boys roamed at night. With Gabriel dead, they could execute their plan.

Packed with ropes and picks and only one lantern, they climbed the slope of the gravel path to Marie Louise's grave. The hooligans wanted nothing from the grave they sought, nothing to sell or savor. Contempt for the girl kept her safe in her coffin. They would seal her identification from all and bid her farewell forever. They weren't grave robbers. The young men lusted for only one thing: to obliterate the offensive pockmark on their city.

The cement slab had not been carelessly plopped on the ground. The sexton had seen to that. The marker was massive and ponderous, but it was never durable in the perpetual sense. Rain would eventually level its words, but the young men knew nothing of that.

So at the risk of being discovered, the broken chunks of the monument banging about in a wooden cart, the youths formed a second funeral procession to a remote bluff over the St. Johns River. Piece by piece, each chunk of stone hefted from the cart by at least two trembling sets of arms slid down the embankment. The broken parts of the girl's last calling card pressed down the bluff leaving the young men gasping for breath. The chunks splashed into the currents below, burrowing and settling onto a floor of light, shifting sand.

A moving calendar should have swept the theft into oblivion. But secrets are for the dead. Otherwise they're never kept. Marie Louise's grave would have been simple untouched dirt but for rumors of the gravestone theft.

Reduced to murmurs, shoved forward, the story was a tiny thing curled in the crests of the years. Sometimes the story swelled until it reached the light, and when it did, it became etched forever in remote places such as this.

Acknowledgments

Years ago, I crossed the Matthews Bridge in Jacksonville, Florida heading west over the St. Johns River. When my red Camaro slid to a stop at the bottom of the exit, I looked to my right and spotted a small Victorian cemetery. Built on a slight rising above sea-level, the cemetery installation was lovely, but I was unprepared for this artistic offering among the declining industrial stretch. The anachronism startled me.

I drove in on a rutted dirt road, parked, and walked through the small burial ground. Old City Cemetery as it had come to be known, the soil first turned in 1852, entered the world as a suburban garden cemetery in the Parisian style, i.e., Cimetière du Père Lachaise, Pere Le Chez. Many of the graves, erected by Jacksonville's affluent of the time are now surrounded by rusty and broken iron fencing, topped by rusty symbolic cornhusks and acorns. These symbolized either the harvest of death or heavenly spiritual growth. A personal choice. Many Gatos and Huaus, subjects of this book, are interred there.

I have been writing this book a long time and following the lives of its characters even longer. I want to thank all the folks who introduced me to the people about whom I have written. Without them I would be standing empty handed without a book.

The little cemetery soared with ideas. A book, dramas, a tour. In 1999, The Port of Jacksonville Pilot Club, a women's service club to which I belonged, began offering tours of Old City Cemetery as a fundraiser for causes related to brain injury. They continued nearly 15 years. The grave of Marie Louise Gato, who was departed by gunshots in 1897, became a popular spot on the tour. The Pilot Club in a small ceremony placed a flat memorial at her gravesite, which had previously been unmarked. If it had not been for this group of women, and others mentioned herein. This book would never have come to fruition. Thank you, Ladies. It was a trip, wasn't it?

After making inquiries in Jacksonville regarding Marie Louise Gato whose murder in 1897 is the heart of the book, *Fatal Switch*, I was introduced to someone also interested in finding the Gato family. Cynthia Anderson, a great-granddaughter who lived in Texas deep in the heart of her family research looking for Gato ancestors. She was lucky enough, as a member of the Church of Latter-Day Saints, to have assembled an extended trail of her forebears including her great grandparents. Cynthia pointed me to a couple of Gato grandchildren in Tampa and Atlanta and shared names of others whom she had traced.

While rolling old newspaper film on a microfilm reader in the Jacksonville Public Library, up popped a photograph of Marie Louise Gato among the flaring headlines of her murder in 1897. I saw the original photo later in Tampa at the home of Gabriel and Enriqueta Gato's granddaughter, Mercedes Calero. While I was there to interview Mercedes she showed me other early photographs of family members and shared stories her mother, Dolores, who had told her about her Gato grandparents. For instance, Gabriel was a stern father and Enriqueta was considered very sweet. Mercedes was reticent to have her picture taken but finally consented. I was most appreciative as it was something she rarely did. She and her husband, who are both deceased, were very kind gathering pictures from the 1800's and sharing their insights of the family. I learned things I would never have learned elsewhere.

Using Cynthia's prior research, we slid up to Atlanta to visit Catherine Huau Clark, Jose Huau's granddaughter. Her father was Polly Huau and Catherine was a niece of Enriqueta Gato, Jose's sister. Catherine Huau Clark was the most excited of the contemporary living descendants to meet us and the most informative and anxious to share what she knew of the family. We had several visits and corresponded after sharing family anecdotes. I appreciated her kindness and her seriousness about the project. She told us how Jose had escaped Cuba to the United States with family members in 1869. He also became one of the foremost cigar men of Florida and was also the leader of the Florida Cuban Junta fighting for Cuban independence from Spain. Her father, Hypolito (Polly) Huau, the youngest son of the Huaus, also played a part in the War of Cuban Independence.

It was sad that Catherine who was so proud and excited about this book did not live to see it published. I knew it would happen. Her age was advanced when we met and I knew the accomplishment of this book would be years completing. Catherine directed me to her much younger first cousin, once removed, Jose and Catalina Huau's great-granddaughter, Stella Huau Mouzon. Stella Mouzon was named after her grandmother, Stella Huau, the youngest child of Catalina and Jose. Both Stellas lived in Jacksonville until the older woman passed away.

Stella Mouzon, a medical administrator currently living in Tennessee, remembered as a youngster visiting her grandmother who lived in Springfield. Her grandmother, a slightly tan lady who spoke without an accent was educated in the United States and spoke English in their home. Catherine, Stella Mouzon's older cousin, nearly failed Spanish in her high school years because her father, Polly, allowed only English spoken in the home.

Stella Mouzon had a hefty collection of memorabilia ranging from the 19th to the 20th centuries. It included copies of original deeds of La Favorita tobacco store. I sat for hours with my ratty little copier and began to feel I knew the households well, even those members who had transitioned years before. The Huau and Gato family lines were brought together by the marriage of Enriqueta Huau and Gabriel H. Gato. Many photos showed the Gato and the Huau families together in the images of that period, lives intertwined. I knew the families were close.

So, you may be as surprised as I to find that by the third generation, (grandchildren) no family member of either family with whom I talked had heard of the other. Not even Catherine and Mercedes, the eldest survivors, knew the family tragedies.

This story takes place in Springfield, the first suburb of Jacksonville. The narrative is constructed on the underpinning or infrastructure such as it was in Springfield from 1870 to 1900. I mean by that, the roads, mud roads, corduroy roads, experimentally paved roads, commercial roads used by mules and oxen, shell roads, foot paths, pasture crossings, bridges and ferries which all controlled the destiny of the book's characters. Also directing lives were train tracks, trolley routes, and electric trolley tracks.

Christine Andow-Farley, the maven of Springfield, originally from England, moved to Springfield twenty years ago. Retiring from Crowley Maritime, she traveled the world as she had years earlier as a flight attendant. She thinks in terms of angles, aspects, orientation, bearing, objectives, specifications, geography and guidelines. But also, literature, politics, and history. She was the first woman to chair a shipping conference to set annual freight rates, passenger fares and shipping routes.

Chris led me to structures in Springfield, which stood in the rural countryside in 1897, and explained what one could have seen from those structures. She indicated what had been renovated, where the dairies and the cow paths had been, where the streets lay that disappeared, who walked or rode on them and when. Her knowledge of the physical and chimerical maps she shared with me is the basis of this book, the bones, the foundation, the hammer and nails. Without them, nothing. Thank you, Chris. I can't say it enough. I must have been so tedious.

Then, one of my oldest friends, a librarian, Elsie Jun Oishi whom I looked at one day and thought, "a resource. Yea!" I asked for help and she agreed. Who could imagine the overwhelming help I would receive? By the time she had gathered enough additional research and written enough little essays, assembled extensive folders on every family or individual in the mix of the book, I couldn't shut my office door. She was definitely a detail person and definitely not a quitter. She stuck by me for years as I tried to decide where my chronicle was headed. For a capability to concentrate, an attention to detail, excellent reading and writing skills and an eager personality, I am very glad. Thank you, friend, for all your help and for keeping me on track, so to speak

Rebecca Louise Berg is a retired Elder Law Attorney and a civic leader with abundant time to help others. Always present, routinely confident, and completely able to assist with anything. She always has an opinion. Whenever I ask her for it, she's ready with an answer. Rebecca, thanks for supporting me and encouraging this project through many stops and starts and years.

I received help, assistance and opinions from other friends as well. I participated in a writers' group, Chats Noir, under the guidance of Carol O'Dell, an excellent writing coach with admirable insight and judgment. Many thanks to my talented coach for her years of time and enthusiasm and for the assistance of the other members as well.

I travelled several times to Pittsburg, PA, Carnegie, PA, Tavares, FL, St. Augustine, FL, Savannah, GA and Charleston, SC. In Carnegie, the home of the Pitzer family, Marcella McKee, now deceased, and Carol Dlugas at the Carnegie Historical Society were eager to share information about the Pitzers and their family. Carol drove me by several of the grand houses where some of the relatives had lived. I was also able to find additional information on Edward Pitzer's maternal family, the Cubbages, and the Pitzers at the Carnegie library in Pittsburgh.

I spent time in Tavares, Lake County, Florida researching Alexander St. Clair-Abrams, the town's founder. Lake County was also the homestead and business of the Pitzers for ten years before moving to Jacksonville. The staff at the Lake County Historical Society and Museum were exceedingly obliging in providing resources such as the membership roster of the Pittman Presbyterian Church.

Obviously, I was engaged with the Jacksonville Historical Society and the Jacksonville Public Library where I obtained pictures of the Gato and Huau houses, views of the El Modelo factory, and scenes of historical Springfield homes where family and trial witnesses had lived.

Local churches also offered fascinating stories buried in their archives. The Huau and Fritot families helped carry the casket of Bishop John Freeman Young from the St. John's Episcopal Church to the Old City Cemetery. I found the rental account for the Pitzers' pew at the Congregational Church abruptly suspended at the time of the Pitzer murder trial when the family moved to Pennsylvania. Gabriel Gato held early membership in St. Stephen's Episcopal Church while his funeral was held at his home on Panama Road. St. Stephen's eventually became St. Mary's on Laura Street, Jacksonville. Most of the Gato family had moved to other sections of the state by the time of their demise

Finally, I dedicated this book to my mother, Mary Crooke Warren. I admired her style, her subtle sense of humor, her dignity, her patience, kindness and wisdom. Mary Crooke grew up in Springfield and attended the local schools. I loved her very much. She was a member of the first graduating class of Andrew Jackson Senior High School in Springfield and taught English there years later. She never let the door slam at Springfield Methodist Church where her mother was music director for twenty years. All that was a century ago.

Fatal Switch was constructed with hammer and nails from my mother's instruction coming through the years. "Anything you write must have an excellent framework or the work will fall like a building without nails and there will be nothing. Literature, drama, journalism, poetry, not even a common letter can be constructed without a strong underpinning. Sometimes she spoke of word form, usage, diagramming and the like, and a better metaphor for writing this book could not be found. I hope she's reading this somewhere.

Notes

Prologue

1. George R. Bentley, *The Episcopal Diocese of Florida, 1892-1975* (Gainesville, FL: University of Florida Press, 1989), 8. Photo of Weed with caption, "The Right Reverend Edwin Gardner Weed, Third Bishop of Florida." Weed (1846-1924) served in this capacity from 1886-1924. Louise Stanton Warren and Mavaleni Bessette co-wrote "From Our Past: Episcopal Bishop Weed," *The Florida Times Union*, June 11, 2005.

Part One—The Murder

Chapter 1—Marie Louise Is Shot

1. *1878 Jacksonville City Directory*. After initially working for Jose Huau, his brothers-in-law headed up their own cigar manufacturing companies. Among them were those of Henry M. Fritot at 23 E. Bay, G. H. Gato & Co. at 17 W. Bay, and Huau & Co. at 52, 54, and 56 W. Bay Street. Huau's company was the largest of these before being eclipsed in the 1880s by the El Modelo Cigar Manufacturing Company with Gabriel Gato as its manager.

2. "Assassin Shoots Miss Gato," *The Florida Times Union*, April 21, 1897. *The New York Times* also carried Marie Louise's shooting headlined "Jacksonville Girl Shot", April 21, 1897.

3. Roland H. Rerick, *Memoirs of Florida: Embracing a General History of the Province, Territory and State* (Atlanta, GA: Southern Historical Association, 1902), 1:630. Neal Mitchell is "one of the most prominent and popular physicians in the State of Florida."

Chapter 2—Police Arrive at Pitzers'

1. Jacksonville's Sheriff Office, *Law Enforcement in Jacksonville, 180 Years of Service* (Paducah, KY: Turner Publishing Co., 2002), 14. Chief of Police, John Keefe, 1886-87, 1892-1894, 1895-1897. Photo of John Keefe.

2. "History of Madison County, Iowa, and Its People," accessed June 15, 2010, http://www.archive.org/stream/historyofmadison. John A. Pitzer was "doubtless the first white man who thoroughly explored the county, lived here longer, and was more continuous and permanently identified with its affairs than any other." After surveying the north part of Madison County, he settled permanently in Winterset in 1849. Photo of John A. Pitzer.

3. V. Robert Agostino, *A Track Through Time: A Centennial History of Carnegie, PA, 1894-1994*, graphics by Marty Wolfson

(Pittsburg, PA: Wolfson Publishing, n.d.), 69. "Carnegie Pennsylvania Neighborhoods New and Old" diagram showing the town's subdivisions, including Cubbage Hill, one of the neighborhoods where coal mines were located.

4. Cubbage Memories: Anna Mary Mosscroft Dewhurst's Recollections of Her Grandmother, Jannet Gilfillan Cubbage," accessed July 27, 2006, http://freepages.genealogy.rootsweb.com/~nikinono/cubbgmry.html. The important role that the Cubbage family and their relations played in their community also found in: "History of Cubbage Family," a typewritten account compiled by James J. Dempsey (circa 1971) found in the files of the Historical Society of Carnegie (PA).

Chapter 4—Pitzer Surrenders

1. "Bullets for Miss Gato," *Daily Florida Citizen*, April 21, 1897. "He [Pitzer] was undoubtedly laboring under great mental excitement and acted much as if insane."

Part Two—Past Experiences

Chapter 1—Pearl of the Caribbean

1. Francisco Xavier de Santa Cruz y Mallen, conde de San Juan de Jaruco, *Historia de Familias Cubanas* (Miami, FL: Ediciones Universal, 1985), 7: 199. Hidalgo-Gato family (pp. 192-206).

2. "Narciso Lopez," *Encyclopedia of World* Biography (2004), accessed August 11, 2019, http://www.encyclopedia.com/people/history/cuban-history-biographies/narciso/lopez. Lopez fought to liberate Cuba from Spain and was publicly garroted in Havana on September 1, 1851.

3. Aisnara Perera Diaz and Maria de los Angeles Merino Fuentes, "Yo, el Notario: Breve Reflexion Micro Historica Sobre el Poder de la Escritura," *Boletim de Historica Demografica*, ano XI, no. 33 (Septembro de 2004), 10.

Chapter 2—Jose and Catalina

Chapter 3—Jacksonville 1880s

1. Wanton S. Webb, ed. and comp., *Webb's Historical, Industrial and Biographical Florida, Part 1* (New York: W. S. Webb and Co., Publishers, 1885), 151. "Huau & Company" profiled with a description of the business and brief personal background.

2. *Florida Daily Times*, November 12, 1882, "One of the nobbiest establishments in town is Huau & Co.'s cigar stand at the Everett Hotel."

3. Webb, 151. "Dr. Hipolitis Cadorette-Huau" entry.

4. "The Yacht Club Hop," *The Florida Times Union*, December 22,

1893. Mentions Alphonso Fritot and his cousins, Henry and Katie Huau, one of the "fairest flowers of Jacksonville society."

Chapter 4—Springfield

1. 1870 U. S. Federal Census," s.v. "Gabriel G. Gato," Ancestry.com. First census that Gabriel Gato is recorded as living in Jacksonville in the household of John Garcias, cigar maker.

2. *The New South Semi-Weekly,* August 1, 1874. *La Favorita,* originally owned by Gato, was known for its impressive soda fountain, superior ice cream, and Vichy water.

3. A Big, New Cigar Company," *The Florida Daily Times,* December 13, 1883. Announcement that the El Modelo Manufacturing Company is open with Herman Myers of the firm of H. Myers and Bros. of Savannah as president, Sigo Myers as secretary/treasurer and Gabriel Gato as manager.

4. S. Paul Brown, *The Book of Jacksonville: A History, Being a Series of Descriptive Articles, Historical, Industrial and Biographical of Jacksonville, Florida* (Poughkeepsie, NY: A. V. Haight, 1895), 103. Cigar manufacturing named as the second most important industry in Jacksonville in respect to number of people employed and the capital involved. "At present there are fifteen regularly established cigar factories ... and the largest of these is El Modelo."

5. "Encyclopedia of Southern Jewish Communities, Savannah, Georgia," Goldring/Woldenberg Instutute of Southern Jewish Life, accessed May 22, 2018, http://www.isjl.org/georgia-savannah-encyclopedia.html. "The Myers Brothers - Herman, Frederick and Sigmund - distilled bourbon and rye whiskey at a site in Kentucky [and] they also owned a tobacco works in Richmond, Virginia and cigar factories in Jacksonville, Florida and New York City." Herman Myers was Savannah's first Jewish mayor, serving almost continuously from 1895 through 1907.

6. Robert Ingalls and Louis A. Perez, Jr., *Tampa Cigar Workers: A Pictorial History* (Gainesville, FL: University Press of Florida, 2003), 81. Photo of a lector (reader) in a Havana cigar factory, circa 1890.

7. *The Florida Times Union,* December 29, 1883. Gato lured workers from other factories with the promise of paying $9.00 per 1000 for making "laundry" (*Los Londres*) cigars but later said he could only pay $8.00, causing the workers to strike.

8. Wayne W. Wood, *Jacksonville's Architectural Heritage,* rev. ed. (Gainesville, FL; University Press of Florida, 1996) 92. The three-story structure was one of only a few buildings in the business district to survive the Jacksonville fire of 1901. Located at 501-513 W. Bay Street, it was listed on the National Register of Historic Places in 1980 ("El Modelo Building: From Cigars to Hotel to Law Offices" by Sandy Strickland, *The Florida*

Times Union, March 12, 2017) and has had many uses through its 130-year-old history but is "probably best known as the old El Modelo Cigar Factory."

Chapter 6—Domingo Herrera

1. "Spies Watching Cubans," *The Florida Times Union*, September 30, 1896. Spies, furnished by the Pinkerton agency, are thicker than ever and every Cuban being shadowed.

2. Rerick, *Memoirs of Florida*, 1:540-541. Alphonso Fritot, a traveling passenger agent for the Florida East Coast Railway and union ticket agent, was also partial owner of the *Dauntless,* and commodore of the Yacht Club.

3. "At Home and Abroad," *The Florida Times Union*, May 26, 1895. Dance at the Florida Yacht Club honoring officers, which included Domingo Herrera as one of three men from Havana.

4. Willis Fletcher Johnson, *The History of Cuba* (New York: B. F. Buck and Company, 1920*)*, 4: 315, accessed May 25, 2018, http://www.gutenberg.org/files/33848/33848-h/33848-h.htm. Domingo Herrera is listed among the notable soldiers under the leadership of Mario Menocal, a military leader under the command of General Calixto Garcia in the Cuban War of Independence.

Chapter 8—Dinner and Duel

1. "In and About Town," *The Florida Times Union*, January 15, 1896. Eddie was shot by a tramp and came to town with his arm in a sling.

Chapter 9—Marie's Letters

1. "Ed Pitzer from the Stand," *The Florida Times Union*, May 1, 1897. Marie's three letters to Eddie after his duel.

Chapter 10—Three Friends

1. Edward A. Mueller, *St. Johns River Steamboats* (Jacksonville, FL: Edward A. Mueller, 1986), 116-140. "The Governor and His Steamboat" chapter about the *Three Friends* with photos.

2. Ibid., 124-125

3. Gene M. Burnett, *Florida's Past*, vol. 2, *People and Events That Shaped the State* (Sarasota, FL: Pineapple Press, 1988), 109-111. Chapter 27, "A Florida Shipwreck Inspires a Classic." Crane's experiences aboard the *Commodore*, the filibustering boat which struck a sandbar on New Year's Eve, 1896, became the inspiration for Stephen Crane's famous short story, "The Open Boat."

4. "Stephen Crane's Own Story: He Tells How the *Commodore* was Wrecked ... "accessed on July 4, 2018, http://ponceinlet.org/images/content/openboatnewspaper.pdf. This account by Crane first appeared on the front page of the *The New York Press* on January 7, 1897.

5. "In and About the City," *The Florida Times Union,* July 27, 1897. Huau's cigar store known throughout the United States as the "filibuster hatchery," which was a room in the back of La Favorita cigar store where meetings to plan sending arms and aid to Cuba to defeat Spain occurred.

6. Richard Rickenbach V., "Filibustering with the 'Dauntless'," *Florida Historical Quarterly* 28, no. 4 (April 1950), 231. "Through the indefatigable efforts of Jose A. Huau and Alphonso Fritot, Jacksonville was an active center of filibustering to Cuba in the years 1895-1898." Emphasizes Alphonso Fritot's importance in his filibustering role with Huau by saying "it would have been all but impossible for the revolutionaries to be successful had they not had the aid of Fritot, for he was the joint agent of all the railroads running into Jacksonville. He had the power of being able to secure a special train or a private railroad car almost at will—an invaluable resource."

7. "Three Friends Return," *The Florida Times Union*, March 23, 1896. Subhead of article, "They laugh slyly when you mention filibustering."

Part Three—The Second Murder
Chapter 1—Lt. William Gruber

1. "1860 U. S. Federal Census," s.v. "Joseph Museak, *Ancestry.com*. Misspelled as Museak, Joseph Marzyck, born in Austria, came with his family to South Carolina by 1860. He served in the Civil War and lived in Charleston until moving by 1870 to Jacksonville ("1870 U. S. Federal Census").

2. "Charleston Orphan House, Charleston, South Carolina," taken from *History and Records of the Charleston Orphan House*, vol. 2: 1860-1899 by Susan L. King, accessed January 28, 2011, http://www.genealogytrails.com/scar/Charleston/Charleston_orphan_house.htm. Located at 160 Calhoun Street and established in 1790, it was the first municipal orphanage in the United States. There is no complete listing of children admitted there.

3. W. Chris Phelps, *Charlestonians in War: The Charleston Battalion* (Gretna, LA: Pelican Publishing, 2004), 212. Listing for C. A. Gruber, Company B, Private, enlistment date: 3/24/1862.

4. *The Florida Times Union*, November 4, 1890. Edwin, 21-month-old son of Mr. and Mrs. Gruber, died on November 3rd. This son was the fourth son of the couple to have died in early childhood as reported in earlier years.

Chapter 4—Search of the Murder Scene

1. "62 Years Old Yesterday," *The Florida Times Union*, July 15, 1903. Dubbed the "Big Judge" in this article, Dzialynski served as municipal

judge in 1897. A Confederate veteran, he led a drive to build a Jewish house of worship in the city and was Jacksonville's only Jewish mayor, serving two terms (Glickstein, *That Ye May Remember*, 20-21).

2. "Murders in Springfield," *The Florida Times Union*, April 30, 1897. Three murders within ten days in the same area of the city.

3. "Lieut. Gruber Assassinated in Springfield," *The Florida Times Union*, May 1, 1897. Gruesome description of the crime scene and theories advanced as to the perpetrator of the crime.

Chapter 5—Gruber Inquest

1. "Verdict of the Jury," *The Florida Times Union*, May 5, 1897. After reconvening the inquest into the death of Lt. Gruber, the coroner's jury concluded that the officer came to his death at the hands of a person or persons unknown.

Part Four—Pitzer Trial

Chapter 1—Trial Opening

1. Wayne W. Wood, *Jacksonville's Architectural Heritage: Landmarks for the Future*, rev. ed (Gainesville, FL: University Press of Florida, 1996), 54-55. The 1886 Duval County Courthouse in which the trial took place was destroyed in the Jacksonville fire of 1901.

2. Jacksonville Sheriff's Office, 13. "Napoleon Bonaparte Broward: The Sheriff Who Lived Up to His Name," pages 55-60.

3. "Long Illness Proves Fatal to Hartridge," *The Florida Times Union*, June 29, 1949. When appointed State Attorney for the Fourth Judicial Circuit in 1893, Hartridge became "at that time the youngest man in the history of Florida ever to hold the position [and] he held the office for 16 years and was aptly trained for it by his service under Judge Rhydon M. Call."

4. Percifer Frazier Smith, *Notable Men of Pittsburg and Vicinity* (Pittsburg, PA: Pittsburg Printing Co., 1901), 404, accessed September 30, 2009, http://archive.org/bookreader/print.php?id=notablemenofpitt00smit&server=ia34100. Photo of Hosack with caption "Bridgeville Coal Company, Carnegie."

5. "Hosack Family Geneaology," taken from the *History of Allegheny County Pennsylvania* (A. Warner & Co., 1889), accessed on May 14, 2009, http://mygeneaologyhound.com/.../hosack-family-geneaology.html. Hosack married Sadie Cubbage, daughter of Joseph Cubbage, "of an old and representative family in this section of Allegheny County."

6. "Went on the Bermuda," *The Florida Times Union*, April 29, 1896. Refers to J. A. Huau as the well-known cigar manufacturer and representative of the Cuban Junta in Jacksonville. The Cuban Junta,

headquarters in New York, were Cuban revolutionary leaders representing the Cuban Republic outside Cuba to promote the overthrow of Spanish rule in their country.

7. "Population of Jacksonville," *The Florida Times Union*, December 12, 1896. Total population reported as 27, 761 (12,461 white, 15,300 black).

8. "Pitzer's Trial Begun," *Daily Florida Citizen*, May 26, 1897. The jury was made up of farmers, many who had never read accounts of the murder. A father and son were among the jurors sworn.

9. *World Heritage Encyclopedia*, s.v. "Alexander St. Clair-Abrams," accessed July 6, 2021, http://www.self.gutenberg.org/articles/Alexander_St._Clair-Abrams. Referred to as the "volcanic Creole," born in New Orleans, served in Civil War as a private ("U. S. Civil War Soldiers, 1861-1865," s.v. "Alexander S. Abrams," Ancestry.com) and was a newspaperman in New York and Atlanta before coming to Florida. He was a Senator in the Florida legislature and practiced law in Orlando and Jacksonville. Today he is mostly remembered as the founder of the town of Tavares in Lake County, Florida in the 1880s. Alexander St. Clair-Abrams (1845-1931).

10. *New Georgia* Encyclopedia, s.v. "Nineteenth Century Georgia Newspapers," accessed August 3, 2009, http://georgiaencyclopedia.org/nge/Article.jsp?id=h-644. St. Clair-Abrams "brought the sensational techniques of yellow journalism to Atlanta in 1872, when employed for the *Atlanta Herald*."

11. Rerick, *Memoirs of Florida*, 1:468-469. Rhydon M. Call graduated from Washington and Lee University with a law degree in 1878. He was a member of the Jacksonville City Council for six years, U.S. District Attorney for the Northern District, and then judge for the Fourth Judicial Circuit Court of Florida in 1893. Judge for the Southern District of Florida, 1913-1927.

Chapter 2—Neal Mitchell, M.D

1. Pleasant Daniel Gold, *History of Duval County, Florida* (St. Augustine: Record Company, 1928), 323. President of the Duval County Board of Health during the yellow fever epidemic of 1888 and President of the Duval Medical Society. He practiced with his father Dr. Joseph Mitchell and his brother Dr. Sollace Mitchell, also prominent physicians in Jacksonville.

Chapter 3—Trolleys Passing

1. T. Frederick Davis, *History of Jacksonville, Florida and Vicinity, 1513 to 1924* (St. Augustine, FL: Record Company, 1925), 373. "Pine (Main) Street Line" entry. The street car line on Pine Street from Bay to Eighth Street in Springfield was chartered in 1882 and began operation within a year.

Chapter 5— Mrs. Eliza Huau

1. Interview with Catherine Huau Clark. Eliza, the second wife of Jose Alejandro Huau, was referred to as the English woman.

Chapter 6—Georgia Gato

1. "A Cuban Coming," *The Florida Times Union*, June 1, 1897. Article of the *Detroit Free Press* that Jose Carbonne, a Lt. Colonel in the Cuban army lately engaged to Marie Louise Gato, is coming to Jacksonville to find her murderer.

Chapter 11—Ernest Benton

1. Wayne W. Wood, *Jacksonville's Architectural Heritage*, 206. "Old Waterworks Building" entry. Photo of the original 1896 building in Springfield at Waterworks Park.

Chapter 15—An Additional Ante Mortem Statement

1. Gustavo J. Godoy, "Jose Alejandro Huau: A Cuban Patriot in Jacksonville Politics," *Florida Historical Quarterly*, vol. 54, no. 2 (October 1975), 196.

Chapter 16—Defense Direct Rebuttal Witnesses

1. "The 'Ys' Organize," *The Florida Times Union*, March 1, 1896. Tillie Pitzer helped organize the Young Women's Christian Temperance Union. The initial membership of 12 girls expanded to 35 when reported by the same newspaper on March 20, 1896 ("WCTU Meeting"). Eddie was an "honorary member," the group's mascot ("The Pitzer Case," *Daily Florida Citizen*, May 2, 1897).

2. "Dignity of the Court Was Disregarded," *The Florida Times Union*, May 29, 1897. Stephens, who was a member of the Jacksonville Rifles club, testified that Pitzer, whom he knew from school, joined the group about two weeks before the murder.

3. "Presbyterian Church Pittman, Fla." From the collection of the Lake County Historical Society in Tavares, Florida. Tillie Pitzer is listed as a member in minutes from church sessions, 1884. John L. Pitzer and brother are listed as Pitzer Brothers Hardware in the *1887. Orange County, Florida Gazetteer and Business Directory*, 284. S. L. Reed (Sarah) and daughter M. M. (Mabel) Reed, defense witnesses in Pitzer trial, recorded in 1885 Florida census for the area.

Chapter 17—William Arpen

1. W. T. Cash, *The Story of Florida*, vol. 2 (New York: American Historical Society, 1938), 662. "Abrams was elected State Senator from the Lake County district in 1892. Resigned the following year over a

controversy concerning the location of the Lake County Courthouse." St. Clair Abrams is described by some in the state legislature as "erratic, selfish, egotistical, unscrupulous" with another saying, "he is an extremist and incapable of giving anyone justice whose views do not coincide with his" ("Let Us Have the Facts," *The Florida Times Union*, July 15, 1893). This article defends St. Clair-Abrams. "Senator Abrams may be unscrupulous and egotistical, but can his accusers point to one single vote during the entire session which was detrimental to the interests of the people?"

Chapter 18—Lycurgus Bigger

1. *1891 Jacksonville City Directory*. Pitzer and Bigger, general merchandise, 2 Everett block.

2. "U.S. World War I Draft Registration Cards, 1917-1918," s.v., "Edward Pitzure Bigger," *Ancestry.com*. Edward Bigger was born on April 14, 1894. Middle name was misspelled on his draft registration card.

3. "Noted Jacksonville Lawyers," *The Daily News Herald*, December 4, 1887. Cockrell was associated with his father in the law firm of A. W. Cockrell and Sons. He had a career as a lawyer and judge in his native Alabama before coming to Jacksonville. Described as a "courtly and amiable man."

Chapter 19—John Bigger

1. S. Paul Brown, *The Book of Jacksonville: A History, Being a Series of Descriptive Articles, Historical, Industrial and Biographical of Jacksonville, Florida*. 183-184. Fletcher's political career included being President of the City Council, member of the state legislature, and Mayor of Jacksonville (1893-1895). Fletcher would again be elected mayor and serve during the rebuilding of Jacksonville after its 1901 fire. Fletcher is remembered for being the longest serving U. S. Senator from the state of Florida, being elected in 1909 and serving until his death in 1936.

2. "Noted Jacksonville Lawyers," *The Daily News Herald*, December 4, 1887. "The earnest and thoughtful face of Duncan U. Fletcher inspires one with confidence in his ability to faithfully and ably defend any cause which he may espouse."

3. "Stones of Remembrance, John Dinsmore Bigger," *Christian Friends of Korea Newsletter* (November 2001), http://www.cfk.org/Newsletters/Nov2001/November%202001%20Activity%20Report.pdf. "It was in August 1911, that Dr. John D. Bigger arrived in Korea to begin his missionary service as a physician with the Northern Presbyterian Mission."

Chapter 22—Mrs. Rachel Bixler

1. *1897 Jacksonville City Directory*. R Bixler and Son, proprietors of the River View Hotel, 218 Riverside Av.

2. "City Items," *The Florida Times Union*, February 9, 1897. Announcement that Ernest Bixler became an agent for the Travelers Accident Insurance Company of Hartford, Connecticut.

3. "Ernest Bixler's Fatal Leap/Meets Watery Grave," *The Metropolis*, September 24, 1903). Bixler committed suicide jumping off a steamer on the St. Johns River.

4. "Ohio Deaths, 1908-1953," s.v., "Rachel Bixler," *Familysearch.org*. Rachel died in Ohio at 60 of "senile dementia" at a state hospital on September 22, 1910.

Chapter 29—Hartridge's Closing Rebuttal

1. "Pitzer Case Undecided," *Daily Florida Citizen*, June 4, 1897. Hartridge spoke for 3.5 hours and his address was "devoid of any effort of oratorical display." In a 1939 interview when asked about his most interesting case, Hartridge cited the State vs. Eddie Pitzler (misspelled), saying the accused was freed because of perjured testimony ("Jacksonville FL History," accessed on March 5, 2010, http://bigelowsociety.com/rod8/jackville.htm).

Chapter 30—Judge Call's Jury Instructions

1. "Lorraine-Huau," *The Florida Times Union*, July 9, 1896. Marriage of Kathryne Huau to Henry Kessler Lorraine with A. W. Fritot as best man. No Gato cousins were in attendance. The bride referred to as "one of Jacksonville's prettiest young ladies."

2. "A Horrible Accident," *The Florida Times Union*, February 9, 1894.

3. "Pitzer Case Undecided," *Daily Florida Citizen*, June 4, 1897. Some thought the charge to the jury favored the defendant, but the defense felt the charge of the court was fair and impartial.

4. "Dead Lieutenant Buried," *Daily Florida Citizen*, May 3, 1897. Supported by family friend Joseph Marzyck, Kate Gruber, wife of the deceased, repeatedly used the word "faithful" in her outcries at the funeral in reference to her husband.

5. "Florida Marriages, 1837-1974," s.v. "Joseph Marzyck," *Familysearch.org*. Kate Gruber (recorded as Kittie Gruber) and widower Joseph Marzyck married on May 20, 1901.

Chapter 32—Verdict

1. "Eddie Pitzer Leaves Town," *The Florida Times Union*, June 7, 1897. Edward Pitzer left Jacksonville for Pennsylvania shortly after his trial. Weeks later his father and mother also left Jacksonville for Pittsburg to reunite with their son ("In and About the City," *The Florida Times Union*, July 30, 1897).

2. "Guarded by Guns," *The Florida Times Union*, April 8, 1898. *La Favorita,* often referred to as "Cuban Junta headquarters," was protected against invasion by two small brass howitzers.

Epilogue

1. "Death of G. H. Gato," *The Florida Times Union*, August 8, 1898. Cause of death was catarrh of the stomach. "Aside from his business, he was a large property owner in North Springfield and did much to develop that section of the city." Obituary listed his age at 48, saying he was born in 1850, but his probable birth year was either 1846 or 1847 per his passports or family tree records.

2. A rumor of what might have been Marie Louise's gravestone inscription at Old City Cemetery.

BIBLIOGRAPHY

Fortunate as I have been to meet people with firsthand memories and personal knowledge of Jacksonville's Cuban population of the 19th and early 20th centuries, I was able to repurpose many of their stories, written an oral, into this narrative history of an important part of Jacksonville's past. Short articles, records and opinions about Marie Louise Gato's murder in Jacksonville, Florida, 1897 also appeared randomly and added greatly to my understanding. Not for want of trying, to reference them all would be impossible, but the items listed below can be utilized easily, if desired. Especially in dealing with the individuals involved, the creation of this book has been most pleasurable. I enjoyed searching for the families. I enjoyed finding them and I greatly enjoyed getting to know them.

Books

Agostino, V. Robert. *A Track Through Time: A Centennial History of Carnegie, PA, 1894-1994*. Graphics by Marty Wolfson. Pittsburgh, PA: Wolfson Publishing, n.d.

Barclay, Juliet. *Havana, Portrait of a City*. Photographs by Martin Charles, foreword by Eusebio Leal Spengler, introduction by Francisco de Borbon y Escasany. First paperback ed. London: Cassell, 1995.

Bentley, George R. *The Episcopal Diocese of Florida, 1892-1975*. Gainesville, FL: University of Florida Press, 1989.

Black, Henry Campbell. *Black's Law Dictionary*. Rev. 4th ed. St. Paul, MN: West Publishing Co.,1968.

Brown, S. Paul. *The Book of Jacksonville: A History, Being a Series of Descriptive Articles, Historical, Industrial and Biographical of Jacksonville, Florida*. Poughkeepsie, NY: A. V. Haight, 1895.

Buker, George E. *Jacksonville, Riverport-Seaport*. Columbia, SC: University of South Carolina Press, 1992.

Burnett, Gene M. *Florida's Past*. Vol. 2: *People and Events that Shaped the State*. Sarasota, FL: Pineapple Press, 1988.

Cash, W. T. *The Story of Florida*. Vol. 2. New York: American Historical Society, 1938.

Cohen, Stan. *Images of the Spanish-American War, April-August 1898*. Missoula, MT: Pictorial Histories Publishing Co., 1997.

Collins, Leroy. *Forerunners Courageous: Stories of Frontier Florida*. Drawings by Wallace Hughes. Tallahassee, FL: Colcade Publishers, 1971.

Davis, T. Frederick. *History of Jacksonville, Florida and Vicinity, 1513 to 1924*. St. Augustine, FL: Record Company, 1925.

Drane, A. H. (Hank). *Hank Drane's Historic Governors...Their Impact on the Sunshine State*. Ocala, FL: Ferguson Printing, 1994.

Foley, Bill and Wayne W. Wood. *The Great Fire of 1901*. Jacksonville, FL: Jacksonville Historical Society, 2001.

Glickstein, Natalie H. *That Ye May Remember: Congregation Ahavath Chesed, 1882-1982*. St. Petersburg, FL: Byron Kennedy and Company Publishers, 1982.

Gold, Pleasant Daniel. *History of Duval County Florida*. St. Augustine: Record Company, 1928.

Howard, Mary-Louise, comp. *Old City Cemetery, Union Street, Jacksonville, Florida*. Jacksonville, FL: Southern Genealogist's Exchange Society, 1993.

Hyman, Ann and Ron Masucci, photo ed. *Jacksonville Greets the 20th Century, the Pictorial Legacy of Leah Mary Cox*. Gainesville, FL: University Press of Florida, 2002.

Ingalls, Robert and Louis A. Perez, Jr. *Tampa Cigar Workers: A Pictorial History*. Gainesville, FL: University Press of Florida, 2003.

Jacksonville Sheriff's Office. *Law Enforcement in Jacksonville, 180 Years of Service* (cover title: *Jacksonville Sheriff's Office, 1822-2001*). Paducah, KY: Turner Publishing Co., 2002.

Johnson, Willis Fletcher. *The History of Cuba*. Vol. 4. New York: B. F. Buck and Company, 1920. Accessed May 25, 2018. http://www.gutenberg.org/files/33848/33848-h/33848-h.htm.

Kidney, Walter C. *Pittsburg Then and Now*. San Diego, CA: Thunder Bay Press, 2004.

Marks, Henry S. *Who Was Who in Florida*. Huntsville, AL: Strode Publishers, 1973.

Martin, Richard A. *A Century of Service, St. Luke's Hospital, 1873-1973*. No publisher or date.

Martin, Richard A. *The City Makers*. Jacksonville, FL: Convention Press, 1972.

Merritt, Webster, ed. and Joseph Lowenthal, associate ed. *Duval County Medical Society, Hundredth Birthday, 1853-1953*. Jacksonville, FL: Duval County Medical Society, 1954.

Montalvo, Maria Luisa Lobo. *Havana History and Architecture of a Romantic City*. New York: The Monacelli Press, 2000, 2009.

Mueller, Edward A. *Along the St. Johns and Ocklawaha River*. Charleston, SC: Arcadia Publishing, 1999.

Mueller, Edward A. *St. Johns River Steamboats*. Jacksonville, FL: Edward A. Mueller, 1986.

Mueller, Edward A. *Steamboating on the St. Johns: Some Travel Accounts and Various Steamboat Materials, 1830-1885*. 2nd printing. Melbourne, FL: South Brevard Florida Historical Society, 1984.

O'Brien, John. *A Captain Unafraid; the Strange Adventures of Dynamite Johnny O'Brien as set down by Horace Smith*. New York: Harper, 1912.

Paine, Ralph D. "The Log of a Filibuster Correspondent (1903)." In *Tales of Old Florida,* edited by Frank Oppel and Tony Meisel, 127-132. Secaucus, NJ: Castle, 1987.

Paine, Ralph Delahaye. *Roads of Adventure.* Popular ed. Boston, New York: Houghton Mifflin, 1925.

Pettengill, George Warren. *The Story of Florida Railroads, 1834-1903.* Reprint with additions of Bulletin 86 (1952) of the Railway and Locomotive Historical Society. Jacksonville, FL: Southeast Chapter of the Railway and Locomotive Historical Society, 1998.

Phelps, W. Chris. *Charlestonians in War: The Charleston Battalion.* Gretna, LA: Pelican Publishing, 2004.

Proctor, Samuel. *Napoleon Bonaparte Broward: Florida's Fighting Democrat.* First paperback ed. Gainesville: University Press of Florida, 1993.

Rerick, Rowland H. *Memoirs of Florida: Embracing a General History of the Province, Territory and State.* 2 vols. Atlanta, GA: Southern Historical Association, 1902.

Rickenbach, Richard Vernon. "A History of Filibustering from Florida to Cuba, 1895-1898." Master's thesis, University of Florida, 1948.

Rinhart, Floyd and Marion Rinhart. *Victorian Florida: America's Last Frontier.* Atlanta, GA: Peachtree Publishers, 1986.

Santa Cruz y Mallen, Francisco Xavier de, conde de San Juan de Jaruco. *Historia de Familias Cubanas.* Vol. 7. Miami, FL: Ediciones Universal, 1985.

Ward, James Robertson and Dena Elizabeth Snodgrass. *Old Hickory's Town: An Illustrated History of Jacksonville.* 2nd ed. Jacksonville, FL: Old Hickory's Town, Inc., 1985.

Webb, Wanton S., ed. and comp. *Webb's Historical, Industrial and Biographical Florida, Part 1.* New York: W. S. Webb and Co., Publishers, 1885.

Wood, Wayne W. *Jacksonville's Architectural Heritage, Landmarks for the Future.* Rev. ed. Gainesville, FL: University Press of Florida, 1996.

Journals/Bulletins

Appel, John C. "The Unionization of Florida Cigarmakers and the Coming of the War with Spain." *Hispanic American Historical Review* 36, no. 1 (February 1956): 38-49. Accessed September 23, 2008. http://www.jstor.org/stable/2508625.

Carson, Ruby Leach. "Florida, Promoter of Cuban Liberty." *Florida Historical Quarterly* 19, no.3 (January 1941): 270-292.

Cornelison, Tom. "Crime Without Punishment," *Jacksonville Magazine* (August 2008): 43-45.Cova, Antonio Raphael de la. "Cuban Filibustering in Jacksonville in 1851." *Journal of the Jacksonville Historical Society* 3 (1996): 17-34.

Cova, Antonio Raphael de la. "Cuban Filibustering in Jacksonville in 1851." *Journal of the Jacksonville Historical Society* 3 (1996): 17-34.

Godoy, Gustavo J. "Jose Alejandro Huau: A Cuban Patriot in Jacksonville Politics." *Florida Historical Quarterly* 54, no. 2 (October 1975): 196-206.

Perera Diaz, Aisnara and Maria de los Angeles Merino Fuentes. "Yo, el Notario: Breve Reflexion Micro Historica Sobre el Poder de la Escritura." *Boletim de Historia Demografica*, ano XI, no. 33 (Septembro de 2004): 1-25. http://historia_demografica.tripod.com/bhds/bhd33/notario.pdf.

Rickenbach, Richard V. "Filibustering with the 'Dauntless'." *Florida Historical Quarterly* 28, no. 4 (April 1950): 231-253.

Government Publication

National Archives/Depository, National Archives at Atlanta. Immigration Records. RG unknown: 1869 Jose and Catalina Huau, Matilde and Charles Fritot with Alphonso and Henry, children.

US Department of the Interior, National Park Service. "El Modelo Building, 501-513 W. Bay Street," prepared by Carolyn Hamm. *Historic American Buildings Survey* (HABS No. FL-345), August 1975.

Newspapers

Microfilm rolls of Jacksonville newspapers were viewed at the Main Library of the Jacksonville Public Library System and at the University of North Florida Library. I learned a great deal researching the papers page by page as no indexes were available:

Daily Florida Citizen, aka *Florida Daily Citizen or Daily Citizen*, 1895-1897
The Daily Florida Union, aka *Florida Daily Union*, 1876
The Daily News Herald, 1887
The Daily Sun and Press, 1877
The Evening Telegram, 1891
The Florida Daily Times, 1881-1882
The Florida Dispatch, 1878
The Florida Times Union, 1883-1905
The Metropolis, for specific events in years 1901, 1903, and 1905
The New South Semi-Weekly, 1874

The murder of Marie Louise Gato and the murder trial of Edward Pitzer described in this book are primarily based on the contemporary accounts of the newspapers covering the events in 1897. The Pitzer trial was reported by the *Daily Florida Citizen* and *The Florida Times Union* from May 26th thru June 5th, 1897. These daily accounts are the basis of the trials' testimony.

Jacksonville City Directories

The earliest surviving Jacksonville city directories in bound volumes are found in the Special Collections department of the Main Library of the

Jacksonville Public Library System and were searched for these dates: 1876-77, 1878-79, 1882, 1887, 1889, 1891, 1895, 1896, 1897, 1899, 1904, and 1905.

On-Line Databases, Genealogical and Historical

Court records, county, state and historical society compilations of marriage, death, birth, divorce, city and church directories and newspaper indices were searched before they were bought and combined by Ancestry.com. Searches primarily focused on the states of Ohio, Illinois, Pennsylvania, Kansas, Florida and Georgia. Many of the original websites I visited, especially of historical societies, no longer exist online.

Ancestry.com was extensively searched and was the primary source of genealogical information, especially researching its collections in these categories: Birth, Marriage and Death; Census and Voter Lists; Immigration and Travel; and Public Member Trees. Examples of specific sources in these categories are: "Florida Marriage Collection, 1822-1875 and 1927-2001"; U.S. Federal Census (1870, 1880, 1900 and 1910); "U.S. Passport Applications, 1795-1925"; and family trees of the major characters in the book.

Civil War records were searched in the Soldiers and Sailors Database, which is maintained by the National Park Service (https://www.nps.gov/civilwar/soldiers-and-sailors-database.htm).

Other Sources of Information

Interviews and correspondence

The author interviewed the following descendants of the Gato and Huau families and from them obtained invaluable photos and information about their ancestors.

Cynthia Anderson, great-great-granddaughter of Gabriel H. Gato. Email correspondence, 2003- present, and interviews in Dallas, Atlanta and Tampa.

Mercedes Calero (1922-2013), granddaughter of Gabriel H. Gato. Interview in Tampa on 12/09/2006.

Catherine Huau Clark (1916-2011), granddaughter of Jose A. Huau. Letters, 2004-2010, and three interviews in Atlanta, one on 10/25/2008.

Joe Huau, great-grandson of Jose A. Huau, interview in Jacksonville, 2011.

Stella Capers Mouzon, great-granddaughter of Jose A. Huau. Email correspondence and an interview in Jacksonville on 9/15/2008.

Places Visited

The author's research included visits and tours of geographical locations for background information. The following is a list of places visited:

Jacksonville, Florida
Arlington Congregational Church
Duval County Courthouse (marriage/probate records)
El Modelo Building
Evergreen Cemetery
First Presbyterian Church (formerly Ocean Street Presbyterian Church)
First Coast Model Railroad Club (Lomax and Park Street)
Jacksonville Historical Society
Jacksonville Public Library, Main (Florida Collection, Special Collections)
Landmark Title Company (Gato, Huau and Fritot real property transfers and holdings)
Old City Cemetery
St. John's Cathedral (formerly St. John's Episcopal Church)
St. Mary's Episcopal Church
Southern Genealogist's Exchange Society (loose page of Old City Cemetery burials) University of North Florida Library

Fernandina, Florida
Nassau County Courthouse (Gabriel H. Gato's passport)

Tampa, Florida
Marti-Colon Cemetery
Tampa-Hillsbrough Public Library (city directories for Gato relatives)
University of Tampa/MacDonald-Kelce Library
Woodlawn Cemetery

Tavares, Florida (and nearby Lake County communities of Altoona and Pittman)
Historic Tavares Courthouse Building (317 W. Main St.), housing the Lake County Historical Society and the Lake County Historical Museum.

Savannah, Georgia
Georgia Historical Society (vertical files, newspaper indexes, photo collection) Live Oak Public Libraries/Bull Street Library (Savannah city directories, 1858-1879)

Carnegie, Pennsylvania
Andrew Carnegie Free Library and Music Hall
Chartiers Cemetery
Historical Society of Carnegie (Cubbage, Hosack and Pitzer families)

Pittsburg, Pennsylvania
Carnegie Library of Pittsburg/Main, Oakland (Cubbage, Hosack and Pitzer families)

Contemporary Cousins who contributed greatly to personal family history and photographs for this book.

Catherine Huau Clark,
Huaus' granddaughter,
1916-2011

Mercedes Calero,
Gatos' granddaughter,
1922-2013

Cynthia Gato Anderson,
Gatos' great-granddaughter,
1965-

Stella Capers Mouzon,
Huaus' great-granddaughter,
1956-

INDEX

2nd Street **xii**, 124, 125, 133, 194, 229, 230, 245
11th Street, **xii**, 7, 8, 20, 121, 130, 131, 154, 155, 158, 170, 189, 191, 202, 203, 204, 205, 206, 208, 243, 246
2nd Street Switch, **xii**, **xiv**, 124, 125, 266
Aberdeen, Fritz, 4, 6, 7, 61, 147-9, 150, 184-9, 190, 250, 254
Bay Street, xiv, 11, 42, **44**, **49**, 59, 62, 64, 66, 68, 91, 109, 124, 160, 167, 194, 210, 221, 222, 245, 261, 271, 283, 296
Bejucal, Cuba, 29, 30, 62, 166
Benton, Ernest, 161, 162, 163
Bigger, Edward Pitzer (Pitzure), 193, 204, 246, 255, 91
Bigger, John, 7, 8, 20, 21, 191, 200-208, 243, 246, 250, 251, 254, 255, 267, 289
Bigger, Lycurgus, 190, 193, 198, 199, 200 201, 246, 289
Bixler, Rachel, 215-222, 230, 233-236, 245-247, 254, 251, 255, 262, 271, 290
Broward, Napoleon Bonaparte, 76-79, **105**, 107, 108, 110, 183, 199, 286, 295
Call, Rhydon Mays, Hon., **104**, 109; IV-1, 151, 153, 178, 182, 183, 215, 216, 218, 221, 228, 252, 253, IV-Ch.30 257-264, 269, 270, 287, 289
Carnegie, PA, 11, 12, 109, 164, 197, 281, 282, 286, 298
Charleston Battalion, 85, 285, 295
Charleston Orphan House, 285
Charleston, SC, 46, 84, 85, 86, 287, 294
Cigar Manufacturing, 50, 283, 281
Clark, George, 16, 17, 232
Cockrell, Augustus W., Jr., 112, 195-199, 213, 214, 249, 262, 289 291
Crane, Stephen, 77, 283,284
Cuban cigar workers, 14, 29, 47, 48, 50, 295
Dean, Russell H., M.D. , 7, 8, 9, 10, 120, 177
Dying Declaration, 171, 172, 174, 175, 176, 178, 180, 181, 182, 190, 245, 250, 260, 264
Dzialynski, Morris, Hon., 95, 230, 262, 268
El Modelo Cigar Manufacturing Co., 3, 42, 46, 47, **49**, 109, 209, 271, 281, 284
Everett Hotel, 44, 282
Fernandina, FL, 46, 78, 112, 263, 298
Fletcher, Duncan U., **105**, 112, IV-Ch.19, IV-Ch.22, IV-Ch.24, IV-Ch.27; 248, 249, 260, 269, 284, 289
Florida Yacht Club, 57, 58, 284
Flynn, Charlie, 7, 20, 189, 197, 198, 203, 206, 207
Fritot, Alphonso , ix, 19, **27**, 43, **44**, 57, 58, 78, 110, 112, 175, 176; IV-Ch.-15; 261, 265, 283, 284, 285

Gardiner, Henry, 93, 94, 112, 113
Gato, Elvira, 28, 50, 73, 203, 207, 208, 243
Gato, Enriqueta Huau, ix, I-Ch.1; 20, 21, **25**, **27**, **28**, 44, 45, 48, 50, 51, 54, 63, 64, 65, 110, 137, 143, 180, 187, IV-Ch.26
Gato, Gabriel H. (Hidalgo-Gato), ix, **3**, I-Ch.-1, I-Ch.3, 24, **25**, 29, 34, 43, 45, 46, II-Chs.3, 4, 5, 7, 8; IV-Chs. 13, 24, 25; 293, 297, 298
Gato, Georgia, x, 5, 6, 15, 19, 50, 54, IV-Ch.6; 250
Gato, Marie Louise, I-Chs.1, 3; II-Chs.4, 7, 8, 9; 91, 107, 110; IV; 273-274
Gato, William (Willie), 2, 7, 11, 17, 26, 50, 64, 65, 66, 77, 143, 177, 178, 180, 232, 260, 262, 265
Gruber, C.A. (William Gruber's father), 85, 285
Gruber, William, 15, I-Ch.4; 77, **82**, III-Chs.1, 2, 3, 4, 5; 112, 117, 178, 212, 232, 235, 236, 264, 285, 286
Guinard, Henry, 158, 159
Hartridge, Augustus, **105**, 109, 112, 117, 126; IV-Ch.1-30
Herrera, Domingo, 19, 58, 59, 60, 65, 67, 68, 69, 71, 72, 73, 75, 77, 78, 79, 146, 235, 246, 284
Hearsay, 138, 139, 142, 171, 206, 245, 262
Hidalgo-Gato, Francisco, 29, 30, 31, 32, 33, 34
Hogans Creek, 51, 87, 96, 99, 122, 160, 231, 267
Hosack, George, 109, 110, 223, 286
Hosack, Sarah (Sadie), **12**, 109, 164, 245, 251, 266, 298
Huau, Catalina Miralles De, **26**, **27**, **28**, II-Ch.2; 42, 44, 45, 49, 57, 58, 110, 129, 130, 137, 143, 149, 167, 169, 177, 178, 181, 189, 289, 232, 249, 258, 260, 261, 270, 276, 277, 296
Huau, Eliza, 5, 6, 7, 9, 10, **25, 44, 137;** IV-Ch.5; IV-Ch.12; 185, 186, 187, 245, 250, 290
Huau, Florida (Flora), 76, 77, 78, 234, 258, 259
Huau, Hypolito (Polly), **27, 28,** 44, 77, 278
Huau, José Alejandro, **26**, **36** II-Chs.-2,3; 42, 44, 47, 48, 76, 78, 110, 166, 167, 179, 180, 181, 254, 265, 266, 271, 277, 283, 285, 291
Huau, Joseph Hypolito Cadorette-Huau, **25,** 44, 137
Huau, Louie, 40, 41, 43, 44, 45, 259
Iowa, 11, 281
Keefe, John, Chief, I-Chs.1, 2, 3, 4; III-Chs. 3, 4, 5; 112, 113, 210, 271, 281
El Esmero cigar, **43,** 92
La Favorita, 42, **43,** 46, 48, 67, 91, 271, 277, 283, 285, 291
Laura Street, 6, 14, 20, 88, 127, 130, 131, 132, 135, 154, 155, 156, 158, 160, 161, 162, 163, 168, 183, 203, 206, 207, 208, 209, 230, 243
LaVilla (Jacksonville, Florida), 68, 84, 85, 87, 96, 99
Lector 47, 48, 283
Lopez, Narcisco, 29, 282

Lorraine, Kathryn Huau (Katie), ix, 2, **28,** 45, 52, 54, 55, 62, 110, 232, 258, 259, 261, 262, 263, 283, 290
Los Londres 47, 48, 49, 283
Lulu Lee , 150, 152, 154
Malvina Lockett, 154
Main Street, 2, 20, 42, 95, 121, 122, 124, 202, 229, 265,
Main Street Trolley, **xiv**, 122
Mambises (Gen. Mamby), 30
Marti, José , 47
Marzyck, Joseph, 83, 85, 91, 137, 264, 285, 290
Matanzas, 35, 36, 37, 39, 40, 44
Mitchell, Neil, M.D., 7, 8, 9, 10, 19
Morro Castle, 38, 39, 40, 41
Myers, Herman, 46, 283
Myers, Sigo (Sigmund), 19, 285
Natatorium and Ice Works, 161
Old City Cemetery, 109, 259, 260, 271, 273, 276, 291
Panama Mills, 2, 128
Panama Road, **xii**; 2, 3, 6, 7, 14, 128, 129
Pickett, Cornelia, Miss, 209
Pickett, Cornelia, Mrs., 209
Pine Street (Main Street), **43,** 290
Pigniolo Restaurant, 11, 83, 138, 231, 236
Pinkerton Detectives, 57, 58, 286
Pittman, FL, 189
Pittman Presbyterian Church, 189
Pitzer, George Edward (Eddie), xii, I-Chs.1, 2, 3, 4; 53, 59, 60, II-Chs.5-10, IV-Chs.1-32; **108**
Pitzer, James, 11, 59, 111, 193, 196, 197, 224
Pitzer, John, 11
Pitzer, Tillie (Matilda Jane Cubbage), 11, **12**, 184, 282
Reed, Sarah 187-189, 288
Riverside (Jacksonville, Florida), 216, 217, 222, 224, 289
River View Hotel, 200, 216, 217, 231, 289
Sanchez, Edward, 156
Sanchez, Marie, 156, 157
Savannah, GA, 34, 46, 78, 109, 162, 278, 283, 298
Serena Field and Drucilla Bryant,sisters, 129, 130, 131, 132, 133, 134, 135
Shad, Mabel, 187, 188
Spontaneous Utterance (res gestae), 139, 245, 250, 260
Springfield (Jacksonville, Florida), 2, 51, 87, 92, 96, 122, 128, 229, 230, 235, 245

St. Clair-Abrams, Alexander, **105,** IV-Ch.1-30, Ch.32, 287, 289
St. Johns Episcopal Church, X, 281, 293, 298
St. Johns River, 57, 58, 77, 78, 128, **218**
Ten Years War in Cuba, 1
The Commodore, 78, 284
The Three Friends, III-Ch.-10, 79, 110, 284
The Dauntless, ii, 284
Trout Creek, 2, 128
Vinzant, W.D., 11, 95, 96, 269, 270
Weed, Edwin, The Rt. Reverend , x, 281
Wheelmen, 1, 2
Winterset, Iowa, 11, 281
Wright, A. O., 19, III-Ch.3, 4, 5, **172**, 177, 178, 186, 195, 196, 209, 260, 264
Young Woman's Christian Temperance Union , 184, 188, 288

About the Author

Louise Stanton Warren is a retired attorney and librarian from Jacksonville, Florida, and was a board member of the Jacksonville Historical Society. She wrote and directed scripts for the Port of Jacksonville Pilot Club's annual tours of Jacksonville's oldest cemeteries for 10 years, revealing the stories behind the headstones of Old City Cemetery and Evergreen Cemetery.

A graduate of the University of Florida College of Law, Ms. Warren has long been involved in community causes, especially those affecting women. She served on the Mayor's Commission on the Status of Women and the Jacksonville Area Legal Aid Board, and also as an officer of the Pilot Club International, Port of Jacksonville. She is a recipient of the National Organization for Women Outstanding Service Award, has been a guest columnist for *The Florida Times-Union* and executive director of La Plume des Femme women's theater, and has won several awards for her writing. In addition, she attended Columbia University and Florida State University, and she has a Master's Degree in Library Science.